Wayne's Angel Trilogy-Book 2

BETWIXT

A novel by

Ron W. Mumford

3rd Coast Books
Houston, Texas
2018

Copyright © 2018 by Ron W. Mumford

All Rights Reserved

All rights reserved. No part of this book may be reproduced or transmitted in any form or by any means, electronic or mechanical. This includes photocopying or recording by any information storage or retrieval system, without written permission from the publisher.

3rd Coast Books
19790 Hwy. 105 W. Ste. 1318
Montgomery, TX 77356

www.3rdCoastBooks.com

ISBN's

Perfect Binding — 978-1-946743-19-0
eBook/.MOBI — 978-1-946743-20-6
eBook/.ePub — 978-1-946743-21-3

Project Coordinator — Rita Mills
Editor & Collaborator — Faye Walker
Text Design — Deena Rae
Cover Design — James Price

Printed in The United States of America

CONTENTS

Acknowledgements v
Introduction vii
1 Euphoria   *"What happened next?"* 1
2 *"Not Yet…"*   *A table for two* 13
3 Close Your Eyes   *Revelation* 25
4 On The Fence   *Girls just want to have fun!* 37
5 1 + 1 = 1   *Shameless!* 49
6 The Garden   *Much given, Much expected* 63
7 Helle Guyion, Ph.D.   *High Priestess of Evil* 69
8 Arrival of Darkness   *Close Encounters* 79
9 Look into My Eyes   *Keys to the Mind* 89
10 Divine Warning   *Leave My Chillins Alone!* 97
11 Quack! Quack!   *Mene, Mene, Tekel Upharsin!* 109
12 Mount Zaphon   *The Aspired Throne of Satan* 121
13 Voyeur   *I want Bella!* 131
14 BFFs   *Return of Mama-Che* 147
15 Vengeance!   *Pandora's Box* 155
16 Segue   *Temptations* 169
17 The Moment   *Enjoy it while you can…* 179
18 Houston: We Have a Problem!   *Altered States* 191
19 Warrior   *"I AM the Storm!"* 203
20 "Go and Sin No More!"   *Debt paid!* 215
21 World War III   *You will call him…* 225
22 I'm Pregnant! I'm Pregnant!   *Me Too!* 235
Looking Forward 243
About the Author 245

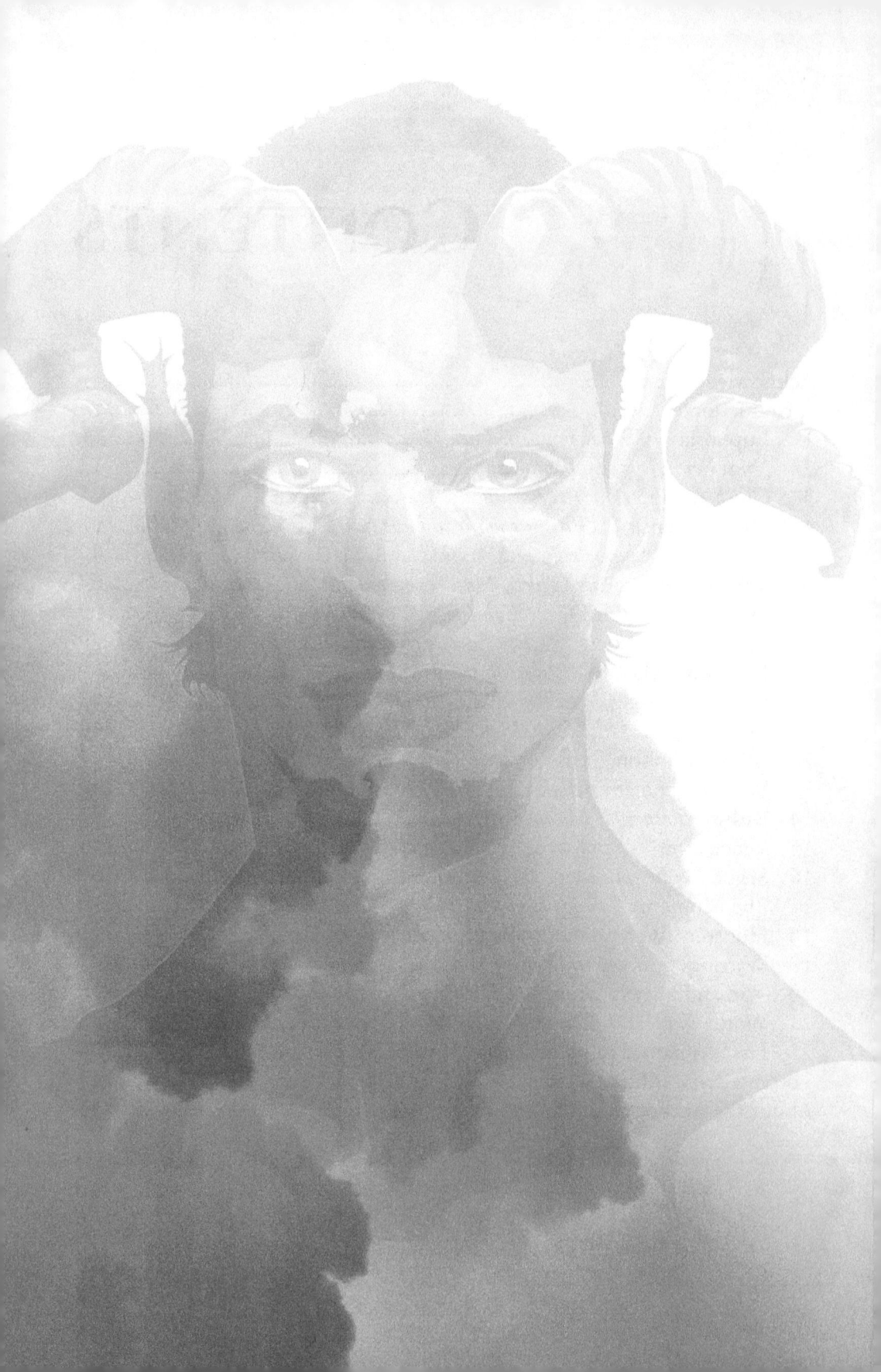

ACKNOWLEDGEMENTS

Always first and foremost, I want to thank my Good Lord for giving me this story to honor Him. After all, where do thoughts come from? Then I have to thank my family who has supported me through this process of writing a *way out* book. A writer and his thoughts can get very lonely when left alone without any encouragement for long periods of time wrestling with demons, organization, characters and voices of each one to make them completely unique, just as God creates us to be unique individuals.

In a sense, an author is a creator of fictitious characters and has to decide who becomes heroes and heroines, protagonists and antagonists. And who lives and who dies. I can tell you that killing one of your characters is like losing a member of your family. Tough to do.

Also, accolades to those who were beta readers, Kimberly Herald, Marshall Wayne Sealey, who is writing his own great book with P.K Ott entitled, *Jesus, Justice & Gentlemen's Clubs*. Book one of the Wayne's Angel trilogy won a silver medal from Maxy Awards for Best Fantasy, book 2, *Betwixt,* will surely be in the running for a gold. I tried my best to make each successive book better than the first. **Betwixt is *Wayne's Angel* on steroids!**

Finally, I want to thank my editor, Faye Walker, Ph.D., the best editor ever (fayewriter@yahoo.com) and Rita Mills, my publisher with 3rd Coast Books.com, Deena Rae for the beautiful text flow and e-book conversion with E-bookbuilders.com along with James Price for his brilliant cover designs at www.aepbookcovers.com. One more talented person to thank, Mario Rosales, 3rd Coast Books' IT Director and master author website builder (www.techlifeblanace.net).

A final thanks goes out to the Global Literary Community, www.ReadersCloud9.com. I would highly recommend my readers and their friends to go to that site and sign up and become part of this world-wide group of authors, writers, book clubs, readers, bloggers, book reviewers and post a review on that site. It's Free!

I couldn't end my thanks until I thank every reader who reads this book. You will get a blessing for doing so. And, as for as the reviews, write what you will…Reviews are in the eyes of the reader.

Be Blessed,
Ron W. Mumford

INTRODUCTION

Book one of the Wayne's Angel trilogy ended with Wayne Tyler winning his battles against his seven demons and experiencing, seeing and feeling what love is in a beautiful, supernatural way. However, it came at great risk and continuing consequences. He has ask Abby to marry him but she has conditions from her lady-pleaser future hubby. How about a honeymoon in the Garden of Eden? Who is the lady that made Daddy Hank's world stand still at the end of the book?

This second book **is Wayne's Angel on steroids.** More supernatural, out of this world sequences, visits to *Betwixt*, the very dimension where demons and their master, Satan, hangs out. In other sequences the reader will get a whole new meaning of *Pandora's Box,* that scares the living daylights out of many of the world's most gifted scientists while they scramble to find the missing element in a doom's day bomb that can destroy an entire continent. It begins a global arm's race like no other in the history of the world.

Bella continues to be her wild-child crazy self and will be one of the main characters in this second book of the trilogy. Actually, her character just cracked me up as if she demanded to be a star in book two…and she is. More Bella, more cheap shots, more telling it like it is, according to her. She may have met her match in book two. Can an independent, confident, smart, beautiful lady like Bella be humbled or completely scared out of her wits? And if so, who will be there to rescue her from her fears?

Tequilaville is on a decline. Can Wayne keep filling the room with his fans when he can barely walk, much less drive the ladies crazy with his moves? Will Daddy Hank accept his new son-in-law or will the feud continue?

And talk about evil, Dr. Helle Guyion will emerge as **the most evil woman in the entire world** with powers never before seen and cannot be harnessed, even by the U.S. government.

More understanding of Wayne's visit to Between, then Betwixt will be revealed in bits and pieces as each character remembers a little more about the event. In book two, the characters will experience more of the supernatural in everyday life, right before their eyes. No one, not even N.A.S.A. scientists can come close to an explanation of what they are seeing and experiencing.

Ron Mumford

Forget reality! In book 2, *reality* takes on a brand new meaning. Some can grasp it, others will not. Put the coffee on and strap yourself in for one of the wildest literary fantasy rides you have ever experienced. Please share with your friends and…**if you have sighted Wayne's Angel**, either Mr. Elroy or his fifteen foot tall angel form, Gordon, drop me a note at www.ronwmumford.com and let us know where you saw **Wayne's Angel.**

BETWIXT

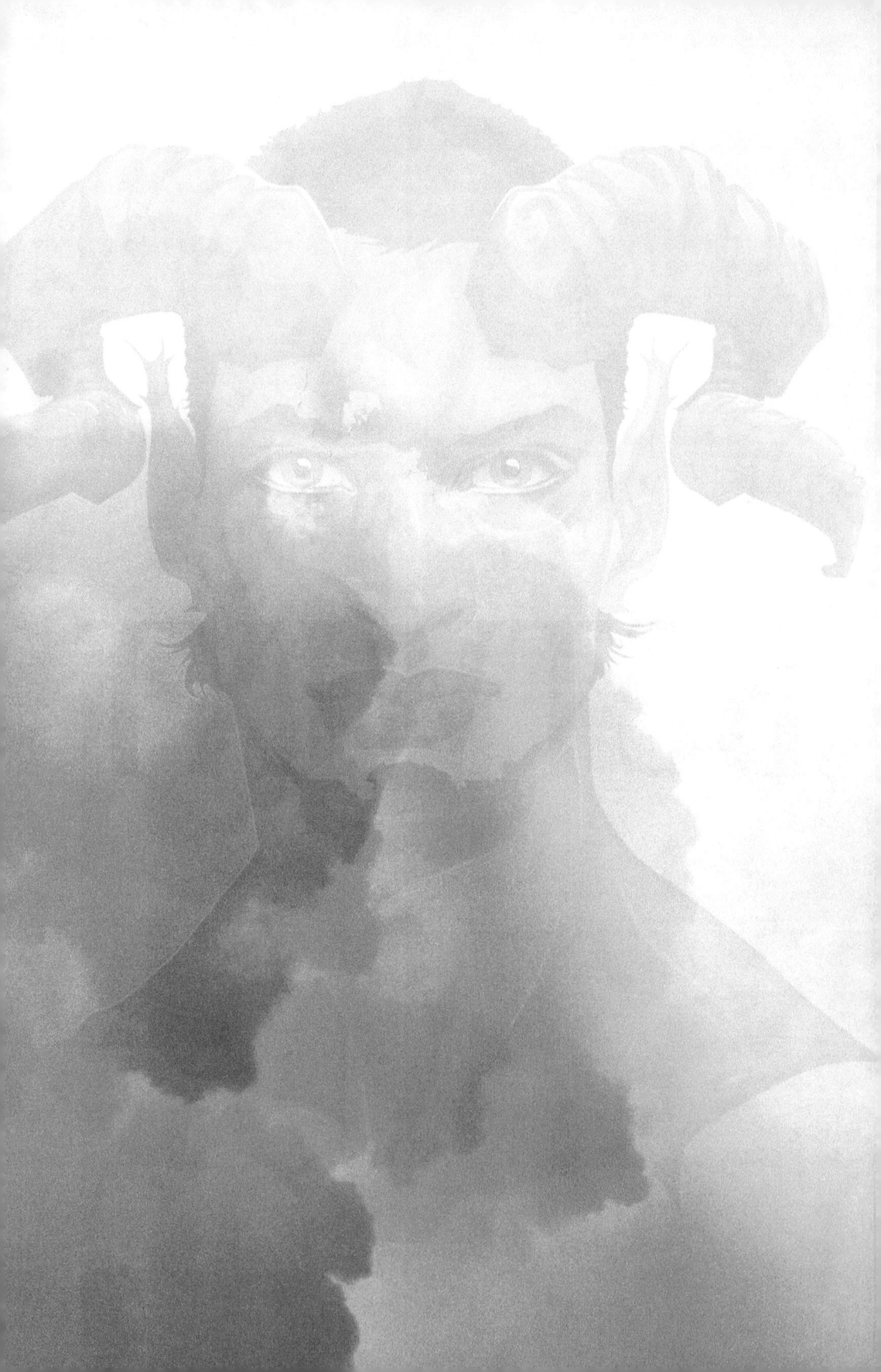

1

EUPHORIA
"WHAT HAPPENED NEXT?"

As Abby and Wayne celebrated their big engagement in the middle of the dance floor at Tequilaville, Hank slid out of his corner booth where his best friends, Robbie Cantrell, her wild-child daughter Bella, and Mary, wife of the bartending staff head, Master Tito, had joined him.

"Mom, I told you Mr. Hank is absolutely mesmerized by that lady on the other side of the room. He's walking over to meet her like a man on a mission. Have you ever seen him do that before?" Bella said to Robbie.

"Never!"

Hank's eyes were fixed on a tall, slender, brown-haired, green-eyed lady who had stood to applaud Abby's acceptance of Wayne Tyler's proposal of marriage. Hank walked across the back edge of Tequilaville's dance floor with reckless abandon, determined to meet this woman.

As he stood in front of her, he forgot to take off his old, beat-up cowboy hat and just blurted out, "Hi, my name's Hank. I haven't seen you here before. What brings you to Tequilaville?"

"Is that the best line you got, Hank?" the lady shot back.

"It's the only line I've got!" Hank was fumbling for words. "You, uh… made my world stand still."

"Wow, it's been a while since anyone said that to me, Hank. Do you say that to all the ladies you meet?"

"Oh, no m'am," Hank said removing his hat. "I'm just, uh…being honest."

The lady smiled at Hank and replied, "In that case, Hank, I'm Elizabeth, but my friends call me Liz. And to answer your other question about what brought me to this club…well, you wouldn't believe me if I told you."

Liz extended her hand to Hank. As they touched for the first time, Hank felt the softness of her skin, saw the joy in her eyes and sensed that she had a gentle but protective nature. She was wearing boots and jeans with a green top accented by a small turquoise crucifix.

"So glad to meet you, Liz." Hank was still stammering for the words to continue their brief introduction. "After what's been going on around here for the past few months, I'd probably believe anything you told me. Oh yeah, that young lady out there on the dance floor is my daughter, Abby. She and I own Tequilaville, and it looks like I'm about to get a new son-in-law. Would you like to meet 'em?"

"Ooh, I'm impressed, Hank. A business owner and a daddy. I'd love to meet them. So where is Abby's mom?"

"In heaven, I hope." Hank couldn't believe he'd said that. "Uh, I've never been married. That's part of the long story. How about you, Liz? Is there a Mister…Liz?She laughed and said, "No, never been married either, Hank. Let's go meet your daughter and future son-in-law."

By this time the entire audience at Tequilaville was standing, applauding the happy couple, who were both on their knees in the middle of the floor. As Abby and Wayne embraced, a TV news reporter stuck a microphone between them to get a final comment.

Hank walked up, nudged the reporter and quietly said, "Could we have a private moment?" The reporter backed off, the camera still recording the event.

"Mom, look! Mr. Hank is actually introducing his mystery lady to Abby and Wayne!" Bella blurted out in typical fashion. "Love is truly in the air. Let's get out there and meet her."

"Bella, give them a few minutes. I'm sure Mr. Hank will introduce her to us when the time is right. Just be still for the first time in your life," Robbie said grabbing Bella's arm. "This is a father-daughter moment between Abby and Mr. Hank."

Abby was trying to help Wayne back into his wheel chair when Hank interceded. "Let me help you." Hank took hold of Wayne's hands and lifted him back into his chair. "I'm so happy for both of you."

Hank extended his hand to Abby, drawing her close to him and gave her a big fatherly hug. Reaching out, he shook Wayne's hand as he whispered in his ear, "Treat her right, Wayne! I love that little girl. She's all I got."

There were tears of joy in all their eyes. A brief moment of peace and acceptance descended.

Abby was entirely in Wayne's world now with no idea what would happen in the future. And she didn't care. As long as they were together with their family around, nothing would be too great to overcome. She knew their love would conquer all.

"Oh, sorry Liz…I got caught up… Abby, Wayne, I want you to meet Liz, uh Liz…"

"Liz Gabriel. I'm so happy for the both of you. Congratulations!"

Abby faced Liz, accepted a little hug from her and then turned toward her Daddy Hank. She noticed a special twinkle in his eyes that she hadn't seen since the day both of them met for the first time when she was eight years old.

"Thank you, Liz," Abby said, smiling. "This is my soul man, Wayne Tyler. Baby, meet Liz."

After the formalities, Hank felt overjoyed that the anxious moment of meeting Liz was over and so far, well, so good. Everyone was happy. Hank led Liz back to her table as news crews, radio announcers and well-wishers surrounded Abby and Wayne. Robbie and Bella, along with the family of Tequilaville staff also crowded around the betrothed couple to offer their congrats.

"Hey, little sister! How'd you like Wayne's song that he wrote for you? Wasn't it great?" Bella just had to grab the moment and be in the spotlight.

"Oh, Bella, the song was beautiful, perfect! It melted my heart and was from Wayne's soul to mine. It was about me and about love…You knew he was going to propose to me tonight, didn't you? Now tell the truth!" Abby said as she hugged Bella and Robbie.

"Well, who do you think picked out the ring? Do you like it? Did I do good or what?"

"It's a beautiful ring. Thank you, but why didn't you tell me? I'm like your sister, remember?"

"Hey, Abby, do you think I'd spoil your big surprise? It wasn't easy not telling you, but hey, you know me. I can keep a secret, right?"

"Sure, Bella. This must be the first time in your life you ever kept a secret, but I'm glad you did. I love you!" Abby said.

Liz touched Hank's hand and motioned for him to sit with her at her table.

"Thank you, Hank. I can see that you are truly blessed. What a great moment. It was my honor to share it with you."

"The pleasure was all mine, Liz. But I'd still like to hear your unbelievable story of what brought you here tonight," Hank said, taking off his hat and flipping his gray ponytail out of his collar.

"I'm curious, Hank. What's your *long story?*"

"Hey, lady. I asked you first," Hank said with a shy smile, hoping this might lead to a second meeting with Liz. He still didn't know who she was, where she was from or if she lived nearby.

"Yes, you did, I'll give you that. Let me ask you a question first. Hank, are you a Christian man?"

"Uh, sort of. I mean, uh, that's part of my long story. Maybe we could have dinner tomorrow night and kind of fill in some details of what's going on in our lives. If you would accept a dinner invitation from an almost complete stranger who has great intentions. I promise you that I'm a complete gentleman, Liz." Hank's stomach was tied in a knot. He hadn't asked anyone out on a date in years.

"On one condition. I'm staying next door at the Bay Hilton. You have to take me to church first, and we can have dinner afterwards. Pick me up about four tomorrow afternoon and you've got yourself a date, Hank."

"Four, tomorrow afternoon." Hank didn't notice that he was grinning from ear to ear. Liz could see Hank fumbling and looking for an exit. He'd had about all the excitement he could stand for one day. Liz let him off the hook gently.

"I've got to get my beauty rest, Hank. See you tomorrow. By the way, what's your last name?"

"Hawkins! Uh, Hank Hawkins. I'll be there."

The night was winding down at Tequilaville. Wayne and Abby loaded up and went home while the house band *South* sung the usual closing song of *Turn Out the Lights, the party's over*…Robbie and Bella headed for the door but not before Bella sucked down a final glass of wine, almost in one gulp.

"Mom, are you jealous that Mr. Hank has found someone? Aren't you afraid Liz will come between you and him?" Bella was the supreme drama queen in the family. If there was no drama going on, she'd make sure to create some.

"Now why would I be jealous of Liz, Bella? Hank is like my brother, just like Abby is like your sister. Are you jealous of Wayne?" Robbie shot back.

"Nah, Mom. I keep my dance card pretty full. I've never been at a loss for attention." Bella smiled, put her hands on her hips, did a little wiggle and flipped her long black hair.

Abby helped Wayne into her SUV to take him back to her home where he had moved in, again. His therapy was progressing and he was strong enough to stand, walk a few steps and lift himself into the passenger seat. Abby was feeling beautiful in her flowing dress. Her mind was racing with thoughts of love and life with him. They held hands on the drive home, saying little, just enjoying the moment and coming down a bit.

As she rolled him into the house, Abby threw her arms around him and said, "Hey you stud muffin, are you burning with desire?"

Instead of making his usual moves on her that Wayne never had a problem with when they first met, he turned his head, winced and seemed to be lost in thought, deep thought. Abby caught on immediately.

"Oh, darling I'm so sorry. I didn't mean…"

"It's okay, Abby. I'm still wrestling with some things. Things we've never discussed."

"I'm pushing too hard, Wayne. Forgive me. I know you still have some physical problems going on and things on your mind. You went through a lot. We all witnessed it. It'll take time, but we have the rest of our lives to deal with them."

Ever since Wayne had gotten out of the county hospital all his friends had just tried to encourage him. No one had asked him questions about what he had experienced during his tribulations at Betwixt so as not to take him back to the ordeals. Wayne was suffering physically, and it appeared he had post-traumatic stress from his own battles. He'd been beaten, defeated and almost raped at that hell hole where demons hang out.

"I know you didn't mean to but when you said the word *burning*, all I could think of was that lake of fire and all of the thoughts that were running through my mind as I was falling into it. I've tried to suppress it, Abby, but I can't compartmentalize some of the events. And there's gaps that I can't explain."

"Wayne, sometimes it helps to talk about it. I'm not forcing you in any way, but when you're ready, I'll try to fill in some gaps with you. Since Daddy Hank, Robbie, Bella, Tito and Mary along with T-Bone and some of the others all shared the same dream, we've tried to write down what we remembered. And yes, there are gaps in all of our recollections of our own time at Betwixt."

"Now's as good a time as any to talk about it, Abby. I don't want to destroy our moment, though."

"Wayne, this could be a wonderfully defining moment that I hope will release you. Okay, if you're ready to talk, let me ask you a question. All of us got to Betwixt in a dream. How did you get there?"

Wayne reached deep into his memory to relive some thoughts that he only wanted to forget. It was like facing his demons once again.

"First, I didn't sleep with Bella, Abby. I want you to know that; I want you to trust me."

"We know. Bella told us everything. Let's just get past that."

"Baby, I wanted so bad to write you a song to make up with you but the words were not there. I had no conception of what love was so I got really drunk that night on the back deck of the club, your dad showed up, broke my nose and I hot-wired a boat and headed out to Red Fish Island.

"When I got there—this is going to be hard, Abby—I ran up on a reef, finished the bottle of tequila, pitched it into the bay and jumped in after it…"

"You tried to commit suicide, Wayne? Really?"

"Yeah, I did. The thought of living without you was more than I could handle."

"What happened next?"

"I really don't know, Abby. That's the truth. I woke up in a foggy mist, I was dry and breathing and there was this fifteen-foot, uh, angel standing in front of me asking me lots of questions…"

"What kind of questions?"

"I really can't remember them all, Abby. Just questions about life, about love, about choices and free will. He said his name was Gordon, like a guardian angel. I told him I didn't believe in angels and he let me touch his hand. I was freaking out big time.

"Then he gave me a bunch of choices. I only remember two of them. He said I could say 'send me back' in my drunken state, fourteen feet under water, or I could face some demons. I began thinking of you, Abby, so the first choice wasn't much of a choice. I'd die. So I picked the second. For the first time in my life, I realized that you meant everything to me and if I couldn't get back to you, well, maybe death would be a better choice."

"Awww!" Abby listened to every word. This was the first anyone had known what Wayne had experienced.

"Where'd you go, Wayne? Did it have a name?"

"Yeah, I remember that well. Gordon said we were at place called Between, a place between day and night, life and death and heaven and hell. And I didn't want to be there. I guess I should have been more thankful. The alternative was pretty grim."

"Go on, Wayne…"

"I also remember asking Gordon if the demons could kill me. He said no, that my soul was eternal. Then I asked him if they could hurt me. He said, 'Yes!' and that was an understatement. The next thing I remember, Gordon flew me to this old Roman coliseum where I saw a platform elevated about two hundred feet above the field below. I heard the shrieks of the demons off in the distance and it scared the hell out of me. I looked down at the grandstands and that's when I saw you there, Abby. Do you remember being there? Were you all really there?"

"Yeah, we were there Wayne, in our dreams. But like the way dreams go, we can't remember everything, either."

Wayne asked Abby to get him a cup of coffee and they took a brief break. When he settled his nerves for a few minutes, Abby tried to lighten up the conversation and said to Wayne, "Honey, do you remember playing music with Stevie Ray Vaughn, Eric Clapton, Garth Brooks, and some of the divas of rock and roll and country music?"

"I did? No, I don't remember that at all, but I sure wish I did. How'd I do?"

"Baby, you were in your element! You played great! You were having a ball!"

Wayne laughed for the first time. Even though it was getting late, sleep was far from them as they continued to put some of the missing pieces of the puzzle together and to grasp the purpose of the experience.

"Thank you, baby, for walking me through this. I love you so much." Wayne reached over and pulled Abby close to him, taking a breath before going back to his memories.

"Hey, let's get out of our pretty clothes and get comfy before going on." Abby got up and changed, emerging from her bedroom in flannel onesie Bugs Bunny jammies with feet in them. Wayne howled with laughter. She helped Wayne change and sat back down on the couch in the family room as they began again.

"Wayne," Abby continued, "do you remember the name 'Ishtar?'"

"Hmm, Ishtar, Ishtar. No, I can't say as I do. Is that important?"

"Not really." Abby was relieved he didn't remember the more than beautiful goddess that almost raped him.

"No! I'm serious, Abby. I want to know about Ishtar. What happened with her or it? Did I do something wrong?"

"No, Wayne, you definitely did something right. You said 'No' to the most beautiful creature you have probably ever laid eyes on. I was proud of you. You told her that you loved me and *me* only!"

"Imagine that, Wayne Tyler turning down a beautiful...whatever she was. But speaking of women, I do remember an old saying coming up during the ordeals. Tell me if this happened or I am just imagining it. Do you remember, 'Hell has no fury like the scorn of a woman?'"

"Oh yeah, Wayne. That happened. What do you remember about it?"

"Not much. I don't even remember the circumstance or who said it. I do remember—and this is weird—being bitten by snakes and stung by big black scorpions. It hurt like hell...oops, I remember something else Gordon told me. He said that every time I used an expletive it was like putting another nail in my coffin and that I should expand my vocabulary."

They both got a chuckle out of that, but the jovial mood changed rapidly as Wayne began to remember more.

"Abby, do you remember Baal?"

"Yes! We all remembered Baal. Tell me what you remember and your thoughts about that event. It was the last of the challenges you faced at Betwixt. We all thought you were a goner and that he would claim your soul for all eternity."

Wayne took several deep breaths. Abby could see him begin to shiver and tighten up before he spoke.

"He was huge! He filled the sky with his enormous size. He was a fire breathing dragon with two heads and claws like tanks." Wayne was talking in phrases and began to hyperventilate.

"I knew that I didn't stand a chance of surviving. I cried out to Gordon to help me and he only said, 'This too shall pass.' I thought that was pretty weak. I felt like Gordon had abandoned me. And then the field below the bleachers turned into a lake of fire like hell itself. I tried to hit Baal with my guitar but he just breathed fire down and burned it up. Then he swooped down on me, ripping my scalp over my right ear and almost tore my shoulder away from my body. I felt pain like I couldn't imagine existed. It was excruciating!"

"It's okay, Wayne. You're here now. You're safe. You don't have to go on…"

"I've got to, Abby. Because that's when you yelled out to Baal and said, 'Take me, Baal. Wayne's had enough.' You were willing to take his wrath for me. You were actually trying to draw his attention away from me. I'll never forget that! Did you do that, baby?"

"Yes. That's true, I did."

"Abby, that's why I decided let go and fall into the flames. I was afraid that if I didn't give Baal what he wanted—my soul—that he would swoop down on you and carry you away. I could never live with that. I was helpless to do anything about it. I had to save you!"

Wayne broke down and sobbed, clutching Abby close to him. She held him and let him get it all out. They were crossing a different type of threshold together that would bond them for the rest of their lives. Wayne was remembering the unthinkable and trying to forget the unforgiveable.

"I'm sorry, Abby. Since I was a kid I was told that big boys don't cry and I never did before…"

"But real men cry. Especially when they finally get in touch with their emotions. Most men never reach this point, but you have. I won't tell anyone. It'll be our secret, big boy. What's important is that each of us was willing to die for the other. There's no greater love than this, Wayne."

"Oh, now I remember another choice that Gordon gave me. Sort of a last ditch choice."

"What choice?"

"Gordon said that I could call upon the name of The Lord. Yep, that was my third choice. I told Gordon at the beginning that I had no idea who 'The Lord' was and why would I call upon someone I never knew. As I was falling into the fire, my life passed before me—every lustful sin that I'd ever committed. The further I fell the more convicted I became. Somehow I felt the flames burning my flesh but it was nothing like the horror I was about to experience. There was something worse in store for me, separation. Separation from love, separation from you and separation from, uh, uh, I guess, the love of The Lord.

"I met Him on the way down, Abby. He was there in the flames with me. He held out His hand and I grabbed it. I surrendered myself to Him, Abby and He forgave me. After that, there's a long gap. Did you see all of this? What happened next, baby?"

Wayne's countenance changed. He was happy again, hopeful. He had admitted his salvation to Abby and how he had to come to the end of himself before he could meet Jesus. He wiped the tears from his eyes but started crying again. The tears washed him clean. He felt wonderful.

"Hey, I've got an idea!" Abby jumped up from the couch and headed for the kitchen. "Since this is turning into an all-night slumber party with just the two of us, why don't I fix us a late night breakfast. How 'bout some eggs, sausage, hot buttered biscuits…"

"With honey, honey. Throw in a cold glass of milk and I'm all in."

Abby wiggled the tail on her Bugs Bunny jammies as she walked away. She was more happy that words couldn't describe.

"Hey, lady. I think you're sexier in that bunny suit than you are in your negligees." Wayne laughed.

"Hmmm. I'm not sure exactly how to take that comment, but for the moment I'll take it as a compliment…I guess."

The late night breakfast was just what they needed to renew their strength. Abby cleaned up the kitchen and put the dishes in the washer as Wayne used his walker to get back to the living room to begin round two of putting the missing pieces of their experience together.

"Where did we leave off, Abby? And thanks for that great meal."

"Baby, do you remember Michael?"

"Who's Michael? No, I don't remember anyone named Michael."

"We asked Robbie about him. She said that Michael was the general of God's heavenly armies, the arch angel. Just before you entered the lake of fire, Michael—and I can't even begin to describe his blinding brilliance, his strength and his authority—actually came down into the arena riding on a lightning bolt. He had a broad sword with eyes all over it and used it to scoop you out of the flames. He waved his other hand and the pit of fire disappeared and the field became a beautiful valley with millions of fragrant flowers. There were lions lying down beside little lambs, both eating green grass and there was no fear. Wayne, it was like a little acre in heaven. The sky above was crisscrossed with hundreds of rainbows containing colors we'd never seen.

"Michael then turned to Baal and banished him from the scene and said something about seeing him again at some place called Armageddon. Then Michael healed you of all your burns and wounds."

"Wow, that must have been a spectacle, Abby. I must have passed out. I don't remember any of this," Wayne said, witnessing the glow of Abby's description.

"Then you probably don't remember Gabriel either, huh?"

"Sorry, Abby. Who's Gabriel? Another angel?"

"Oh yes! Gabriel is another angel. He was beautiful. Robbie also told us about him. He's God's messenger angel."

"So what was his message, Abby?"

"He announced that you were now a citizen of the kingdom of heaven and a new child of God. His voice, Wayne, it was so small and quiet, yet booming. We could hear angel wings flapping above us. Like millions of them. We heard applause and the most beautiful music. I can't come close to telling you the feeling that we had. It was really out of this world."

"Leave it to me to miss all the good stuff. Abby, do you remember seeing a big door there, like a portal?"

"No. What was it?"

"I'll get to that in a minute. This is where I think I woke up and I remember something else that Gordon told me back at Between. He told me that if I made it past the demons—and he doubted that I would—that my prize would be to know what love is. Abby, I had to write a song for you, a love song. But I didn't know what love was…

"Gordon took me up on a mountain and left me standing there. All of a sudden I was engulfed by a warm, wonderful mist. I looked up and saw thousands of broken gold threads going right through me, Abby. It was the most wonderful feeling that I've ever felt. Those golden threads were rays of love that completely impregnated every part of me. I felt, saw and experienced the most perfect love. I can't explain it in words. I didn't want it to go away, but it did."

Wayne closed his eyes and tried his best to capture the feeling once again. He was beginning to remember more and more of the dream. He was also trying to grasp the reality of it. Surely, it had really happened. He hoped against hope that it was real. Abby was on the edge of her seat. She wanted more.

"What happened next, Wayne?"

"That's where the portal came into play. Gordon led me up to it and told me this portal was the doorway to heaven. He said I could walk through it and never suffer pain again. But it would mean ending my life on earth.

"Abby, the only choice that I hadn't taken at this point was to say 'send me back.' I kept thinking about you so I told Gordon to send me back. He reminded me that I was fourteen feet under water in Galveston Bay and that there were no guarantees that I would survive the attempted suicide. He told me I could be paralyzed for life or become a living vegetable…"

"And you chose life, Wayne? Even with no assurances?"

"Yes. I had to take a chance of seeing you again, Abby, and writing that song you wanted. At this point, I go completely blank other than what y'all told me at the hospital when Lt. Stark, my 'streak brother,' went over about the Coast Guard thinking I was a drug dealer and fishing me out of the drink."

"I'm so proud of my brave man! You chose me, you chose life over eternity for me, Wayne. What more could a girl ask for in her betrothed?"

"Uh, uh, Abby. I wanted to talk to you about that. I love you and I hope you know that. But I want our marriage to be blessed. How 'bout I move into the guest room until our wedding night? I want it to be special and…I'm starting to get that burning desire for you again, baby!"

"I can wait if you can, honey. But will you do me a favor?"

"Anything, Abby."

"There's lots more pieces to this puzzle that we don't remember. I'd really like to set an appointment with some psychologist so we can talk it out and find a comfort to all of this. Would you be willing to attend with me?"

"Book it, baby. I'll be there. This ought to be an interesting gig…"

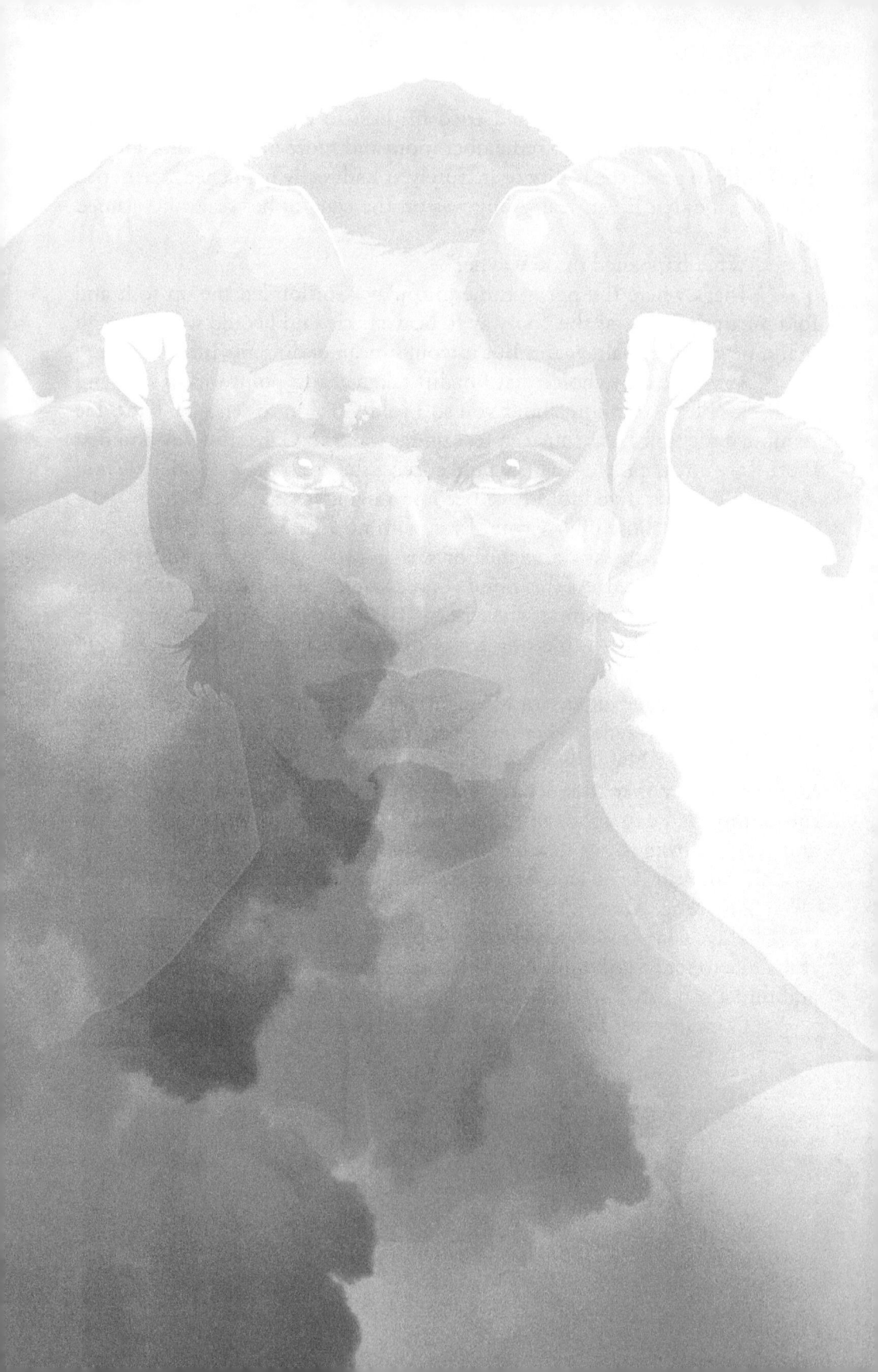

2

"Not Yet..."
A table for two

Hank took an extra-long shower, put on his best starched jeans, lizard boots and decided to put on the only white shirt he owned. After looking at himself in the mirror for a second, he combed through his gray beard and decided to wear a blue blazer and a red tie. He thought to himself, *This is good as I get. I hope Liz likes me…even though I detest wearing ties.* Before walking out of his condo, Hank grabbed his best silver belly beaver cowboy hat from its box in the top of his sparsely filled clothes closet.

As he entered the foyer of the Bay Hilton, next door to Tequilaville, the first sight Hank saw was Liz standing in the lobby wearing raggedy knee-holed blue jeans, rough out boots and a wrinkled orange shirt. He immediately felt over-dressed.

"Hey, Liz, uh, what kind of church are we going to? I wore my Sunday go-to-meeting clothes, " he said with a laugh, pointing to his tie. He walked over and gave her a little greeting hug.

"I should have told you. Forgive me, Hank. We're going to a Cowboy Church. Have you ever been to one?"

"Can't say as I have."

"Just lose the coat and tie and you'll fit right in," Liz said with a giggle.

Hank held out his arm and escorted Liz out of the hotel, opening the door for her and led her out to his truck where he again opened the door and helped her in. Liz could tell that Hank was a true southern gentleman. He was making a great impression on her. Liz gave him directions as they pulled out of the parking lot.

"So, where're you from originally, Liz?" Hank was trying to fill the trip with some active conversation. He had lots of room for improvement.

"Originally from Atlanta."

"Oh, a Georgia peach, huh? A real southern belle!" Hank said with a smile on his face, never turning his head away from the road ahead.

"Pretty much. I had great parents, both dead now, but I was a driven young lady. College just wasn't affordable for a long time after I graduated high school so I worked as a waitress in some of the Atlanta bars until I could afford my tuition. I got my undergraduate degree at the University of Georgia in business—struggling to make ends meet and pay the tuition—then attended New York University on a full academic scholarship. I graduated summa cum laude when I got my M.B.A. Finance."

All of a sudden Hank felt a bit outmatched in the intelligence department. Liz didn't strike him as an intellectual.

"I was in New York when 9/11 happened, though not involved directly in the tragedy. Many of the financial firms were based in the World Trade Center so, unfortunately, they had plenty of job openings after they relocated. I went to work for one of the larger firms as a fundamental analyst…"

"You're losing me, Liz. I've got some investments, but I really don't know much about Wall Street and all the terminology." "Wall Street is chaotic, Hank. Every day it's crazy with all that's going on in the world. The 'Street' is a back-stabbing, crawl over people to go up the ladder to success work environment. Failure is not an option there."

"So, how high up the ladder did you get, Ms. Smarty Pants, and why are you in Clear Lake?"

"After ten years, I was head of all the analysts at the firm. Both technical and fundamental analysts. Sorry, Hank, more street terms."

"No worry, Liz, I'll catch up. Keep talking."

"For a long time working was enough for me. Trying to get my career going, trying to get some degree of financial security for myself. The problem was that I was what is described as a *contra*, someone who goes against the grain. I didn't really believe all the crap that my own analysts were putting out."

"So you've got a little *rebel* in you, huh, Liz?"

"A *little* is an understatement, Hank. I began trading in my own accounts and doing just the opposite of what the firm was recommending to our clients. With salary and bonuses, Hank, I was making seven and eight figure yearly incomes. When I began trading I was dead on. I made another fortune added on to the one I already had in the bank! I hope you're not a gold digger, Cowboy. I've never divulged my success to anyone."

Hank just laughed and shook his head. "I don't want your money, Liz. I got a few bucks of my own. What happened next?"

"At that point, I was investigated by the Securities and Exchange Commission. I did nothing illegal, but my firm showed me the door. I got fired for being successful and going against the establishment."

"Liz, something's still puzzling me. You mentioned security. Why didn't you ever get married? You're beautiful, educated and rich. Surely those guys in New York aren't stupid enough not to notice a woman like you."

"Oh, Hank, they noticed all right. It's just that most of them were only out to put notches on their bed posts and satisfy a momentary physical desire. I was raised in a loving home. My dad was devoted to my mom and vice-versa. I didn't find that kind of relationship in New York, and I wasn't going to settle for less."

"Good for you, Liz. So what brings you to Clear Lake?"

Liz settled back into her seat in Hank's truck. She stared out the window as they drove by the lake that opened up into Galveston Bay. She breathed in the sea breeze coming off the Gulf and took her time to respond, to gather her thoughts before she replied. It had been quite some time since Liz had asked herself this same question. Why was she here? What had changed in her life to change her direction?

Liz sighed a long sigh.

"When I left New York, I had no place to return to. No close friends, no relatives, no place to go. I began feeling an emptiness. An emptiness in my heart, in my life and in my soul. Besides feeling secure at home with my parents, the only other place that I ever felt secure was in college. So to seek that secure feeling again, I decided to return to school for another degree. I had to change careers—not that I needed the money—I just needed something to fill that emptiness. I had no direction. I had no clue of what path I would pursue. But Hank, deep down inside of me I knew I had a purpose to fulfill."

Hank could see the deep thought that encompassed Liz. She was a thinker. He didn't interrupt her and knew she was figuring things out as she continued to tell her story. He felt privileged to be the one to hear it.

"I still had three months to go on the lease of my Fifth Avenue apartment, so I just settled in and began searching the internet to see what interested me. I was really searching for purpose. I Googled that word and a book title popped up, *The Purpose Driven Life* by Rick Warren. I bought it, read it and I'll never forget the first line on the first page: *It's not about you!* Have you ever read that book, Hank?"

"No, I haven't. I've heard about it, though."

"After reading it, I began referring to it as *the Bible for dummies like me*."

"Liz. Ms, Summa cum laude, I wouldn't say that you're exactly a dummy. How did you decide that?"

"Hank, I knew about investing, making money, working hard, avoiding heartache, but I didn't know much about life. Life was hitting me squarely between my eyes. I was a failure at life and living it. When you have no purpose, Hank, you have no life."

"One of those bad *ah hah* moments, huh, Liz?"

"Totally bad, Hank. I was crushed. I felt defeated, like I had wasted my life on things that didn't matter."

"Keep going, Liz. I'm intrigued about what you're going to say next."

"I finally decided to enroll in a small seminary."

"You were going to be an ordained minister, Liz?"

"I didn't know what I was going to be. A minister, a missionary. I just felt like I was in a desert, thirsting for a reason to be. Trying to make my life matter."

"Are you an ordained minister now, Liz?" Hank was really intrigued with this woman, her life and her thoughts. He hoped they had time before arriving at the Cowboy Church for her to finish the story.

"No! I'm not. As a matter of fact, I got kicked out of seminary."

"Kicked out? Why?"

"Hank, I told you that I was a contra-type of person. The theology that they were teaching was really deep. I didn't fully understand it. I began reading the Bible and discovered that it was written in such a simple language that the poor and uneducated could understand it. The learned Pharisees and Sadducees of that ancient age never got it. It was so simply and literally written that the scholarly theologians just flat missed it.

"I began writing class assignment papers that voiced my disapproval for trying to complicate simple Christian doctrine. I got "F" after "F" and lots of negative comments from the professors. I was losing the small faith that I had. I needed faith in something so I decided to put my faith in God's Word instead of theological opinions. Besides, the Bible says that God laughs at the combined wisdom of all of mankind. I agree with God. As far as I was concerned, these professors could stuff their legalistic opinions and their man-made rules."

Liz sat up in her seat. Her face was turning red and she began to show her anger. Hank liked the spunk she was showing. He'd been a warrior himself and didn't always approve of what people thought of him, either.

"Hank, it's not a sin to drink! It's a sin to drink too much. It's not a sin to dance! David danced. It's a sin to dance lewdly and cause others to sin. So I just went face-to-face with the professors in class and told them to kiss my butt! Not very Christian, but it sure made me feel better. I left that bunch of *holier than thous* who wanted to beat everyone over the head with the Bible and keep them on some kind of a guilt trip for ever having been alive.

"I got on my soap box and told that professor that if God had the power to create the heavens and the earth, He certainly wasn't going to allow Himself to be misquoted in His word and He sure as heck didn't need them to explain everything. That's when they showed me the door. And I felt alive when I walked through it. I knew the truth and like the Bible says, 'The truth set me free!'"

Liz took a deep breath, trying to calm down. She was angry and it showed.

"Take the next right, Hank. We're here."

As Hank steered into the crushed shell parking lot where he saw many beat up pick-up trucks and he noticed a line of motorcycles parked in a row with helmets hanging on one handle bar and leather jackets bearing MC colors hanging from the other. The church was a large barn-like building. A big white cross hung on the front and to one side stood a silhouette of a horse standing in front of the cross with a cowboy down on his knees. On the other side, was a silhouette of a motorcycle with its rider, wearing colors, down on his knees.

Hank went around to open the door for Liz. He'd never seen a place like this and looked forward to the experience. He could identify with these ordinary, extraordinary people.

"As for why I am here, Hank. I planted, funded and help build this church. Now you know. This is my purpose for being…"

There was a crowd outside the church foyer consisting of what appeared to be hard-working people. It was evident by their dress. Some were shrimpers, pipefitters, welders, plant workers, some fishermen evidenced by their fishy aroma, some were actually cowboys working at local ranches and others were biker gang members. There were lots of children taking advantage of the free donuts and teenagers wearing whatever they wanted to wear. No one judged anyone here.

As Liz and Hank walked into the main sanctuary, Hank was amazed at the rustic décor. The walls consisted of course, un-sanded, natural wood. A rail around the top edges of the room resembled an old saloon in TV cowboy movies. There were no church pews but rather folding chairs all in a row. Hank guessed there was seating for several hundred people.

At the front of the sanctuary was a stage where a country and western band began playing *The Orange Blossom Special* to welcome the guests that

Sunday afternoon. Behind the stage was an old rugged cross made from almost rotted wood with holes in it. The lighting consisted of several wagon wheels suspended from the high ceilings with kerosene-like lanterns fitted into the spokes. Just to the left of center stage was a horse trough filled with water.

Bikers, cowboys, men and women all walked up to Liz to greet her and gave her hugs. She was well-known in this place.

After the first few songs from the C&W band, two of the ushers helped an old black man carrying a Fender Stratocaster up to the stage. Everyone in the congregation began to applaud.

Church pastor Randy Harrison walked up to the microphone. He wore simple boots, jeans, a Stetson hat and sported a huge silver belt buckle with a cross on it.

"Please welcome our own beloved Mr. Elroy," Pastor Randy said. "He's got a couple of blues tunes he'd like to play for you."

The old black musician looked to be at least a hundred years old. He moved very slowly but carried himself fairly upright with a little help from the ushers. He plugged in his guitar and began singing an old Ray Charles tune entitled, *You Don't Know Me*. His voice was raspy and clear. He played that guitar as if he'd taught Stevie Ray Vaughn to play. Mr. Elroy mixed in some new words to the songs he sang that just resonated the love of Christ in them. Everyone knew he had a special, ageless talent.

Pastor Randy then stood before the congregation of about 250 people and delivered his simple message, "No matter your past, come to the Lord. He will forgive you of your sins…"

After a very short closing prayer by one of the bikers in the crowd, a line began to form on the left aisle of the church. Hank saw about fifteen people, ranging in age from ten to eighty, standing barefoot wearing old clothes, some in bathing suits, others in leotards while many just wore jeans and a T-shirt.

"Watch this, Hank," Liz whispered, "these people are about to be baptized in that horse trough."

One by one, each person stepped into the trough while Pastor Randy knelt down behind it, asking them if this was their free will decision to accept Christ and receive the Holy Spirit. In the middle of the group was a twenty-something girl wearing black shorts, a black T-shirt, black hair and painted nails and heavy black eye shadow. She seemed to be very anxious about what she was planning to do. She had tattoos on both arms and legs. After Pastor Randy baptized her in the water, she emerged with a huge smile of joy as the black goth-like mascara ran down her face.

"Unbelievable!" Hank said to Liz. "That young lady looks like she's been rode hard and put up wet…She's beaming with joy. I can see it in her eyes."

"Hank, her burdens are gone. She's a new woman with a new future in front of her. No one looks down on anyone here. People are accepted just as they are—sins and all."

"I'll never forget that young lady, Liz. I could see the track marks in her arms. She's obviously a junkie, but a happy one."

"She's the ole lady of one of the biker bosses. He forbid her to come, but hey, she's here and probably for the first time in her life made her own life changing decision. She's free now."

Liz introduced Hank to Pastor Randy and his wife, Pat. Hank kept staring at Mr. Elroy, who was surrounded by a large group of people. He felt that he knew him from somewhere and was especially impressed with his music.

"Liz, could you introduce me to Mr. Elroy?"

"Sure, Hank. Everyone wants to meet him. We'll have to wade through his fans first."

Mr. Elroy was such a humble old man. His white teeth smiled like a beacon from his dark, wrinkled skin. He loved everyone and everyone loved him.

"Mr. Elroy! I'd like you to meet my new friend, Hank Hawkins." Liz gave the old blues singer a big hug.

"My pleasure, Mr. Hank."

"Oh, Mr. Elroy, the pleasure is mine. I've never heard anyone, anyone, play and sing like you. If you ever need a gig, you can play at my club anytime."

"Well, uh, thank ya, Mr. Hank. I been practicing for some time and I do sings a bit."

After the formalities, Hank escorted Liz from the church and back to their awaiting chariot.

"Liz, where does Mr. Elroy live? Seems he should be in a nursing home or something."

"Mr. Elroy lives with Pastor Randy and Pat. They've taken care of him for a long time."

Hank had a simple dinner planned for the rest of his date with Liz. On the way back, Hank still had some questions before he faced the obvious questioning that he knew was coming from her.

"Hank, is all this religious stuff too much for you?"

"Not yet. Just taking it all in. Part of getting to know you, Liz. It seems to be who you are. So tell me, again, what brought you to Tequilaville last night? Who knows, I may even believe it."

Liz laughed. "Here goes, Hank. I was driving my rental car back from the church and just before I got to the hotel, the wheel turned left right out of my hands and I found myself in your parking lot. No further explanation."

"Is that the best line you got, pretty lady?" Hank smiled.

"It's the only line I've got. I'm just being honest," Liz shot back with a smile. "Do you believe in fate?"

"Never thought about it much, Liz. I guess I do now."

"Hank, I got out of the car, walked into the club just in time to hear one of the most amazing, beautiful, heart-felt songs I've ever heard—when Wayne was singing to Abby. I got to witness an accepted proposal of marriage and then you walked into my life. All in all, I'd say that was fate.

"So where are you taking me to dinner? Do I need to go back and change first?"

"Not necessary. You're dressed just right for the occasion."

Driving back from church, Hank looked over at Liz and said, "Pardon me one second," grabbed his cell phone, made a quick call and said, "Five minutes." Then hung up.

Liz noticed that the hotel was near and was hoping that Hank wasn't going to take her to the restaurant there. She'd just about gone through the entire menu and really wasn't looking forward to more hotel food.

Just before arriving at the Bay Hilton, Hank took a quick left into the Tequilaville parking lot. This didn't set too well with Liz, either, as she waited with some apprehension thinking Hank was taking her back to that cigarette-smelling club for a free barbeque meal. *How cheap,* was running through her mind. Her taste buds were geared for sea food. Hank opened the truck door for Liz and walked her around the club to the back deck.

Hank had been busy that Sunday morning preparing for his special date with Liz. He'd asked Tito and Mary to prepare a seafood meal and to set up a table on the back patio of Tequilaville. In Hank's mind, there was no more beautiful view of the lake at night. Mary wanted it to be extra special and brought in a clear canopy with small twinkling lights around the edges.

She placed the table and awning strategically close to the new man-made rock water fall and wading pool that Abby had installed out on the deck a couple of months earlier. Boaters' kids loved to play in it and there was a small shower for water skiers to wash the salt water off their skin before sitting out on the deck to order dinner.

The table was prepared for two only with a white table cloth and a candelabra in the center. Fresh roses finished the décor. She and Tito would serve the meal and then disappear to come back later and clear the deck. The club was always closed from Sunday through Tuesday.

When the moon was high and bright as it was tonight, Clear Lake turned into a moving, silver, glistening lake, adorned by the twinkling lights of the coast line across the water. The setting was simple, beautiful and very romantic. Mary was pleased with her planning. Mr. Hank hadn't had a date since she and Tito could remember, much less invite his family to meet this woman who had just walked into his life.

When Hank and Liz got to the back patio, Liz's eyes lit up.

"Oh Hank, this is beautiful. A table for two, under the moon light. Candles and roses…You are such a romantic! I love it." She reached over and squeezed Hank's hand as he helped her into her seat. Now there was a magic in her eyes.

In front of them was a garden salad, a bread basket with hot rolls and an array of seafood—fried, boiled and baked—that would satisfy the hunger of many more than two. Fresh oysters on the half shell lay on a platter alongside a pitcher of tea, a water pitcher and a small carafe of coffee heated by sterno. The place settings were perfect with all the knives, forks and spoons in order set next to white starched table napkins. Liz had dined at the finest New York restaurants but had never experienced the type of outdoor atmosphere that Hank had planned for her. She was beyond impressed with this simple man who sat across from her with the gray pony tail and close-cut beard.

After they finished eating, Liz became very pensive and said nothing for a few minutes.

"Hank, I've always known that I have the gift of perception. Being able to see beyond a person's thoughts. At the risk of offending you, and I don't mean to do that, could I tell you what I see in your eyes?"

"Sure, go ahead."

"I see sadness in one eye and joy in the other. Could you tell me about your sadness and joy?"

Hank told Liz about being a Marine Recon member and his two tours in Vietnam. He left out the horrors of war stories. Then he told about his one-night stand with Abigail Greene in San Francisco, Abby's mom, and how eight years later he'd received a call from California Child Protective Services confirming that he was the father of Abby. He went on to tell how Abby had been abused in foster care and how he'd brought her home to Clear Lake.

"Touching story, Hank. That explains the sadness and the joy. Your sadness was losing the love of your life. The joy was in finding Abby. Am I close?"

Hank wasn't used to sharing his emotions and was having trouble dealing with them.

"Yeah."

"Hank, do I remind you of Abigail?"

"Since the moment I laid eyes on you, Liz."

"I'm not Abigail. I can't become or compete with a ghost, Hank. And, if that's your unbelievable story, well, it's not that hard to believe. It's a beautiful story."

"Liz, that was then. I'm glad it's just the two of us sitting here talking. The story that I'm about to tell you happened just a few months ago. This may take a while because the story is incomplete. Do you have to be back anytime soon?"

"I'm all ears, Hank..."

Hank began telling Liz about a dream their entire family group experienced on the same night. He prefaced the dream with background details, telling Liz about how Wayne Tyler had shown up at Tequilaville with his many talents, got into a relationship with Abby, a big family squabble concerning Wayne's thought-to-be affair with Bella, how he, himself, had broken Wayne's nose and fired him.

"After Abby kicked Wayne out, he got drunk, hot-wired a friend's boat and cruised out to Red Fish Island in Galveston Bay. That's where the story and the dreams began..."

Hank went on to tell Liz about being in a place—barely remembering the name of the dimension as being Betwixt—where there were angels and demons. He told her about a fifteen-foot angel named Gordon who was Wayne's guardian angel and how Wayne had chosen to face several demons. Hank couldn't remember how many.

"Liz, this was the craziest dream I have ever had in my life. What was really strange was that everyone in our family group had the same dream. We were all there. We even got together later to try and put the pieces together. Like all dreams, some of us remember certain parts but no one could remember everything. It was horrifying what happened there, Liz. It scared the hell out of me, and I don't mind admitting it."

"Keep going Hank. What you are describing is called an epiphany, maybe a theophany, which is a close encounter with God, Himself. What did this place look like?"

"Like an old Roman coliseum. It was huge and Wayne was pretty much on his own while the rest of us sat in the stands. He was elevated on a circular platform about two hundred feet above the ground below—which was constantly changing. Sometimes it was full of snakes and scorpions, sometimes it looked like the pit of hell itself. I told you it was frightening."

"Hank, you're describing how the Christians were murdered by Caesar Nero in Rome. It's written in the Bible."

"Well, Liz, I don't know much about the Bible. I'm just telling you what we all experienced."

"Please continue, Hank."

Hank was uncomfortable even trying to recall the experience. He fidgeted and got up from the table to gather his thoughts.

"You know, Liz, most of these demons were not what a normal person would conceive a demon to be, not like they are depicted in the movies. Some were downright funny, some were manipulative, all were conniving and every one of them was trying to steal Wayne's soul. And we were helpless to go to Wayne's aid. I don't remember all of their names but all of us remembered the name of Baal. He appeared as a huge two-headed, fire-breathing dragon that absolutely demoralized Wayne. If it hadn't been for another angel named Michael, Wayne would have fallen into a pit of fire."

At the sound of *Baal* and *Michael*, Liz knew in an instant that their dreams were true dreams.

"Hank, Baal was a very powerful false god that the Israelites worshipped. He demanded the sacrifice of children and drew God's wrath upon the Israelites. And Michael, well, Michael is the archangel that is God's general over all of heaven's armies. He replaced Lucifer as the archangel when God cast him out of heaven. One third of the angels followed Lucifer, who God renamed Satan. They were the fallen angels mentioned in the Bible. They exist. They are very powerful and all bad. What else happened?"

"There was another angel but I can't remember his name..."

"Hank, there are only three angels called by name in the Bible. The third one is Gabriel. Does that sound familiar?"

"Yeah! That was his name. Hey, that's your last name, Gabriel."

"Coincidental, Hank. Gabriel is God's messenger angel. You and your group of friends are so blessed to have seen them. What did they look like?"

"I wish I could tell you, Liz. I just don't remember all the details. We tried to get together and write down what we remembered, but there are so many gaps.

"The next thing we recalled is that we got a call from the Coast Guard about rescuing Wayne from Galveston Bay. They thought he was involved in some kind of drug deal. They helicoptered Wayne to the county hospital in Houston where he was in a coma for a while and came down with bacterial meningitis. That's why he's in a wheel chair. Did you notice that white streak of hair over Wayne's right ear?"

"I saw it but didn't really think anything about it. Is that significant, Hank?"

"Very! He didn't have that…mark until he came back. There's also someone you haven't met yet, a Lieutenant Stan Stark who is a chaplain in the Coast Guard, who has the same mark and told us that he, too, had a similar experience when he was eighteen years old which began in the same place, Red Fish Island."

"Is there more to this story, Hank?"

"Yeah, Liz, there is, but we'd be here all night. It's frustrating not to be able to put everything together. It's also draining. All we know is that Wayne came back a changed man. He kept saying that he knew what love was and tried to describe it but couldn't. I guess the end result of the whole experience we all shared was that Wayne wrote Abby that song you heard and they're getting married. What more do we need to know?"

Hank walked out to the edge of the deck looking across the lake. Liz walked up beside him and took his hand.

"Thank you for sharing that with me, Hank. I know it wasn't easy."

With Hank's hand in hers, she faced him and looked right into his eyes. The moment was almost overwhelming for Hank.

"Liz, I haven't kissed a woman on the lips since I can remember but I'm getting the urge to hold you close to me and kiss you. Would you mind?"

Liz released her hold on Hank's hands and placed them on either side of Hank's face. Pulling him down to her level, just as their lips were about to meet, she smiled and said, "Not yet…"

3

Close Your Eyes Revelation

Abby put in a call to her friend Hattie Lang at the NASA accounting office.

"Hey, girlfriend, this is Abby. How's the space business doing?"

"It's slow. With all the budget cuts, we don't have a lot to do. What's up with you?"

Abby wasn't sure how to get into the conversation she wanted to have with Hattie, about finding a psychologist for Wayne, so she just dove in. Hattie had been a trusted friend for a long time and had been present at Wayne's birthday party at the rehab center when Lieutenant Stark showed up and spilled the beans about Wayne's ordeal. Hattie had heard a lot about the dreams and knew who had been present at Betwixt but had never breathed a word to anyone.

"Hattie, I think Wayne is suffering from some sort of PTSD from his, uh, trip that we all talked about. Would you happen to know anyone, like a psychologist, who deals with this sort of thing? Wayne needs some help. He's so different these days…"

"Funny you should mention this, Abby. Just yesterday I was having lunch with Belinda Sealy. She's the assistant to Dr. Eric Palmer. He's the leading parapsychologist in the whole United States, maybe in the world. He's got an MD in Psychiatry with a Ph.D. in Parapsychology. He counsels our astronauts about unexplainable things they see in space. We lovingly refer to him as NASA's 'ghost buster.' If he's not too busy, I'll ask Belinda if he'd be interested in talking to you and Wayne. How's that?"

"That would be great, Hattie, but I'll have to trust you to be discreet. I don't want people to think we're all crazy. Don't tell him everything you know. Just give him my number and I'll talk to him."

"Abby, if you only knew some of the things our astronauts have seen, and I don't even know, it's so top secret. Dr. Palmer can be trusted. If there were ever any sightings of 'little green men,' he would know about it but no one else would. He's been vetted by the F.B.I. and has the highest security clearances."

"Thanks, Hattie. I'll await his call."

Hattie put in an inner-office call to Belinda and began briefly telling her about Wayne and Abby's experience in that unknown dimension. Belinda was intrigued and told her that might be right up her boss's alley. She'd talk to him and get back to her.

Within ten minutes, Dr. Palmer called Hattie.

"Ms. Lang? Dr. Palmer. Tell me more about your friends, uh, Mr. Tyler and Ms. Hawkins. Belinda tells me they and several other people claim to have gone to another dimension in space and time in some kind of a joint dream they had…"

"Dr. Palmer, it's the wildest story you've ever heard. Wayne, uh, Mr. Tyler, came back with a white streak over his right ear that'd never been there before and was a completely changed man from the experience. If you're interested, I'll give you Abby Hawkins' cell number. She's engaged to Wayne."

"I'm more than interested, Ms. Lang. I need to publish some white papers for my profession and since everything at NASA is classified, well, this would be an interesting project for me. And, I'll counsel with them on a *pro bono* basis if it amounts to anything."

Hattie gave Dr. Palmer Abby's number and within a few of minutes, he was talking to her.

Abby began her story hesitantly, telling Dr. Palmer about several of their friends dreaming the same dream on the same night and witnessing some terrible events in an unknown dimension.

"Dr. Palmer, some of the things our group can't figure out, even after we met and wrote down everything each of us remembered. Even though we all witnessed the same things, we saw the events through our own eyes and if I recalled something, it didn't necessarily cause anyone else to remember it. It was like we all had our versions. Each of us remember bits and pieces of the events, but no one remembers it all."

"Ms. Hawkins…"

"Please call me Abby, Dr. Palmer."

"Abby, I can give you my personal email address. Would it be possible for you to write down the names of everyone you remember who was present and send the list to me along with the notes that your group has written down?"

"I'll have to get their permission, Dr. Palmer. I don't know who will talk about it and who won't. I know Wayne and I will be happy to meet with you. Can you give me a few days on the email?"

"Sure, Abby. But I would like to get a complete list…"

"Including the angels and demons?"

"Angels and demons? Are you telling me that all of you actually saw angels and demons?"

"Yessir. We certainly did. Dr. Palmer, do you believe they exist? And will you agree to keep this confidential? My dad, Hank Hawkins, and I, own Tequilaville across the street from NASA. If this got out, it could hurt our business if you know what I mean…"

"I assure you, Abby, it will be highly confidential and if I do write a paper on this, I won't mention your names. I have a non-disclosure and confidentiality contract that we can all sign even though there is always a professional doctor/patient privilege clause that is accepted by law. Will that be enough for you?"

"Probably. I'll check with the rest of my group. Dr. Palmer, you didn't answer my question about believing in angels and demons."

"Abby, I'm a scientist. I believe in facts, but I do keep an open mind. I have to in my profession."

Sara begin playing on Hank's cell phone.

"Hi, Sweetie Pie. How's everything with you and Wayne? How's his rehab coming along?"

"Daddy Hank, that's what I called about. Wayne and I had a long talk. He's, uh, I don't know how to put this…He's different. I think he may be suffering from some sort of PTSD and need some help in dealing with what happened."

"Different? In what ways, Abby?"

"Don't get me wrong, Dad. Wayne's changed for the best, but I think he's lost his passion for music and performing…"

"That's not good, Abby! He's our headliner, our draw, our main attraction at the club."

"Yeah, I know. Not too good for business, Pop, but Wayne's about to be my husband. Right now he can't walk, he certainly can't perform and I need to get him some professional help to get him back to whatever his new normal is going to be in the future."

"So what's your plan?"

"Pop, I called Hattie Lang over at NASA. She referred me to a Dr. Eric Palmer. He counsels the astronauts. He's interested in talking to all of us as a group. Would you be willing to attend a meeting with everyone? He's doing this on a *pro bono* basis so it won't cost anyone anything."

"If it will help you and Wayne, I have no problem showing up. He's not going to play with our heads, is he?"

"Don't know what his plan is, Dad. I'm just trying to get a meeting set with him. He'll keep everything confidential."

"I'm a little skeptical about shrinks, Abby, but I'm willing to show up. Let me know when and where and I'll contact the others who were there."

"Great Dad. So how was your big date with Liz?"

"She's interesting. She kind of makes my life come to life again. I'll tell you more later. Don't want to kiss and tell…"

"Did you kiss her, Dad?"

"Not yet."

"But you wanted to didn't you, Dad? When are you going to see her again? You know that women want to be pursued. I'm excited!"

"Slow down, Abby. We'll just see how this plays out. Let me know about Dr. Palmer. I'll call the others and you may want to ask the doctor if we can meet here at Tequilaville."

"Will do, Pop. And thanks!"

At the club, Hank met with Tito and Mary, T-Bone, Scott Wood, and put in calls to Robbie and Bella, along with Lieutenant Stan Stark. They all agreed to an initial meeting with Dr. Palmer, but several of them had reservations about what he wanted to discover and what they wanted to share with him. If it would help Wayne, they would attend, but most of the group, without actually admitting it, didn't want to revisit their out of body experience again.

On the day of the meeting, one-by-one the non-employees of the club drifted in. Robbie was wearing scrubs, Bella made her usual entrance as if the meeting were being held in her honor…

"Hey, all you spooks! Let's get this party rolling. I've got houses to sell! I can't wait to hear what all's going on. How's it hanging, Mr. Hank?"

"Bella! My gosh! What a thing to say. You're going to be the death of me, child!" Robbie shot back.

Lieutenant Stark arrived in his Coast Guard uniform, looking very sharp and reserved.

"I love a man in uniform, Lieutenant Stan. We should get together sometime!" Bella was always looking for a new adventure.

Lieutenant Stark smiled at her and gave everyone a hug trying to escape the embarrassment of Bella's very forward, obvious advance.

Wayne entered the club walking on his walker, Abby by his side. It was apparent that the months of physical therapy were having a positive effect on Wayne. He could take several steps before having to depend on his rolling support apparatus and was close to walking on his own. Abby was all smiles as the women wanted to get a closer look at her engagement ring. She was beaming; she was happy and it showed.

The last to arrive at Tequilaville was Dr. Palmer and his assistant, Belinda Sealy. After introductions and credentials were presented, they agreed to go by first names for simplicity's sake. Dr. Palmer assured them of complete confidentiality and everyone signed the Non-Disclosure and release forms he had brought with him.

"I'm so glad to meet everyone. I've heard a lot about your experience and sincerely hope that I can help each of you fill in some gaps. Abby has graciously sent me the notes that your group took about your journey into the unknown and I've had a chance to go over them. I have to say that I'm very intrigued."

"You're sure not what I expected you to look like, Dr. Palmer!" Bella blurted out.

"I'm sorry, uh, Bella, is it? How did you envision me to look?"

"Oh, like some bushy-haired Einstein look-alike with little round glasses. I think all the brainy types at NASA look like that." Bella found Dr. Palmer attractive and immediately gave him a little flirty wink.

Dr. Palmer looked as though he was in his late forties or early fifties, a distinguished looking man about average height, with graying light brown hair, trim and. Wearing a blue shirt and red tie, he had lots of pens and pencils in his shirt pocket.

"Sorry to disappoint, Bella." Palmer returned the glance. "Today I would just like to get to know all of you and try to reach a comfort zone with everyone. I'm open to any questions you may have."

Hank spoke up and asked Dr. Palmer to explain to the group how he was going to conduct his investigation.

"Good question, Hank. Today I'm trying to establish a time-line of the events like when each of you went to bed on the night in question and the earliest recollection of the time that you awakened from the dream.

"I have a small office suite with a conference room just down the street. We can meet there if that is convenient. I want to meet with everyone individually, but Wayne and Abby are first so I can concentrate on his experience. That will give me more insight to work with Wayne, who seems to be the center of attention in this dream you all had. My assistant, Belinda

Sealy, can set up each appointment. She'll give you her card with all of the contact information."

"Dr. Palmer, I have another question." Hank was always direct. "Are you planning on using hypnosis as part of this discovery process?"

"If necessary, Hank. I use hypnosis on the astronauts all the time. It often leads to things we can't recall and can yield a lot of information in a short amount of time. Have you ever been under hypnosis before?"

"No, doc, and I'm not sure I want to go there."

"Understandable, Hank. I assure you that you're free to bring a witness or a friend to the sessions if you so choose and my assistant will always be present to give you a higher comfort level."

"Good enough, doc."

Belinda scheduled all of the appointments an hour apart for Mondays and Tuesdays while the club was closed. Dr. Palmer studied the groups' notes very carefully. When Wayne and Abby had a conflict due to Wayne's therapy sessions, Palmer chose to interview Lieutenant Stan Stark first since the notes revealed that he had visited Betwixt twice in his life. Palmer was also intrigued with the white streak of hair that Wayne and Stark shared. This could be a baseline of proof that the experience was real.

As a standard operational procedure, Dr. Palmer always began each session asking the participants to give a brief back story on themselves. This helped to create a comfortable setting to go forward and it also gave him much needed cultural, ethnic and religious backgrounds from which to get greater insight into their educational levels, past life experiences and other outside influences that may cause each person to respond differently to his questions. He was trained in F.B.I. psychological profiling and planned to profile each patient.

Stark entered the office suite wearing his civvies, jeans and tennis shoes and an old wrinkled denim shirt. Belinda Sealy was present and took notes for the doctor.

"Tell me, Lieutenant, what was the most memorable picture in your mind of your two trips to this unknown dimension?"

"Hell."

"Hell? Describe what it looked and felt like to you."

"Horror, complete horror. The heat was so intense I don't have words to describe it. If Gordon hadn't been there to protect us, we would all have been completely burned up. The pit was like a crevice opening in the ground, like in an earthquake that had an endless bottom. It reeked of the smell of sulfur. I'm telling you, Dr. Palmer, hell is real, it exists. I saw it twice."

Dr. Palmer could see the grimace on the lieutenant's face and how uncomfortable he was talking about the experience. That puzzled the parapsychologist since Lieutenant Stark was an ordained minister in the Coast Guard.

"But of course, Lieutenant, you would believe that hell exists if you studied the Bible and believe what's written in it. Wasn't that part of your training at your seminary?"
"Yes it was, Doctor. But reading about it, believing in something I've never seen is one thing. Actually viewing it, feeling it and smelling it is another thing. I'm telling you, hell is real! Are you a Christian, Dr. Palmer?"

"Let's just say that for the present I'm an agnostic, a scientist who seeks the truth. Tell me about the white streak of hair over your right ear. How did that happen and did you have that trait before your first experience with Betwixt?"

"I can't explain it, Doctor. When I went to Betwixt when I was eighteen years old, I didn't have the streak. When I returned from that experience, I did have it. No explanation that I know of."

"With your permission, Lieutenant, I'd like to take a sample of the white hair and run some DNA tests through our data bases."

"Fine with me."

Dr. Palmer cut a small segment of hair from the white streak and placed it into a small zip-lock bag and ended the first session. It was time for his next appointment, Bella Cantrell, who arrived alone.

Lieutenant Stark bumped into Bella in the foyer of the office suite as he was leaving.

"Hi, Lady!" Stark said with a smile.

"Hey, you handsome hunk of man, you!" Bella said in her usual flirtatious manner, walking over to Stark and giving him a close, sensual hug. She'd had her eye on the lieutenant since they first met. "Are you ever going to call me? I'm open for dinner any time you are. Here's my card."

Bella was wearing her work clothes, a very expensive dark suit, spike heels and a low-cut blouse clearly showing her cleavage. Her long dark hair and makeup were perfect. She gave the lieutenant a little wave as she walked into Dr. Palmer's conference room. For a brief moment, the good Lieutenant had to remember he was a chaplain. Bella had certainly gotten his attention. Until now, he hadn't thought about asking her out, but he was single and the opportunity was certainly presenting itself—clearly presenting itself, or herself.

Bella has such a great personality, Stark thought to himself… *Yeah, right! It's her personality I'm interested in!*

"Have a seat, Bella. I see that you didn't bring anyone with you. You know my assistant, Belinda?"

"Hey, Belinda. have you ever thought of a new do for your hair? It's okay now, but my hairdresser could do wonders for you."

Belinda had curly red hair usually pulled back in a loose pony tail and wasn't exactly a slave to fashion. She maintained her professional look with bland colored suits and horn-rimmed glasses. A little overweight, she hadn't dated anyone in years and made her career at NASA her life. She smiled sheepishly and passed off the small insult from Bella.

Dr. Palmer could tell that Bella was a free-spirit type and immediately gave her a quick once-over glance. She was gorgeous, smart, quick-witted and would probably be easier to open up than the rest. He looked forward to the session with her.

"So, Bella, tell me the most memorable event you can recall about this place called Betwixt."

"That's easy, Doc…"

"Do call me Eric, Bella. Please continue."

"Well, Eric, and by the way, you never asked me for my phone number. When are we getting together?"

For a moment, Belinda felt like a third party on a date but regained her professional composure, sitting silently and continuing to take notes. She decided that Bella was the most forward woman she'd ever met and began to dislike her.

"Maybe later, Bella. You were saying, 'That's easy…'"

"Yeah, Eric." Bella's expression turned to a quick serious face, which was totally out of character for this flamboyant, young, beautiful lady. "It scared the hell out of me. I still have bad dreams about it. Hey, maybe you could counsel me about those dreams…say, over a couple of drinks sometime. And since you're not going to ask me for my number in front of your secretary, here it is."

Bella pulled out her realtor's card with her contact information on it and slid it across the table to Dr. Palmer.

Belinda couldn't believe the audacity she was witnessing and looked over at Dr. Palmer to see how he was going to react. He just smiled back at Bella and put the card in his shirt pocket.

"What or who scared the hell out of you, Bella?"

"Hell! I saw it and I can't get the memory of it out of my mind. I mean it was hot, it smelled terrible, even though I think I was wearing my best perfume, and well, I just don't want to talk about it anymore."

"Okay, let's move on. What was another thing you remember about the experience?"

"I remember Ishtar, that slutty witch. She thought she was sooo gorgeous and beautiful. She wasn't in my opinion. All she wanted to do was seduce Wayne right there in front of my little sister, Abby."

"Who was Ishtar, Bella?"

"I think she said that she was Satan's main squeeze or something. Like a concubine…whatever that is. I just wanted to pull her hair out by the roots. Oh, I almost forgot, she had a tail."

Dr. Palmer and Belinda were both holding back horse laughs that they almost couldn't contain. Bella was a trip. Her descriptions were so off the cuff and basically honest. That began to concern Palmer. He believed she was telling the truth just from the spontaneous emotions and expressions on her face.

"Thank you, Bella. That should be all for today. Our hour is just about up. I'll have Belinda contact you for our next appointment."

"You better call me yourself, Eric. I'm not one for waiting; besides, I want you to help me with those bad dreams. No offense, Belinda."

Next on the appointment list was Tito, the karate master, services manager at the club and his wife, Mary. Both Latinos. Dr. Palmer was interested in getting their views on the experience since he guessed that they were Catholic. When they entered the conference room, T-Bone, the six-foot-seven, 285-pound bouncer and former motorcycle gang member was with them along with Scott Wood. They had a lot of work to do at the club and asked Dr. Palmer if they could all come at once.

"No problem. If you all feel comfortable talking in front of each other, I can do a small group session; however, in the future I would like to meet with you separately. Since you are all here together, I want to make sure that one person's answer to my next question is not an influence on anyone else's answer. Take a minute and think of the main thing you remember most about your time at Betwixt and write a one word or, at most, a paragraph answer on the sheet of paper in front of you and give it back to me."

For a brief moment, they all looked at each other. This was exactly why Dr. Palmer didn't like to begin his research with more than one or two people present.

One by one they handed their written answers to Dr. Palmer. Tito wrote: The Lake of Fire. Mary wrote: Hell. T-Bone wrote down: The Pit. Scott wrote on his piece of paper: The Abyss.

"Thank you. Now who would like to go first and tell me about what you have written down?" Palmer was amazed that they had all described the same horrific memory.

"I'll start off," Tito said with a firm look on his face. Mary gripped his hand in hers. "It was bad, doctor. This place was solid bad, scary and I'm not scared of much…"

Tito was fidgeting and took a long deep breath.

"Go on," Palmer said.

"The thing that I remember most was that lake of fire."

"Yeah, me too!" T-Bone chimed in. "The pit. It scared even me."

"Count me in on that one, Doc," Scott Wood added. "I never want to experience that abyss again. I have bad dreams about it and can't get it out of my mind."

"We're all having bad dreams, Doctor," Mary said with a frightened expression on her face. "I was raised Catholic, just like Tito and T-Bone, and we've always believed in a purgatory. We didn't see any purgatory. And Wayne never had any choice of purgatory. It was just going up or going down if you know what I mean. I thought for sure Wayne was going to wind up in hell. We almost lost him."

Dr. Palmer observed the true fright in each of their eyes. "What choices are you talking about? Who had choices and who gave them the choices?"

"That's part of what none of us can remember, Doc," Scott said. "We all remember Gordon talking about free choice and free will, so there must have been choices for Wayne to make. We've all gone over this in our minds for quite some time trying to figure it out. When we only have pieces to the puzzle, like you, doc, we try to fill in the gaps. So far none of us has been able to do that.

"We all saw Wayne falling into the pit but none of us can figure out what he did to avoid it. He was just falling and then the pit was gone and angels started showing up."

"What angels? What did they look like?"

Now Mary was excited and had a hopeful look on her face. "It was Michael, the arch angel. He came down on a lightning bolt and had a sword in his hands that had eyes all over it. He cleared away the pit and the tribulations were over. He was a mighty angel and was very powerful, brilliant, muscles, glowing. That's all I remember, Dr. Palmer."

"Anything else anyone would like to add about what you remembered?"

"The stage!" Scott was opening up and his dark expression changed. His own life and dedication to music set him on fire. "The stars on the stage were like holograms, uh, I can't really put it into words…Images of some of the greatest musical artists, past and present, who had been music divas. Garth Brooks, Stevie Ray Vaughn, Eric Clapton and some others I didn't know. Some were already dead and gone, others are still here today. It was confusing and it was spectacular, the sounds were so clear, mesmerizing. It was the greatest musical performance ever. Wayne was up there on that stage jamming with them…"

"Interesting and descriptive, Scott," Dr. Palmer added. "Was there a reason for this that you can remember?"

"You bet I remember. There was some demon who said he was a star god. He promised Wayne stardom, fame, money, women, anything he wanted if he would sign a contract with him. You should have seen this demon's office. He had Platinum and Gold record plaques all over the walls."

"Could you see the names of the recording artists on the plaques, Scott?"

"Nah. We couldn't read the names…something about a privacy clause in the contract."

"Scott, did Wayne sign the contract? And what was his price for stardom? Do you remember that?"

"Yessir, I do. Wayne had to sign his soul over to the demon. But, I gotta tell you something about Wayne. He's a purist when it comes to his music. He wouldn't sign a record contract before all of this happened because he didn't want a record label to own his life so he wouldn't sign the demon's contract. I respect Wayne Tyler for that."

Since the group of four that had just left his office created some time before his next appointment with Hank Hawkins and Robbie Cantrell, Dr. Palmer had a chance to think about what he was hearing and the obvious similar accounts that each person had given. He could tell this was a tight-knit group of people and wondered if they had just made up the story collectively.

"Belinda, you've been with me while we interviewed some of our astronauts and heard some of their experiences in outer space. What do you make of this so far?"

"Dr. Palmer, I don't know what to make of it. They all seem to be sincere. They all have such diversified personalities with their own ways of explaining their views. I mean, I only have a Masters in Psychology but for the life of me, their stories don't fit into any known quadrants of truth or lies that I know about. Compared to the astronaut stories we have heard, I'd put this experience at the top of our list of the most *out there* stories ever. What do you think? I'd really be interested to hear your views."

"I'm still taking an objective view for now, Belinda. There's so much more of this to hear and understand. If they're lying, I'll catch them sooner or later. If they are telling the truth, this could be one of the greatest studies known in my field. I mean, just imagine…people actually going to another dimension in time and space and living to tell about it. We've got astrophysicists and theoretical physicists working on these areas now.

"I can't wait to get the DNA samples analyzed from Lieutenant Stark and Wayne's streaks of hair. I hope he'll allow me to take samples. They could tell a separate story all their own. Is it time for Mr. Hawkins and Ms. Cantrell's appointment?"

"They're both right outside, Dr. Palmer. Are you ready for them?"

4

On The Fence
Girls just want to have fun!

Hank and Robbie walked into Dr. Palmer's conference room. Robbie immediately took a seat across from Belinda Sealy while Hank strolled along the wall reading all of Dr. Palmer's degrees—M.D. Psychiatry, Ph.D. Parapsychology, F.B.I. Profiling Certificates, signed letters and pictures from astronaut patients and former Presidents of the United States.

Dr. Palmer waited patiently for Hank to finish his review, not wanting to rush things. He sensed that Hank might be difficult about divulging much of his experience and made some mental notes about asking Hank about his background.

"I hope I measure up to your expectations, Hank," Palmer said. "Are you ready to get started?"

"I have no expectations, Doc. I'm ready if Robbie is." Degrees or no degrees, Hank was skeptical when it came to shrinks.

"Could you both tell me a little about yourselves? What you do, how you got to Clear Lake, about your kids? Just a brief back story on yourselves if you don't mind."

Robbie went first, telling Dr. Palmer about being a widow, being careful to leave out the details of her husband's death for obvious reasons. She went into detail about her nursing background and the love of her life, her daughter Bella, describing her as a *free spirit, beautiful wild child* that listened to no one and cut her own path.

"I've talked to Bella, Robbie. She is indeed unique in her outlook on life. You should be proud of her."

"I'm very proud of her, Dr. Palmer. She's got some rough edges, but time should take care of that. I've got faith that it will."

"Could I ask what your relationship is with Mr. Hawkins just so I can understand…"

"We're like brother and sister. We raised our daughters together and they're like sisters. Hank sort of provided fatherly guidance to Bella…"

Hank laughed and broke in, "Yeah, Robbie, I tried but I'm not so sure how effective I've been as a father figure to Bella."

"…and I've tried to be a mother figure to Abby. They are both so different."

"In what ways?" Palmer asked.

Robbie pondered a moment then said, "Abby is so grounded, disciplined, responsible, very deep in her thinking at times…Bella is just the opposite but each is unique and Hank and I love both of them equally."

"So you have raised your girls as mother and father without being married?"

"Correct," Robbie said. "Hank and I are BFFs. He's my rock and I'm his confidant. It's a great relationship and we love each other deeply." Robbie reached over and squeezed Hank's hand.

Belinda made notes during the conversation being careful to be almost unnoticed. She never interrupted Dr. Palmer as he continued his probe into this mystery.

"Robbie, what is the main thing that you remembered from your dream?"

"This experience confirmed my faith as a Christian."

"How so, Robbie?"

"I read my Bible, go to church and hear sermons. What I experienced confirmed everything that I've read. I saw hell and I saw a little bit of heaven's glory. I saw hate in the demons and I saw saving grace at the end of Wayne's ordeal.

"When Wayne got to the end of himself and began falling into the fire from that platform, you cannot imagine the terror, the stench of his burning flesh and the hopelessness on his face. It was the single most horrific moment of my entire life…"

"Do you know how Wayne's ordeal ended? What saved him from the fire?"

"I haven't asked him, Dr. Palmer, but the Bible says that anyone who calls upon name of The Lord will be saved. I have to guess that this is what Wayne did just before he entered the pit. There's really no other explanation.

"Can I ask you a question, Dr. Palmer?"

"Sure, Robbie, go ahead."

"Have you read the Bible? I mean, you've already told us that you're a scientist and an agnostic, Doctor, but do you believe in a higher power?"

"Robbie, I have read every holy book of all the religions of the world. I find things that I agree with and things that I don't in all of them."

"Do you believe in a judgment? In a hell?"

"Robbie, I can see that you believe in them, but I'm more interested in the facts surrounding this experience than I am what everyone believes."

All the time that Dr. Palmer was interviewing Robbie, Hank sat silent staring into the doctor's eyes, trying to get a read on him before divulging any of his story to him. Hank appreciated the direct questions that Robbie asked the doctor and began forming a few of his own.

"Very good, Robbie. I've asked each person that I've counseled with to email me any other facts they may remember. Would you do the same?"

Robbie acknowledged that she would.

"Hank, what is the most memorable thing you remembered about your dream?"

"I've got a few questions for you first, Doc," Hank said authoritatively.

"Shoot, Hank."

"You've heard about some of our histories and lives, but you haven't told us anything about you. I like to know who I'm dealing with. Have you ever been married and what is your story?"

"Hank, I'm here to help Wayne, Abby and everyone else who shared this experience. I'm not here to tell you about me. You can see my credentials on the wall…"

"Then I'm not telling you jack, Doc! Credentials don't make the man. Trust is a two-way street. You share, I share. Take it or leave it."

"Fair enough, Hank. I'll tell you what I can since most of it is classified. I was married for a brief time when I was working on my Ph.D. at the University of Edinburgh in Scotland. She, too, was getting her Ph.D. in the same field. She was originally from Norway and her name is Helle…"

"Hell? Doc, her name is hell?" Hank cracked a smile, then added, "I'm no authority on marriage but that should have told you something…"

"No, no, Hank. Helle is a very common name in Norway. It's pronounced Hel-lay, not hell." Dr. Palmer chuckled. He continued.

"After three years, we each went our own way if you know what I mean. Being from a neutral country in Europe, she counseled many of the Russian cosmonauts in paranormal situations just as I have counseled U.S. astronauts in similar cases.

"I've also consulted with Interpol, the F.B.I., NSA and CIA, again all classified. While I was consulting for the F.B.I., I profiled and helped capture many mass murderers and later interviewed them when they were sentenced and went to prison…"

"So you've seen death, Doc?"

"More than I can say, Hank. Humankind can be very barbaric at times. Will that suffice for my back story?"

"Good enough. And how did you deal with all this barbarism that you've experienced, Dr. Palmer?"

"To be honest, death often becomes horrific memories. Men, even like myself, tend to contain bad experiences and place a padlock on them in our minds. In my case, my containers are double padlocked. Have you seen a lot of death and gore, Hank?"

Hank began opening up and telling Palmer about his two tours in Vietnam as a behind-the-lines Marine Recon team member.

"But most of this was classified, Doc. I'm sure you can identify with that…"

Hank continued telling about his one-night stand in San Francisco and the love child that came out of it. He didn't mention that Abby had been abused in foster care; that was their secret. He continued with how he got custody of Abby, brought her to Clear Lake and began working as an electrician. Later, when Abby was grown, they opened up Tequilaville.

"Thank you for your service, Hank. Semper Fi!"

Hank just nodded with little or no emotion.

"Could we get back to my original question now, Hank? What were the most memorable moments that you can recall from your experience?"

"Baal! I remember Baal, Doc."

"Hmmm. Baal was a god that the Canaanites and the Israelites worshipped long ago. He also had other names such as Molech. This god required child sacrifice from his followers. Did you know about this, Hank?"

"Not really, Doc. I haven't studied the Bible much…"

"Hank, are you a Christian?"

"Not yet, but after that dream I'm leaning that way."

"Hank, I can tell by your military background that not much frightens you. You truly have a warrior spirit. But you mention Baal as your most memorable moment and not the fires of hell. Did Baal frighten you and what did he look like?"

"Quite frankly, Doc, Baal didn't frighten me, he just pissed me off!"

"How so, Hank?"

"When we arrived at that place, Betwixt, I had just broken Wayne's nose shortly before thinking he had cheated on my daughter—which we later found out was a false accusation. I watched Wayne face many demons—I can't remember them all—and how they tried to trick him, manipulate him and finally Baal tried to annihilate him by ripping him to shreds, literally. No man should have to face all of this alone.

"Baal appeared as a two-headed, fire-breathing dragon that was big as the sky above. Wayne was by himself up there on that platform and the handwriting was on the wall for him. He couldn't fight this thing. I wanted to go up there and fight with him. I wanted a sword in my hand about fifteen-feet long to cut both the heads off that hellish creature. I actually wanted to come to Wayne's defense, but I was helpless to help him…And that, Doc, pisses me off! I was restrained. Yes, you bet I have a warrior spirit and it was going nuts to assist Wayne. I never want to go back to that place, but if I did, I'd kick some butt! Damn right, Semper Fi!"

Hank's eyes were blazing. Everyone in the conference room could see the veins in his neck begin to tense and the fearless expression on his face.

"Not much scares you does it, Hank?" Palmer said, trying to calm the man's emotions.

"Not much!"

Early the next morning, Wayne and Abby came in for their first individual appointment with Dr. Palmer. Belinda greeted them and led them into the conference room. Wayne had his walker and Abby helped him every step of the way even though it was clear that Wayne would be able to walk on his own with a little more therapy. They took their seats around the conference table as Dr. Palmer began.

"I hear that congratulations are in order for the two of you," Palmer said with a smile. "I hope you both will be very happy with your life together."

"That's why we're here, Dr. Palmer." Abby gave Wayne a kiss on the cheek. Wayne put his arm around Abby.

"Let's start with you, Abby. What's the most memorable thing you remember about your dream?"

Abby closed her eyes for several seconds. As she opened them, a smile came across her face. Palmer thought this very odd after hearing from the others about the ghoulish setting and experiences they had undergone. The doctor waited patiently for her answer.

"I remember Wayne telling me—not by voice, but telepathically when he was about to fall into the flames—that he loved me. I so wanted to hear those words, even knowing that it appeared he was about to die. Those sweet words could have carried me the rest of my life. I wanted to die in his place;

I love him that much, Dr. Palmer." Tears boiled up in Abby's eyes as Wayne was fighting back a few of his own.

"What else, Abby?"

"I remember Gordon, Wayne's angel, telling us that Wayne still had some decisions to make and that there were no guarantees that Wayne would return to us. I didn't understand what else Wayne had to decide or what would happen. Gordon had such a peaceful nature about him and actually gave me peace about what would happen next. Then I woke up from the dream thinking I had to find Wayne. I had the strangest feeling that he was in danger because I didn't really give the dream much thought. I considered it a temporary nightmare.

"When I found out that Daddy Hank, Robbie, Bella and the others had the same dream, I was frantic to find Wayne. Then we got the call from the Coast Guard and rushed to the hospital. Wayne was alive! That's all that mattered."

"Thank you, Abby. Let me know of anything else you remember. I'd like to get to Wayne now. Wayne, how did you get to Betwixt?"

"Gordon flew me there from Between."

Dr. Palmer looked over at Belinda to make sure she was writing this down. Palmer hadn't heard of Between yet.

"What is Between, Wayne? How did you get there and what did it look like?"

"I haven't a clue, doc. I got drunk, hot-wired a boat, putted out to Red Fish Island and fell into the water. Next thing I knew I was in this misty place, dry, breathing normally, not drunk, when I saw Gordon. He said that he was like my guardian angel. I told him I didn't believe in all that stuff so he stuck out his hand and I touched it. That freaked me out, kinda like pinching yourself to see if something is real or imagined. I asked him where I was and he said Between, between heaven and hell…"

"And you don't know how you got there?"

"No, I don't, Dr. Palmer. All I know is that Gordon said I had some decisions to make and to face some demons. If they won, I would be done. If I made it through the ordeals, I would know what love is. That's it. I'm telling you what I remember."

"What made the most lasting impression on you, Wayne, from everything you do remember?"

"That's easy, Doc. I saw, felt and experienced love. That part's hard to explain…"

"Where did that part happen?"

"At Betwixt, on a hill after everyone was gone. I actually went blank from the time I was falling into the fire until after everyone else had left."

"Describe the hill, Wayne. What did love feel like?"

Wayne thought for a few minutes trying to find the words to describe the indescribable.

"When I woke up…the lake of fire, the ghoulish figures on the dark side of the stadium were all gone. Doc, that wasn't that unusual since the field below the platform changed many times from hell pits, to snake pits, you name it. But when I awoke, the field was beautiful. Flowers everywhere, rainbows—many rainbows—all over the sky. There were animals that were normally enemies on the earth, like tigers and goats, lying down beside each other eating grass. It was fantastic.

"Then Gordon led me up the hill to claim my prize of knowing what love is. But, Doc, I can't describe it. It's something you would just have to experience."

"Wayne, it seems part of this big mystery is how you escaped the flames after you fell off the platform. Do you remember that?"

"Sure do, Doc. I saw a hand, an arm reaching out to me from eye level as I was falling. It was Jesus."

"Interesting. How do you know it was Jesus?"

"I don't know, Doc. I just knew. That's the best I got for you. Words just rolled out of my mouth when I saw His hand…"

"What words, Wayne?"

"I said, 'Save me Jesus,' and He did!"

"Just like that, Wayne?"

"Just like that, Doc. I told you there was lots I can't comprehend about this thing. I hope this helps to put the pieces together."

Dr. Palmer realized at that point that he was going to have to hypnotize Wayne and possibly others in the group to get more answers. The borders of this puzzle were beginning to form but still so many pieces missing.

"Wayne, think back. What happened after you came down from the hill where you experienced love. Do you remember what happened next and how you got back from Betwixt?"

"I do remember. There was a portal, a door that was always present at Betwixt. Gordon wouldn't tell me in advance what it was or what it was for until I came down from the hill. Then he told me that this was a portal to heaven and that I could enter it and never again feel pain or suffering…"

"A portal to heaven? That must have been tempting. So what happened next, Wayne? How did you get back to earth?"

"I had to write Abby that love song. If I went through the portal, I could never have written it for her and told her how much I loved her. 'Cause, Doc, I knew what love was for the first time in my life. It's the most wonderful feeling anywhere—on earth or wherever I was. I told Gordon to send me back…"

"Back into fourteen feet of water? Drunk? Almost lifeless?"

"Yep. That pretty much sizes up the situation. Gordon sent me back and the Coast Guard rescued me. That's the best truth that I got, Doc. Believe it or not. I haven't seen or talked to Gordon since."

"Wayne, what an amazing story. I talked to Lieutenant Stark earlier. He said that he had been to Betwixt and came back with that white streak in his hair…"

"Yeah, I noticed. We jokingly call each other *streak brothers*."

"Do you have any idea how that happened?"

"None, Doc. All I know is that Baal almost took my scalp off on one of his swoops down on me, and I came back with this streak of white hair. I don't know how Stark got his."

"Could I take a little sample of your regular hair and a separate sample of the white hair, Wayne?"

"Go ahead. Just don't scalp me, Doc. One of these days I gotta go back on stage."

While Dr. Palmer was carefully taking the hair samples from Wayne, Abby used this opportunity to tell Palmer about some of the issues they were dealing with.

"Dr. Palmer, Wayne going back on stage is part of the reason we need some help. Besides the nightmares he's having, Wayne seems to have lost part of his passion for the music he plays so well. We don't know why. It's been his living and his passion all his life, but now… Could this be part of some kind of PTSD or something?"

"Tell me about this, Wayne, if you feel up to it."

"Doc, I can't explain what I don't feel anymore. That part of my life—the songs, the music, the impersonations, the performing in front of people, the sex, the lust—well, it seems like it was all part of an act, a façade that I was hiding behind. I just don't have that song in my heart anymore. Does this make sense?"

"Wayne, it seems that you've had a traumatic experience. All of you have shared in it. I doubt it is PTSD, Abby. That's a disorder that is caused by a prolonged experience and sometimes takes a long time to show up in a person. I've worked with the Veteran's Administration also, so I'm schooled on PTSD. It's too early in our counseling to make any kind of diagnosis at this time, but I assure you that in time, I will be able to give you a prognosis of what is going on. For the time being, let's continue to talk and get Wayne on his feet again. Belinda can schedule your next appointment. Let's go slow on this…"

After Wayne and Abby left the office, Dr. Palmer gave the samples of hair to Belinda.

"Get these samples off to the DNA lab ASAP, Belinda. Tell 'em to put a rush on it. I can't wait to see the results and compare them to Stark's samples. This is where I'll catch them if all of this is a hoax."

With the exception of Wayne, Robbie Cantrell, Mary and Tito were the only Christians in their family group and it weighed heavily on Robbie that no one else had accepted Christ as their savior, especially in response to the dream they had all experienced. She knew that Dr. Palmer was a very qualified physician and psychotherapist and was bound to probe the minds to find the truth about their trip to the unknown. She wasn't sure how Bella would handle this and put in a call to her.

"Hey, baby, it's Mom! How did your session go with Dr. Palmer?"

"It went better than good, Mom. I think Eric is going to ask me out! And by the way, I bumped into Lieutenant Stark on my way out and he gave me the eye also. Fun, fun, fun! New adventures and I can't wait to date both of them…"

"Bella, is that all you think of? Dates and adventures? When are you going to grow up? I asked you about the session, not your love life."

"Oh, Mom, the session went just fine. I told Eric—he said to call him Eric—that I was having bad dreams, occasional panic attacks and I was having trouble sleeping sometimes. He said he would help me, personally, with these things."

"I didn't know you were having panic attacks and trouble sleeping, baby. Are you okay?"

"I thought everyone was having these problems, Mom. Nothing I can't handle! I just exercise myself through them. Then it gets better."

"I'm not having those problems, baby girl," Robbie said.

Robbie knew that Bella was a strong, determined woman but she also knew that everyone could come to the end of themselves. Being a loving mother, she just wanted to be there when Bella finally fell, if she ever did.

"Well, since we're talking about your love life, I hope you lean toward Stan Stark more so than Dr. Palmer."

"And why is that? Eric is a very important man. He works with the astronauts and he's very respected in his field. I could do worse."

"He's not a Christian, Bella…"

"Neither am I, Mom. At least not yet. I'll get around to those decisions one of these days. Besides, right now—and I have a Bible that I read occasionally—I just want to enjoy the sins of my youth. How's that for Bible talk, Mom?"

"Bella, you're not a *youth* anymore. You're thirty-five years old. Why don't you go to church with me this coming Sunday?"

"Mom, remember that I'm a realtor. Duh! I have to work on Sundays. I'd really appreciate it if you wouldn't bug me about all the religious stuff. I'm feeling like you're trying to put one of your guilt trips on me again. Would you give me a break! I just want to have fun and enjoy my life, if you'll just let me."

"Baby, you're my only child. I love you! I want you to be happy besides being successful. Haven't you ever thought about settling down with a good man and raising a family?"

"Uh, oh, Mom. Here comes the tick, tick, tick of my body clock ticking away. Getting too old for children and all that. I love you, too, Mom, but you gotta let me make my own decisions and quit hitting me over the head with your Bible all the time. And don't start with all of that *left behind* noise. I won't be left behind. I wouldn't miss that party in the sky for anything. Just cool it …"

"I can't promise you that I won't bring it up again, Bella…Hey, do you want to come over for dinner tomorrow night? I'm fixing your favorite!"

"I really don't mean to put it this way, but could I let you know? I told you that I'm expecting calls from Stan and Eric. I'll let you know. Gotta go now, Mom. We'll get together soon…"

Back at NASA, Belinda Sealy was typing up some notes for Dr. Palmer. His door was closed and locked as it often was. She sometimes wondered what he did behind closed doors. Like many of the brainy-types at NASA, Dr. Palmer was not an easy man to get to know. Before Hank Hawkins demanded to know more about Palmer's background, Belinda had no idea that he had been married. It was an even greater mystery to her why Dr. Palmer had bowed to Hank's demands to know more about him in the interviews.

A Fed-X package arrived at her desk. She hit the intercom button on her phone.

"Dr. Palmer, I just got a Fed-X package. I think it may be the DNA results you've been waiting for."

"Please bring them in."

"Uh, your door is locked. Want to unlock it for me?"

Dr. Palmer opened his door with no shoes on, in his stocking feet, rubbing his eyes and looking like he had been grabbing a quick nap.

"Sit down, Belinda. These tests are going to tell us who's been naughty and who's been nice. I can't wait to read them."

5

1 + 1 = 1
SHAMELESS!

"Hey, Robbie, it's Hank…"

"I couldn't have guessed. Caller ID, remember?"

"Yeah..well, uh, I'm not thinking too clearly right now."

"What's the problem?"

"No problem. I need a wedding planner. Interested?"

"Are you getting married, Hank?!"

"No, no. Not me. Abby just called and wants to set the date of her wedding. Sunday afternoon in two weeks. Just a quiet simple wedding at Tequilaville, nothing extravagant, close friends and family. She emailed me a guest list. Could you help us out?"

"Absolutely, Hank. How do you feel about this?"

"If Abby's happy, I'm happy. Time will tell. I'll send you the guest list and you may want to touch base with Abby."

"Who's officiating, Hank?"

"Wayne's 'streak brother,' Lieutenant Stark. I like that young man. Great choice on their part."

"I like him, too, Hank. I wish Bella liked him or he liked Bella. He's just what she needs in her life."

"Bella could sure do worse. Incidentally, speaking of Bella, Abby has already called her and wants her to be Maid of Honor."

"Consider it done, Hank. I'm surprised I haven't gotten a call from Bella, but it sounds just like Abby to have a simple wedding. I've got a few ideas I'll go over with her. How's your relationship with Liz going?"

"I'm seeing her tonight. Wish me luck…"

Hank walked into Tequilaville and saw Scott Wood and the band rehearsing, trying to add to their play list. Attendance at the club had steadily been falling off since Wayne hadn't performed in weeks. Despite their best efforts to fill in for him, it was plain that the crowd around the lake wanted to hear Wayne Tyler perform. His rehab was coming along, he could stand and walk, but his stamina and voice were not up to par.

Hank was worried about Wayne losing his passion for his music. Without passion, there was no music, no performance, no crowd. During their rehearsals, Scott kept turning away from the microphone, sneezing and coughing. He looked like he was coming down with something.

"Scott, are you okay?" Hank asked.

"Mr. Hank, I'm not really feeling well. I'm not sure I'm going to be able to sing Wednesday night. I can call a couple of my friends to see if they can fill in for me just in case. I'm really sorry about this. It's certainly not a good time to get sick with Wayne being out…"

"You can't choose when you're sick, Scott. We've got a couple of days to figure this out. I've got someone in mind. Why don't you go home and get well? I'll handle the rest…"

Hank arrived at the Bay Hilton about 6:30 in the evening for his date with Liz. He'd told her to just dress comfortably, nothing fancy, leaving it up to her. He was in his normal starched jeans, boots and cowboy hat.

"Do you like Cajun food?"

"Crawfish and jambalaya? You bet I do."

"We call crawfish *mudbugs* around here, Liz. They get a little smelly peeling them but it's hard to beat if you have the time to eat enough of 'em along with new potatoes and corn on the cob."

Hank pulled into *The Crazy Cajun* restaurant, one of the many cafes around the lake that had a back terrace leading down to the water. It was a fun place. The very rotund and cheery Chef Boudreaux was a long-time friend of Hank and immediately greeted them and put them at a great table with a view.

"How you are, my friend? Who's dis lucky lady you be with?"

"This is Liz. Liz this is my friend, Chef Boudreaux. He serves the best Cajun food in the world."

The café had such a wonderfully happy atmosphere. Chef Boudreaux insisted in giving them little samples of the entire menu, calling his waiters over and practically ordering for them. The café was filled with old time French Zydeco music that made the patrons want to jump up and dance.

When the food arrived at their table, Hank started to dive in and eat, toasting Liz with his glass of water.

"Aren't you going to bless the food first, Hank?"

"Uh, here? In front of all these people?"

Liz extended both of her hands across the table and gently took hold of Hank's hands.

"Go ahead, Hank. Right here in front of all these people."

Hank removed his cowboy hat, bowed his head and stammered for words.

"Dear God…"

While Liz's head was bowed and her eyes closed, Hank looked up to see if anyone noticed him. He felt very uncomfortable. He'd never prayed in public before and really didn't know what to say.

"…please bless this food. And thank you…"

"In Jesus' holy name we pray…" Liz finished the prayer for Hank and gave him a squeeze with both hands.

"Was that hard for you to do, Hank?"

"I guess I'm just a little out of practice. Thanks for helping me out."

Liz chuckled, still holding Hank's hands in hers and said, "It gets easier the more you do it, Cowboy."

"I liked the holding hands part. You have such soft hands, Liz."

After eating their meal, Hank walked Liz outside to take a short stroll along the waterfront. He told her about Abby and Wayne's wedding plans and wanted to make sure she could attend.

"I wouldn't miss this big day in your life, Hank. Thank you for asking me."

"I wouldn't ask anyone else. There's something else I'd like to talk to you about…"

Hank told her about Scott Wood, their singer at the club and asked her if she could contact Mr. Elroy and see if he would like to play for a few nights at Tequilaville.

"I think Mr. Elroy would be delighted to play. I'll make arrangements to pick him up. Pastor Randy and Pat will probably be there also, but you know they don't drink."

"No problem. I just hope we don't have too rowdy a crowd. Let me know and I'll get the band to rehearse with him a little. I'll pay him well. He looks like he could use a few bucks… I love holding your hand, Liz!"

Keeping her distance, yet pulling his hand closer to her, Liz smiled and winked at Hank. He was really falling for this lady and realized he was possibly opening himself up for a fall, for a broken heart if anything were to go wrong. But it didn't matter. It ran in the family. He was all in…

About noon the next day, Hank and Abby were at the club doing paperwork, payroll, ordering in new beverages and meat for the cooker. Even though it was a day off for most of the employees, Tito and Mary were there checking their inventories, sending new purchase orders to Abby and making sure the wait staff was scheduled.

Scott was on stage with *South*, trying to rehearse and go over new material—looking and singing like death itself—feeling worse today than yesterday.

There was a knock at the front door of the club and Hank went over to unlock it. Liz was standing outside with Mr. Elroy.

"Come in, come in, Mr. Elroy. So glad you could make it. Can I help you with your guitar or anything?" Hank said, trying to help the old man.

Mr. Elroy was wearing old denim overalls with only one of the suspenders hooked, a flannel shirt with several buttons missing and a torn pocket, and some unmatched tennis shoes with the backs torn out so he could just slide into them. His big grin lit up the room as he slowly walked into the club.

"Oh, naw sir, Mr. Hank. Thank ya! Thank ya! I thinks I can manage. Where can I plugs in my guitar?"

Hank motioned to the band to help the old blues singer out and introduced Mr. Elroy to everyone, trying to make him feel welcome.

Dylan, *South's* bass player, couldn't take his eyes off of Mr. Elroy's Stratocaster. He'd never seen one like it and Dylan knew his Fender guitars and the history behind them.

"I've got a chair for you right here, Mr. Elroy. I'm Dylan, the bass player. Would you mind if I took a closer look at your guitar?"

"Sho, go right ahead, Mr. Dylan. My pleasure to meet ya."

The guitar looked ancient, beat up, scarred. Dylan plugged it in to the amplifier and struck a chord on it. The notes were so clear. He then looked for the serial number on the instrument. It read #0001-P-1952.

"That can't be!" Dylan said aloud. "Mr. Elroy, the first Fender Stratocaster didn't even hit the market until 1954. Where did you get this guitar?"

"Look on da back, Mr. Dylan."

Dylan turned the instrument over and there was a small bronze label attached that read, "Thank You, Mr. Elroy, for helping me design my first guitar. The prototype is yours as a gift." And it was signed, "Leo Fender."

"Mr. Elroy, you helped design the first Stratocaster for Leo Fender?"

"Yessir, I did. Taught him to play even before dat." Mr. Elroy broke into another big grin.

Dylan couldn't believe what he was holding in his hand. Years before, a 1954 Stratocaster had sold for over $500,00 at a Sotheby auction in New York. This instrument had to be worth well over a million dollars. After passing the guitar around to the rest of the band members to see it and hold it, Scott handed the Stratocaster back to Mr. Elroy. Before he even played his first song, they all knew they were in for a once-in-a-life time experience.

"Mr. Elroy," Scott broke in, "do you have insurance on this guitar?"

Mr. Elroy chuckled and look over at Scott, "Well, let me put it dis way. I gots all the inshawrence I needs...Hey, do you men know *Born to Play Guitar* by Buddy Guy?" Mr. Elroy began tuning up his instrument.

Dylan smiled back at the old blues singer and said, "Mr. Elroy, it is an honor for us to back you up. You just start playing; we'll catch up."

As the music began, Jett, the drummer picked up the beat and the bustle in the club went silent. Hank looked over at Liz, pulling her close to him and said. "Liz, I had no idea. Thank you so much for bringing us this master to play at the club. He has an amazing gift, truly amazing."

Abby came out of her office when she heard the tantalizing blues guitar and the raspy voice. She stood next to Daddy Hank to listen to the music that filled the room.

"Dad, who is this old man? Where did you find him?"

"I met him when Liz took me to the Cowboy Church..."

"Liz, you got my dad to church? There really must be a God. How did you do that?"

"Oh, it wasn't hard. I forgot to tell you, Abby, that's why I'm in Clear Lake. I plant churches."

"So what's his name, Dad?"

"Mr. Elroy. His name is Mr. Elroy. That's all anyone knows. He stays with the Pastor and his wife at the church."

At the sound of his name, Abby's eyes grew large with disbelief. She temporarily lost her breath and couldn't speak. Hank noticed her about to faint and reached over to help her.

"Are you okay, Sweetie Pie? What's wrong?"

Abby sat down at a table near the dance floor and caught her breath. Liz got her a glass of water.

"I've got to get Wayne down here, Dad. That's the old man that raised him in Austin for six years when Wayne was a kid. Wayne told me about him. He taught Wayne to play his guitar. This can't be happening! I can't believe my eyes!"

Wayne was in Abby's driveway putting a hand wax job on his recently purchased, used yellow Jeep Cherokee. He'd traded in his beat-up old van that contained so many illicit memories that he now wanted to forget. When his cell phone chirped, he wiped the wax from his hands and answered the call from Abby.

"Hey, precious…"

"Wayne, you gotta get down to the club, now!"

"Is anything wrong?"

"Just get here; nothing's wrong. There's someone I want you to meet… again."

Wayne arrived at Tequilaville and walked in the front door. The moment he entered, his eyes centered on the old black blues singer. The sight caught him completely off guard.

"Mr. Elroy?" Wayne said in disbelief.

"Well how ya do, Mr. Wayne. It's been a while."

Wayne walked as fast as he could to the band stand and began hugging Mr. Elroy. Tears flowed from both of them as they embraced.

"This is truly a miracle, Mr. Elroy! I've seen a miracle here today…"

"Oh, Mr. Wayne, miracles are everywhere if you just looks for 'em. You'll probably be seeing some more befo long. I loves ya, son."

"I love you, too, Mr. Elroy. I can't wait to hear you sing and play. Are you going to be filling in for me until I get back to whatever normal is?"

"I'll do my best. What would you like me to play for you, Mr. Wayne?"

"Anything you want to play, Mr. Elroy. How in the world did you get your old guitar back? I hocked it when I bought a new one way back when…"

"Oh, Mr. Wayne, I has a friend at that hock shop that reconized it and he let me buy it back. Long story. Now what can I play for you?"

Dr. Palmer anxiously opened the Fed-X package containing the results of the DNA tests from Lieutenant Stan Stark and Wayne Tyler. Belinda didn't leave his office as she usually did. She, too, was excited to know the results. Palmer systematically divided the two tests into small stacks and began reading the results on Stark first, page by page.

Before uttering a word, Palmer began comparing Stark's tests with Wayne's, studying each graph, each chart intensely. Finally, he rocked back in his big executive chair and took a deep breath.

"Amazing, Belinda. We may have uncovered the second most important scientific find of the twenty-first Century."

"What, Dr. Palmer? What do the tests reveal?"

"Belinda, as you know, *all* human DNA contains twenty-three pairs of chromosomes. Stark and Tyler's DNA have twenty-three point five in the white hair samples, only twenty-three in the regular hair samples. That's impossible! The point five anomalies on their charts are labeled 'Unknown.' And, the results have been run against every database known to mankind…"

"Dr, Palmer, why do you say that these tests may be the *second* most important scientific find of our century?"

"Because these tests may add to and substantiate the Higgs Boson theory that the super collider in Switzerland determined a couple of years ago…"

"Dr. Palmer, I guess I'm not up to speed on that. What's the Higgs Boson theory?"

"I'm surprised at you, Belinda. You should stay more abreast of what's going on in the world of science. The Higgs Boson is commonly referred to as 'The God Particle.' From this moment on, Belinda, you are to treat these tests as Top Secret! Don't breathe a word to anyone. Do I make myself clear?"

"Not even NASA?"

"Not even NASA, Belinda. At least not until we have further confirmation. These tests partially tell me what I wanted to know—that Tyler and Stark did have an event in their lives that defy time and space. I want you to line up more interviews beginning with Stark, then Tyler, alone! I'm going to use hypnosis to seek what we don't know, to find more details, to get to the truth surrounding their experiences."

One of the many reasons that NASA had chosen Dr. Palmer as their chief psychiatrist and parapsychologist was that he had a near photographic memory for facts, dates and information that he had gathered.

"Dr. Palmer, could you fill me in on more of the Higgs Boson information? I mean, I could research it, and I will, but I would rather get your take on it first."

"Belinda, on July 4th, 2012, *The National Geographic Daily News* ran a headline which stated, "God Particle Found," with a question mark after it. On that Wednesday morning in Geneva, the international laboratory CERN Director General Rolf Heuer said that two separate teams working at the Hadron Collider were more than 99% certain they had discovered the Higgs Boson or 'The God Particle.'

"The long-sought particle may complete the standard model of physics by explaining why objects in our universe have mass, and in so doing, why galaxies, planets and even humans have any right to exist. The Higgs Boson is one of the final pieces of the puzzle required for a complete understanding of the standard model of physics which explains how fundamental particles interact with the elementary forces of nature…"

"Pardon me, Dr. Palmer. I'm not a physicist. You're losing me."

"Belinda, this *particle* was proposed in the sixties by Peter Higgs. His ideas were that the universe is bathed in an invisible field similar to a magnetic field. If the Higgs field did not exist, the universe would be a very different place. In other words, no galaxies, no stars, no planets, no life on earth. Can you grasp this, Belinda?"

"Not entirely. So what's the connection with our DNA tests?"

Dr. Palmer turned to Belinda with a very confident and intense look on his face.

"The scientists working at the super collider said that they were *99%* sure that they had discovered 'The God Particle.' These tests may confirm the final one percent. Possibly proof that the universe *may* have been created by divine design rather than by evolution. Our tests, once we have confirmed more thorough hypnosis on Tyler and Stark, could blow even Steven Hawkins' mind and he's thought to be the most brilliant theoretical physicist in the entire world. Are you picking up on how important these tests are, Belinda?"

"Yes, sir! Do you want me to make copies of them, just in case something happens to the originals?"

"No! I'll hang on to them. Not a word to anyone. And, by the way, I want you to find Dr. Helle Guyion. Get her contact information for me. The last paper I read that she published was from Antwerp, Belgium…"

"Your ex-wife, Dr. Palmer?"

"The same, Belinda. She's second only to me in the discovery of the unknown. Get me her phone number, email address and all the information you can gather on her, ASAP!"

Bella was getting frustrated that she had heard from neither Dr. Palmer nor Lieutenant Stark. Not being one to wait and not having the slightest concern with being forward, she put in a call to Dr. Palmer.

"Eric? This is Bella, Bella Cantrell. Remember me?"

"How could I forget one of my favorite patients, Bella? I was just talking to Belinda about scheduling you for another session…"

"To heck with the session, Eric. I have big news. Abby and Wayne have set the date for their wedding and I'm going to be the Maid of Honor. Would you like to escort me to the wedding? And afterwards, maybe you could help me out with my sleepless nights."

"I would love to escort you, Bella. Just let me know all the details and I'll pick you up. Consider it a date. I just happen to be in the mood for some celebrating…"

After talking at length with Abby, Robbie had most of the wedding planned. The staff at Tequilaville had been more than willing to pitch in for *the boss* and make her big day special. The small guest list had received their invitations and only final little details remained.

"Abby? Robbie. Just checking to make sure that you do want the ceremony to be performed inside the club, not outside on the deck?"

"Right, inside the club on the dance floor in front of the stage. Besides not knowing what the weather could be like tomorrow, there's a chance of rain, if we hold it outside on the deck I'm thinking boaters on the lake may think we're open for business and the whole small wedding thing could get blown in a hurry."

"Just checking, honey. It will be perfect. Bella is so excited; we all are! Have you got your dress ready? Need some help primping before the ceremony?"

"Robbie, I'm ready and I want to keep everything simple, even me. Yes, my dress is ready. I'll duck into my office to dress. Just make sure Daddy Hank is in his tux. That will be the biggest challenge. I've already gotten with Scott and Mr. Elroy. They're going to play some very special music before I walk down the aisle."

"Are you nervous, little girl? Need some time with mom before you become an ole married lady?'

"Oh, thank you, Mom. I'd love some girl-talk time with you, but right now I'm running on adrenaline and probably couldn't sit still. I love you. You know that, don't you?"

"I understand, Abby, and I love you, too. See you tomorrow around ten at the club."

Abby had chosen the *Hawaiian Wedding Song* by Elvis Presley as her lead-in music but wanted to include Mr. Elroy since he played such a huge role in Wayne's life. She left the music to Wayne as his part of the wedding and couldn't wait to hear what he had put together. She knew it would be special.

Robbie and Mary, Tito's wife, had prepared a beautiful trellis in front of the stage that was filled with bright flowers. A small white pulpit was centered below it for Lieutenant Stark to perform the ceremony. Candles lined the path of the bride to the altar. There were two red roses on every guest table. Big bouquets of flowers filled the room with a wonderful fragrance, blotting out the smell of smoke and spilled drinks from the club.

Tito and Mary's two young daughters would serve as the flower girls, dropping rose petals down the path to the altar, but Abby had no idea who Wayne had chosen as his Best Man since her dad, Hank, was going to walk her down the aisle. T-Bone had the barbeque cookers going with enough food to feed an army. Tito had champagne glasses ready on each table with bottles of their best beverages ready to serve after the wedding. The wait staff were all dressed in white. Everything was ready.

Lieutenant Stark arrived wearing his white Coast Guard uniform and carrying a red Bible under his arm. As the other guests began to arrive, no one had seen Abby. She had come in from the back entrance and was in her office putting on her dress. Robbie knocked on her door to make sure she was okay.

"Are you ready, baby girl? Oh, you look stunning. What a beautiful dress."

"Mom, I've been ready since the day I laid eyes on Wayne. No regrets."

Hank pulled up to the Bay Hilton to pick up Liz. He adjusted the cummerbund on his tux that kept sliding up. As he walked into the hotel, he could see Liz standing in the lobby. People were passing by her gaping at her beautiful, flowing dress. As he entered, Hank stood there for a moment. Once again his world was standing still as he viewed the most beautiful woman he had ever seen.

"Are your legs working today, Cowboy? I'm not going to come to you."

"Oh, uh, sorry Liz. I was just caught in the moment. You are breathtaking! I got you some flowers. Didn't know if it was appropriate or not. It has been a while since I have bought anyone flowers. Hope you like them."

"Very appropriate, Hank. And they're beautiful. You didn't answer my question. Are you going to be able to walk Abby down the aisle?"

"Yeah, I can do that, Liz. I can walk her down the aisle. It's the giving her away part that I'm having trouble with…"

The moment had arrived. Wayne walked up on the band stand and stood before the microphone. *South* began to play as Wayne began to sing in his best Elvis Presley voice…
This is the moment
Mr. Elroy filled in between Wayne's lines with his own song…
Amazing Grace
Wayne picked up with his song as the two exchanged verses.
I've waited for…
How sweet the sound…
I can hear my heart singing…
That saved a wretch like me…
Soon bells will be ringing…
The small group of friends were stunned at how well the two songs blended into this special moment. Wayne with his Elvis voice and Mr. Elroy with his raspy voice and beautiful guitar accompaniment. When the song was finished, Wayne helped Mr. Elroy, also dressed in a rented tux, down from the band stand and positioned him as his Best Man in front of the altar.

Lieutenant Stark stood under the flowered trellis as Bella made her entrance escorted by Dr. Palmer and took her position as Maid of Honor. She, too, was dressed to the nines, as usual. *South* began playing the wedding march as Abby and Hank emerged from the back of the club.

Even with all of the therapy, Wayne's knees grew weak when he saw Abby. She wore a simple floor-length white gown, a pearl necklace and a wreath of white flowers around her beautiful brown hair that held the small veil over her face. She had a smile on her face that could launch a thousand ships. Hank had tears running from both eyes.

The moment of the bride's walk down the aisle could not have been better. The crowd was hushed as Hank reluctantly placed Abby's hand in Wayne's, giving her a kiss on the cheek and then whispering in Wayne's ear.

"You have my blessings, son. Take good care of my Sweetie Pie."

Lieutenant Stark began with a prayer for God's blessing upon this marriage and then read from the love chapter, 1st Corinthians 13:4-7:

> *"Love is very patient and kind, never jealous or envious, never boastful or proud, never haughty or selfish or rude. Love does not demand its own way. It is not irritable or touchy. It does not hold grudges and will hardly even notice when others are wrong. It is never glad about injustice, but rejoices whenever truth wins out. If you love someone, you will be loyal to him no matter what the cost. You will always believe in him, always expect the best in him and always stand your ground in defending him."*

When he finished, he turned to Wayne and said, "Wayne Tyler, would you like to recite the vows you have prepared for this special moment in your life?"

Wayne took Abby's hands in his, choked by his tears, and began talking to his betrothed from his heart...

"Abby, I tried to tell you what love is in a song, but the words were not enough. I have new words for you now..."

Mr. Elroy stood firmly beside Wayne, needing no assistance. He seemed to glow and remained humble and silent.

"As I walked up on the hill in that unknown place, I was overwhelmed with the feeling of love. My cup runneth over. I couldn't contain it, didn't understand it, never wanted it to go away and had to share it. My love for you, Abby, is more powerful than I can comprehend and worth any consequence to gain it. I couldn't imagine losing it and had to share it with you, my love.

"Love quickened me, strengthened me and empowered me to love you. It was the purest form of righteousness, the only path to happiness and with this presence of love engulfing me, nothing could block it, nothing could stop it and I had to give this gift to you. It was like the key to life itself, the reason for being and to even exist."

Abby's eyes began filling with tears. She was on the verge of completely breaking down in the moment of Wayne telling her of his amazing feeling for the love he had for her. Words that she thought she would never hear, but now being said from his heart with such dignity and clarity beyond what she thought Wayne was capable of.

"Abby, love is a driving force and a guiding light to keep both of us in its path. There is no fear in love, baby, no lust, no greed and no pride. It's like Garth Brooks singing *Shameless*, there is no shame in love. I have no regrets. My love for you consumes me just as I am and I don't need anyone else to explain it to me. Abby, we are perfect in love because love opened my eyes to you. You're my perfect love and I am yours. I know that with every essence of my being.

"It showed me, clearly, what the term 'when two become one' means. It is a perfect blending of two people, two hearts, two souls and two spirits into one. We can't conceal it and we can't contain it. We've got the rest of our lives to nurture it and to share it. Love is like the explosion of the immovable object hitting the irresistible force. Love explodes within you and creates such joy that you just can't even imagine.

"Abby Gale Hawkins, I love you, I love you, I love you!"

Abby's now gushing tears caused her makeup to fade down her cheeks. Her nose was running and she didn't have a handkerchief. She clutched her bouquet and looked over at Robbie, who was quick to hand her some Kleenex. Abby had a perplexed look on her face as she turned to Lieutenant Stark, gripping Wayne's hand tighter and tighter.

"Stan, uh, Wayne's vows have made me absolutely forget mine. Nothing I could say could come close. Wayne, you're my man and my everlasting love..."

Once again Abby turned to Stan Stark.

"Could we just get to the 'I Do' part, Stan? I can't wait another second to marry this man."

"Abby Gale Hawkins, do you take this man to be your lawfully wedded husband..."

"Yes! Yes! Yes! I DO!"

Their passionate kiss, before God and the universe, sealed their vows.

When the ceremony was finished, the festivities began. A big cake was rolled in, photographers took all the pictures of the event and the band, along with Mr. Elroy, began playing lively music.

It was finally time for Abby to throw her bouquet and all the ladies in the wait staff, Bella, Robbie, Hattie Lang, the band's girlfriends along with Liz, standing at the back of the crowd, joined the group. Abby turned her back and pitched the bouquet high in the air and it came down squarely into Liz's folded hands.

Everyone cheered, crowded around Liz and began making remarks about the future possibilities of Liz and Daddy Hank. There was laughing and applause. Applause from everyone but Bella. She was not happy at all. She couldn't believe that her *sister* Abby would throw out her bouquet to anyone but her and hollered over to T-Bone...

"T-Bone! Could you bring me about four tequila shots? I'm having a bad day."

"Bella, this is Abby and Wayne's special day. Please don't blow it for them." T-Bone was trying to be diplomatic and avoid a scene.

"Fine! I'll get them myself. Put' em on my tab." Bella went behind the bar, poured the shots and sucked 'em down before returning to her table. Turning to Dr. Palmer, she blurted out in a loud voice…

"Are you ready to get me out of here, Eric? As far as I'm concerned, this party's over."

But the celebration was far from over…

6

THE GARDEN
MUCH GIVEN, MUCH EXPECTED

As all of the well-wishers huddled around Abby, looking at her ring, hugging her and wishing her well, Wayne slipped away and sat at Daddy Hank's corner table away from the crowd. He was physically exhausted and had something on his mind. Abby's sixth sense told her something wasn't right; she was missing her man's presence and nearness to her on this special day in her life.

Her eyes panned Tequilaville, searching for her new husband. Finally, she caught a glimpse of him sitting in the darkness of the corner table and made her way over to him.

"Wayne, are you okay? You're not leaving me yet, are you?" she said jokingly.

"No way, Mrs. Tyler. I faced hell itself to win you over. I just wanted to let you have your special day…"

"Wayne, you *are* my special day. What's wrong?"

"Uh…just a little something bugging me…"

"What? Are you worried about tonight?"

"No, no, Abby. I'm just exhausted and…"

"And what, baby?"

"Abby, I want to start our marriage off right. I have so much to be thankful for and there's one more thing I have to do. Right now!"

"Anything, baby. Just name it."

"Okay, here it is…I want to be baptized by Lieutenant Stark."

"Then let's do it together, Wayne. I'm so proud of you, baby."

"Abby, you don't have to do this…you're all dressed up in your wedding…"

"I've got jeans hanging in my office. You've got some in there, too, Wayne. Let's do this in the wading pool out on the patio. I'll tell Stan."

Without drawing attention, Abby and Wayne changed clothes and met Lieutenant Stark, Daddy Hank, Liz, Mr. Elroy, and Robbie out on the patio while the rest of the crowd continued the celebration inside.

"Wayne Tyler, Abby Gale Tyler, do you both take Jesus Christ to be your Lord and Savior?" Lieutenant Stark asked them.

In unison, Abby and Wayne said, "Yes," as the Coast Guard Chaplain dunked them below the water.

"How do you two feel?" asked Stark.

"Wet! Saved!" Abby was twisting the water out of her now destroyed wedding day hair-do. "How do you feel, husband? That sounds so good to call you that, Wayne."

"I know this may sound crazy, but I feel lighter."

"What do you mean lighter?" Abby asked with an expression on her face suggesting Wayne was kidding. She could tell by the look on his face that he was not kidding at all.

"Lighter. Like all the baggage and sins I have been carrying around with me are gone. I feel lighter."

Abby and Wayne hugged each other, grabbed a towel and walked into the club to change back into their formal attire. Mr. Elroy was smiling. He knew things that others present didn't know. Abby and Wayne were going to have a divine wedding night like only two others.

Dr. Eric Palmer walked a very tipsy Bella to his car and began driving to his huge house in nearby Taylor Crest. The living quarters were built above a four-car garage where he housed an old restored Maserati and a Lexus SUV. He held on to her as he walked her into the elevator on the first floor of the three-story house overlooking Taylor Lake. As they entered his luxurious living room, he dimmed the lights and put on some soothing music.

"Beau-ti-ful house, Eric! Could you pour me a couple of shots of tequila?"

"Let's get you to the couch first, my lovely. How're you feeling?"

"Wonderful, da link!" Bella replied with a sexy smile. She leaned over and gave Dr. Palmer a passionate kiss.

"Bella, I'd like to see more of you when all of the therapy is over…"

"I thought you'd never ask, Eric." Bella, bombed at this point, rose and started to sway with the music and began unbuttoning her blouse…

"Uh, Bella. That's not exactly what I had in mind. You are beautiful…"

"Yes, I am beau-ti-ful, Eric, and I'm about to give you an eye full, the greatest night of your life and I doubt seriously if you can handle all of me!"

"Bella, I can't do this. You're my patient. I could lose my license. How do you like your coffee?"

"Coffee? I don't want your coffee, Eric. I want YOU! NOW! It's pretty sad when a great looking girl like me can't even get laid. I'm definitely having a bad day. Now come on, Eric…"

Finally, the festivities of the wedding were over and Abby helped Wayne into her car for the trip back to her home. Both were a little tired. Abby was still looking forward to their wedding night consummation and tried to engage Wayne in some happy conversation, giggling at everything Wayne said. When they pulled into the driveway, Wayne struggled to get out of the car and reached back for his walker.

"Mrs. Tyler, I'm not sure that I can physically carry you over the threshold…"

"Then I'll carry you," Abby said, reaching down, unlocking and opening the door. She picked Wayne up and carried him into their house, high heels and all.

"That isn't right, Abby. Wow, you have been working out. Now put me down so I can kiss you, Mrs. Tyler."

It was almost midnight when they hung up all of their clothes and got ready for bed. Abby wore a sheer lilac negligee. Wayne just stripped down to his cleanest pair of brief underwear as they pulled back the covers to their bed, which Abby had adorned with rose petals for the big night.

"Are you ready to close this deal, Mr. Tyler?" Abby said with a big smile.

"Uh…ummm, Abby, I'm really tired and a bit anxious. I love you, baby but I'm not sure I'm ready for this, physically, if you know what I mean. I told you that this may happen. Could you give me a little time?"

"Wayne, my beloved, we have the rest of our lives to consummate this marriage. Just snuggle up to me, hold me, give me a good night kiss and rest. I love you, baby, in sickness and in health. Now let me kiss you to sleep…"

As they drifted off into the twilight of a deep dream, holding each other, loving each other, they suddenly awoke in a strange and beautiful place.

They were naked but not ashamed as the first images they saw were two thirty-foot-tall cherubim angels holding long flaming swords, guarding a gate that was opening before them. Hand-in-hand they entered the gate without fear. The garden inside was overwhelmingly beautiful. The fragrance was mesmerizing, pleasant, perfect. The light inside was brilliant white, not like sun light, and there were no shadows anywhere.

A crystal river ran through the garden with fruit trees on either side bearing every type of fruit known to mankind. Wayne and Abby walked deeper into the garden, hand in hand, feeling the green grass beneath their feet that led them to the shores of the river.

Animals were everywhere: elephants, lions, tigers, dogs, cats, giraffes, monkeys, leopards. There were birds of every color flying above, singing wonderful songs in unison. A sparkling swarm of unthreatening mosquitoes sung high-pitched notes as they mingled with swarms of bees which filled in their wonderful songs of never-before heard falsettos. There was no fear among the animals nor did Wayne and Abby fear them.

The sky above was endless, as if they could look up and see heaven itself. There were many rainbows with colors they had never seen before. A sense of warmth and love permeated all their senses. This was a garden of complete perfection. Nothing could have made it better.

Wayne and Abby breathed deeply and felt like they were sixteen years old again. The wonderful air seemed to cleanse their inner souls as the brilliant light above healed their outer appearances. They, too, were perfect in every way, without blemish, without wrinkles. Their faces shown like fine porcelain images of unbelievable beauty transformed by the air, the water, the sky, and the beautiful surroundings.

As Wayne and Abby looked back, the gate was closing behind them. Before them stood Gordon, Wayne's angel.

"Welcome to the garden," Gordon said in a booming, majestic voice. "This is your honeymoon gift from the Almighty."

"We thought we'd never see you again, Gordon," Wayne said, smiling up at the fifteen-foot angelic being.

"Wayne and Abby, you both risked your lives to be together. Now you will experience unconditional love in this place. Be fruitful and multiply. To whom much is given, much is expected…"

"Gordon, this is so beautiful and I thank you so much, but, since this is obviously a wondrous dream, and our honeymoon, will Wayne and I remember this? It is our important day. Will we retain these memories?" Abby asked holding Wayne closer to her.

"You are granted three days, earth time, for your gift in the garden. I will speak to you before you leave. Time in the entire universe is frozen for your special moments here. Be of good cheer." Gordon disappeared right before their eyes.

Locked in a deep embrace, Wayne kissed Abby passionately, feeling her love in him and his love in her. With their eyes closed, their nude bodies touching, they both felt a furry being rubbing up against them. It was a large, white male lion with a thick mane and eyes of gold. It spoke to them.

"Wayne, Abby, follow me to your wedding bed. I will be your pillow."

"Well, hi there, big fellow," Wayne said. "What's your name? I didn't know lions could talk."

"I'm called Judah. I will be your guide here in this garden. I'll never leave you."

Judah led the barefoot couple down to a three-foot-thick bed of rose petals bordered by honeysuckle vines and orchids.

"This is your wedding bed. Enjoy. Be fruitful and multiply," Judah said as he crawled over the border and lay down at one end to be their furry pillow.

Mr. and Mrs. Wayne Tyler stepped into the bed, snuggled into the rose petals and consummated their marriage vows. The two became one.

For what seemed like endless times, Wayne and Abby, led by the magnificent white lion, Judah, played in the garden taking advantage of all the wedding gifts that were before them there. They rode giraffes, horses, camels, elephants and zebras. They flew above the garden on wings of eagles. They ran for miles and did not grow faint, nor did they perspire. There was no night, no time in the garden.

"Hey Abby, how about a swim in the river? Are you up to it, baby?"

"Wayne, I'm up for anything. Don't you wish this could last for eternity?" Abby was having the time of her life as she laughed and threw her hands up in the air in sheer joy.

As they walked into the crystal river, they were lifted up by male and female hippopotamuses that took them on a tour of the river, speaking to them in deep guttural voices to point out the sights along the way. When the tour of the river was complete, Abby and Wayne were returned to the awaiting Judah who led them into a great forest.

The cedar forest had a wonderful aroma. The trees were home to every type of bird which sang songs while the newlyweds walked along the many paths with Judah. When Wayne and Abby felt the need for nourishment, which was not often, they would reach up and pick fruit off the trees and eat. The leaves were even tasty and seemed to heal them from within.

This was a divine honeymoon that all the money in the world could not buy. There were no wedding coordinators, no caterers, no limos, no hotels and no photographers. Their only memories would be what they would be allowed to recall. For the moment, their lives were perfect, their love was perfect and they were both in a perfect place with perfect peace of mind.

Like all good things, their honeymoon had a time limit in this timeless place. Two days later, Gordon appeared to Wayne and Abby once again. They found themselves outside the gates, fully clothed, as the cherubim guards with the flaming swords closed the bejeweled gates behind them. Judah stood just inside the gates looking so majestic and waving goodbye to them with his huge paw.

"I will never leave you," were Judah's parting words.

"Oh, Gordon, is our time really up? So soon?" Abby said, looking up at Gordon.

"Time to go back and begin your lives together," Gordon replied. "You have been blessed and you will remember fragments of this time in the garden, enough that you will never doubt. But these are memories that you cannot share with another living being. Is that understood?"

"Yes, Gordon, we understand. Thank you!" Wayne held Abby close to him.

"Don't thank me, Wayne and Abby. These are gifts from the Almighty. Always praise Him."

Wayne and Abby turned around to take one last look at the garden, to try to get the image firmly seated in their memories that they hoped would last forever.

"I told you that to whom much has been given, much is expected." Gordon became even more brilliant as he spoke. "Now go back to your bed and arise. Wayne, you have been healed of all of your afflictions. Walk in the light."

Once again, Gordon disappeared from their sight. Time resumed throughout the entire universe as Wayne slowly woke up, pulling Abby close to him in their bed. Abby nestled closer to him, wrapping his arm around her.

"Hey, baby, you want to try this consummation thing again? Somehow I feel stronger than I've ever felt in my entire life," Wayne said, pulling back her long hair and giving Abby a good morning kiss behind her ear.

"Oh, yeah, Mr. Tyler. Let's seal this deal!"

7

HELLE GUYION, PH.D. HIGH PRIESTESS OF EVIL

Dr. Eric Palmer was anxious to speak to his ex-wife, Dr. Helle Guyion, and called his assistant, Belinda Sealy, into his office to get the results of her research on how to contact Helle.

"Belinda. What have you found on Dr. Guyion? Do you have her contact information for me?"

"Uh, Dr. Palmer…yes, I do have her contact information but even though it wasn't easy, I've got a lot more information on your ex that you may not want to hear."

"What do you mean that it wasn't easy?"

"Dr. Palmer, it is almost like she doesn't exist. I had to get some of our NASA hackers involved. Hope you don't mind. You told me to keep this a secret."

"Hackers? Why did you have to hack the info, Belinda?"

"Dr. Palmer, when I Googled Dr. Guyion there was no and I mean *no* information on her. Not in Norway, not in Scotland where you both got your doctorates in parapsychology. She isn't even listed as ever having been in Scotland or any documentation on her doctorate."

"Hmmm. So where is she now?"

"Antwerp, Belgium. I found that from passport information which was almost impossible to get. Hence, I used hackers."

"So what's this information you found out that I may not want to hear, Belinda?"

Belinda Sealy presented a thick dossier to Dr. Palmer. It contained classified information of Dr. Guyion's involvement with top European, Russian and Chinese leaders. Not only had she been a parapsychologist for Russian cosmonauts, she had also been very active in world leaders' personal lives.

"I know this may be painful, Dr. Palmer, but it seems that Dr. Guyion has slept with many very influential people, both male and female."

"Go on, Belinda. We've been divorced for many years. She can't hurt me anymore. I'm only interested in her professional life now. She is very intelligent and somehow has great insight into the unknown. That's what we're dealing with here, the unknown. I need her help. Continue with your findings."

Belinda spent a couple of hours showing Dr. Palmer that Dr. Guyion was, quietly, a very powerful woman. Even though her net worth could not be fully determined, it was suspected that she was many times over a billionaire. She had fleets of jet aircraft, owned many sea-going transport ships. Most all of her correspondence with world leaders was encrypted and very difficult to break the codes. Although she had never been indicted, Dr. Guyion was suspected of arranging drug shipments from Antwerp, Belgium—called the "drug gateway" into Eastern Europe and Asia. She was not on any "Do Not Fly" lists with the U.S. or Interpol and could travel easily anywhere she desired to go. She was on all of the "must invite" lists of practically every State department in Europe and Asia.

"Great research, Belinda. Thank you."

"Dr. Palmer, if you don't mind my saying so…you're playing with fire with this, uh, lady. Do you still want to involve her in this research?"

Dr. Palmer rocked back in his big leather chair. He was silent for a few minutes, then finally spoke.

"This doesn't surprise me, Belinda. Helle was always a different type of person. Beyond a free-spirit. She seemed to have a power that went beyond my imagination. She even scared me a time or two when we were married."

"At the risk of prying into your past life, Dr. Palmer, and since I am obviously going to be working with Dr. Guyion, would you share a little more information about your life with her? I'll promise my loyalty to you and keep anything you tell me confidential."

"Okay, Belinda. Get us both a cup of coffee and have a seat. This is going to take a while and it *will* remain confidential."

Dr. Palmer began telling Belinda about his one-year marriage to Dr. Guyion when they were in Glasgow, Scotland, and both received Ph.D.s in parapsychology. He told of how Helle used hypnosis to get whatever she wanted.

"Helle could hypnotize people faster than anyone I ever met. I even think she hypnotized me a couple of times when I didn't realize it. She very seldom attended the conferences required with the doctorate board and to tell you the truth, that's when infidelity crept into our marriage. I honestly believe that she slept with every member of the board, both male and female members, but I couldn't prove it. She wrote her dissertation on the 'Powers of Darkness.'

"That dissertation could have been a horror novel. It vividly outlined the power of the Satanical realm and what could be accomplished using this dark side power. I think she planted post-hypnotic suggestions into the board's minds, violating every ethic known to medical science. She was questioned very little on her dissertation and got the highest marks ever given by them. To me, that was cheating. I had to work hard for my doctorate."

"Was that the final straw in your marriage, Dr. Palmer? I'm sorry to dive deeper into this, but I need to know." Belinda was feeling very uncomfortable and squirmed as she sipped her coffee, sitting in front of Dr. Palmer's desk with his door closed.

"No. There was much more since Helle always had an excuse for all of my suspicions. She manipulated me, she lied all the time and even at the height of my anger, she'd smile at me and the anger just seemed to go away. I'll admit, Belinda, I was a slave to her beauty and her intelligence. She's an albino. Did your research point that out?"

"I suspected that, Dr. Palmer. But I couldn't find any pictures of her."

"She had long blondish white, straight hair, light blue to pinkish eyes, a figure that would make a bulldog break his chain and she was sexy. My gosh, she was sexy. She had a spell on me from the first moment I laid eyes on her."

"So what was the final straw, Dr. Palmer? What caused the break up if it wasn't infidelity, lying, manipulation and the lack of professional integrity? I mean, any of those things would make most people file for divorce."

"I'm not most people, Belinda!" Dr. Palmer had a stern look on his face speaking directly to his assistant. He was once again establishing his own position and integrity. "It was later in our marriage. The part that actually scared the hell out of me…"

This time it was Dr. Palmer who was squirming in his chair, sipping feverishly at his coffee, trying to gather his painful thoughts and put them into words.

"One night while I was studying late, before either of us received our doctorates, I was a bit brain dead and began feeling amorous. Helle did that to me. Making love to Helle was constantly on my mind. So I walked into our bedroom to take a little sex break with my wife and that's when it happened…"

"What happened, Dr. Palmer? Was she asleep? You didn't wake her up to have sex did you?" Belinda giggled to sway Dr. Palmer's mood back to a lighter conversation even though she could see he was dying inside.

Palmer took another long breath and sighed. "This is where it gets really weird. Belinda, you can either believe what I'm about to tell you or not. But it's the truth.

"I walked into the bedroom and all of the lights were out. It was dark… except for two red laser-like beams emanating from her eyes, looking straight up at the ceiling. Like she was in a trance…"

"That's scary, Dr. Palmer!"

"That's not the half of it. It startled me. That's when I turned on the light next to the bed. Helle was under the covers but was levitated about a foot above the mattress, suspended in midair."

"Oh, crap, Dr. Palmer! Like in *The Exorcist*?"

"Yes. The same scene, except it was real."

"What did you say to her?"

"Nothing. I just stood there, gawking at her. When I turned on the light and she noticed my presence, it didn't bother her at all. She just looked over at me, smiled and beckoned me over to her as she lowered herself onto the mattress. It was what happened next that blew me away."

Belinda was on the edge of her seat, straining to hear more of this unknown story.

"It was if I, too, were enthralled in a trance. I stripped down, crawled into the bed next to her and she went nuts! She was all over me. It was like I was completely at her will. We made such violent love it seemed like it would never end. She scratched me from head to foot, forcing me into positions that were completely unknown to me. This was not making love by any human standards. It was absolute painful barbaric animalistic lust, fornication, sadistic and masochistic madness. She was literally, savagely, raping me. I tried to get away but couldn't. Her physical strength was beyond my capacity to understand it. I was her sex slave and I felt like she was about to kill me in bed. She would choke me to the point of my passing out and shriek out words I had never heard before like a banshee in the night. It scared the living hell out of me, like I was in hell itself."

Dr. Palmer was hyperventilating as he told the story to Belinda, not caring whether or not she believed anything he was saying.

"Oh my gosh, Dr. Palmer! How did you get outta there?"

"I did pass out finally. When I awoke, Helle had turned over and gone into a deep sleep. I immediately felt the pain of the scratches and bruises that she had inflicted on me, got up, went into the bathroom and began applying antiseptic to the now-bleeding wounds.

"While she slept, I packed a small bag and left. I felt like I was running for my life. I never saw her again—even at the divorce proceedings. That's it, Belinda. That's how we split."

Palmer sheepishly unbuttoned his shirt and displayed thin, tiny ever-present scars that were still on his body from that night as proof that the night really happened.

Belinda gasped as she looked at the bevy of tiny scars still remaining on Dr. Palmer's chest.

"I have scars all over my body, Belinda. That's why I rarely go swimming or expose my body to others. Too much explaining to do."

Belinda walked over to Dr. Palmer, buttoning his open shirt and giving him a comforting hug. "I'm so sorry, Dr. Palmer. I believe your story. All this may explain the next piece of information that I found for you."

"Belinda, don't try to protect my feelings and don't drip this information out to me. Now what else did you find?"

Belinda dug down into her folder of files on Helle and pulled an article she found in a small-town newspaper in Europe telling about a Satanical rally to be held where the High Priest of Satanical Worship would speak. It mentioned no names and there were no pictures. The article did mention an albino woman who would be delivering the address.

A follow-up article to the event written by the same journalist, who said he had been present at the rally, mentioned how mesmerizing the albino speaker had been. It also said, "Curiously, every attendee at the rally, consisting of about 5,000 people from all over the area, had emptied their wallets as donations to the cause on their way out of the rally. Many of the people attending found themselves without train fare back to their homes… Imagine that!"

"She hypnotized them, Belinda and put a post-hypnotic suggestion in their heads to give her every dime they had on them. She probably walked away with a couple million—in cash! She's self-centered, very narcissistic and could care less how they got home."

"Dr. Palmer, do you really want to go forward in getting Dr. Guyion involved in our investigation? There's no telling what she can do if we bring her into this."

"I appreciate your concern, Belinda. Have you ever read *The Art of War* by Sun Tzu?"

"I've heard of the ancient book, but I've never read it."

"One of the first points this Chinese author points out is to 'Know your enemy.' Helle is not, at this point, the enemy but we must respect her knowledge into the unknown. She obviously knows things that we don't. She is also completely unscrupulous, immoral, will lie, cheat and do anything to get her way. She could be one of the most powerful women on earth. We must respect this and learn from her knowledge without telling her everything we know. Be on your guard at all times around her, Belinda.

"I'll call her and ask her a few key questions before making up my mind to bring her to the States. Now where's her cell number?"

Since Bella and Dr. Palmer had left the wedding celebration early and Bella seemed to be not only drunk but mad at the world, Robbie placed a call to her to see if she was all right.

"Hi, Mom," Bella blurted out with frustration. "Are you checking up on your little girl again? I'm pretty busy; so what's on your mind?"

"I noticed you left the wedding early. You missed a great event."

"Like what, Mom?"

"Lieutenant Stark baptized Wayne and Abby in the wading pool on the deck of Tequilaville. It was such a beautiful scene. So sorry you missed it."

"You mean Abby got her hair wet and was dunked in her wedding dress? That's just crazy! Did you hear angels sing and fire come down from the sky?" Bella said facetiously.

"Bella! How rude! That was a major moment in their lives. I can't believe you're being so obnoxious about this…"

"Like I said, Mom, I'm real busy. I'm happy for them; so what else?"

"Did Dr. Palmer get you home okay? Are you all right?"

"Obviously I got home, you're calling me here. And, yes, I guess I'm okay. I tried my best to seduce him but he said something about me being his patient and professional ethics…just a bunch of crap. It's pretty bad when a girl like me can't get a little amorous every now and then."

"Bella, I'm your Mom and I love you, but you've got to change your ways. When are you going to accept Christ and be baptized?"

"Don't start on me about that! I will when I decide to do so and not a minute sooner. It's my life and I'll live it the way I want to before getting old and gray like you. Good-bye. Great conversation, Mom." Bella hung up.

When Wayne and Abby returned from their honeymoon, Wayne placed a call to Hank to see how things were going at the club. As best he could, he also let Hank know of his miraculous recovery and regaining his vocal skills. He was ready to return and get back to earning his living. Hank told Wayne how well the club was doing with their newest draw, Mr. Elroy.

"I can't explain it Wayne, but we're getting a different crowd here at the club. We've lost some of the rowdies that usually drop in but we've gained more families. Mr. Elroy's playing and strange lyrics that we've never heard before are packing the house."

"Hey Hank, I'm not losing my job, am I?" Wayne said with a chuckle. "No way. If you and Abby didn't sign a pre-nup, you're a quarter owner of this place now. Besides, I kinda like the new crowds we are getting in here. They don't drink as much but food sales are going off the chart."

"Hank, if we can afford to pay and keep Mr. Elroy a little longer, I would like to jam with him and learn some new material. Like I mentioned to you, I've kinda lost my passion for some of the other music I've been playing. Maybe Mr. Elroy can teach an old dog like me some new tricks. What do you think?"

"Wayne, we can certainly afford him. Mr. Elroy will not accept a single dime of pay from me. He said he has everything he needs. Hard to figure, he seems old and destitute, but he's the happiest man I've ever known and very talented. He's here every night we're open so just come on in and jam. I think our new customers will like that. Is everything okay with you and my daughter?"

"Better than good, Hank. She's truly an angel. How are you and Liz doing?"

"She's another angel, Wayne. I'm not very good at expressing my sentiments, but she's got my heart. I just hope she doesn't beat me to death with it. I'd marry her in a second. The problem is she has some strict boundaries, but I really like holding her hand and all the conversations we have every night. That's where we stand and it's just fine with me, at least for now."

Dr. Palmer placed a call to Dr. Guyion's cell phone. It was screened and answered by her assistant, Natasha Patski.

"Hello, Dr. Palmer, this is Natasha, Dr. Guyion's assistant. We've been expecting your call. I'll put you through to her."

"Hello, lover! I've been patiently awaiting your call. Long time no see!"

"Helle, I'm not your lover. You seem to have plenty of those…"

"I get around, lover. So tell me about your life and you're work at NASA."

"If you were expecting my call, Helle, you tell me. Have you perfected extrasensory perception?"

"Way beyond ESP, lover. I'll just take a guess and say that you want to consult with me on the DNA tests that you've been working on recently. Am I close?"

"You could not have known about those tests, Helle! What gives?"

"Oh, nothing supernatural, my love. When your hackers hacked into my accounts, I had my hackers hack into the NASA lab tests that you requested. They're on my desk now. I've been going over them with great interest."

"Helle, you've got to keep those tests highly confidential. I haven't breathed a word to anyone about them. Not even NASA! Are you trying to steal my research?"

"Not at all, lover. I knew you would call me. So what did you have in mind? How can I help you?"

Dr. Palmer was trying to pry into Helle's knowledge of the supernatural realms that Wayne and Lieutenant Stark, among others, had mentioned to him in their therapy sessions. One word would determine if he would bring Helle to the States to assist him. That word was 'Betwixt.'

"What do you know about supernatural dimensions? Their names, where they are and how people get there?" Palmer began his probe knowing that nothing was mentioned in the DNA reports about this realm.

"Oh lover, let's stop playing games," Helle said like she was laughing at Dr. Palmer. "Eric, you want to know about a place called Betwixt, don't you?"

Palmer was stunned. He took a deep breath and tried to regroup.

"So…how do you know about Betwixt?"

"I was waiting for you to finally stumble upon this glorious realm, Eric. Have you been privileged to have visited there?"

"Me? No! Have you?"

"Of course, Eric. I've been there several times. It is where my master hangs out."

"Your master? Who would that be?"

"Satan, of course! Want to go there with me sometime, lover?"

"Helle, I didn't think you were into religious mumbo jumbo. I've always considered you somewhat like myself, a scientist, believing only in facts, not fictitious conspiracy theories."

"Oh Eric, I'm not religious. But I do believe my own eyes. Do you?"

"So you can get me to Betwixt? I can see this realm with my own eyes? How will you do that? Do we have to be blasted into outer space on some Russian rocket ship?"

"My no, lover. That would take way too long. We'll get there by my master's mighty power and will travel at the speed of thought. Intrigued? So when can I come and visit? And who are the people that tipped you off to this realm? Do I sense a little bit of supernatural happening that you cannot accept or explain?"

"Maybe. I still can't believe you knew anything about this place...even though you say you've been there. Do you guarantee that you can take me there, Helle?"

"Guaranteed, lover. I've already got a whole floor of the Bay Hilton rented for a month or two..."

"Helle, NASA cannot pay you or your expenses while you're here. I just wanted to make that clear..."

"Lover, I could buy NASA and the Bay Hilton. I don't need your money. I just want to see you again after all these years, maybe fool around a little and have some fun. I can't wait to meet your clients and get all the details that you're unable to obtain on your own. And, 'no' I'm not trying to steal your research. I only want to expand your mind. You could be useful to me, also. I'll be there in three days."

Dr. Palmer called Belinda into his office. She could see the look of complete disbelief on his face.

"What happened with your talk with Dr. Guyion?"

"She knew! She has the DNA reports! She was the one that mentioned 'Betwixt' before I even brought it up. She said that she has been there and can get me there!"

"Uh, oh, Dr. Palmer. I'm thinking we're in for a wild ride. Are you sure about this? When is she arriving?"

"In three days, Belinda. Not a word of this to anyone. Start blocking out some time for me here at NASA and begin rescheduling some appointments at my off-site office with Wayne Tyler and the Lieutenant."

"How long do you think we can keep all of this a secret, Dr. Palmer?"

"I have no idea. This could be a career-changer for you and me both. Belinda, are you in or out?"

"I'm in for the whole ride, Dr. Palmer. What can I do to assist the preparations of Dr. Guyion's visit?"

"At this point, I don't know, Belinda. Just put on your spurs and dig in..."

8

ARRIVAL OF DARKNESS
CLOSE ENCOUNTERS

A solid black Airbus A330-300 circled Houston Hobby airport. The "N" number issued to the aircraft by the Chinese government was N-666-66, written in red on the back fuselage of the huge airliner. Originally designed for a long-haul passenger aircraft with three tier seating for 400 passengers, Helle had the interior of the plane re-designed with conference rooms and sleeping quarters to accommodate her staff of about thirty professionals—security guards, tech experts, communications personnel, research analysts, medical staff, along with her own financial and logistical group. The craft had the name "*Darkness*" written in large red script on both sides of the nose.

Dr. Guyion's passport was that of an official Belgian diplomat which meant she didn't have to go through customs by immigration officials upon landing. However, she loved to display her powers to her employees at every opportunity. As they entered the customs area of international flights, she feared nothing and presented her passport to officials and allowed them to inspect all of her cargo.

In one large trunk there was over $30 million in U.S. cash. Another trunk was packed with automatic weapons and ammunition used by her security team. As the immigration authorities opened each piece of luggage, Dr. Guyion smiled at them, exposed a more-than-a-glance view of her cleavage, touched their hands with a single finger and told them, "Just shoes and clothes."

The inspectors, looking down on the cash and weaponry smiled back and replied, "Shoes and clothes. You're free to pass. Have a pleasant stay in Texas…" as Helle planted a vision of shoes and clothes in their subconscious minds.

A large tour bus transported her staff and luggage to the Bay Hilton. A black limo leased for several months carried Helle, her assistant Natasha Patski and two security guards to the hotel just across the street from the NASA facilities in Clear Lake.

When Dr. Guyion's entourage arrived at the hotel, her security team met with hotel management instructing them not to allow anyone on their floors without permission and had the hotel seal off the stairway entrances which was strictly against local fire restrictions. Once again, Dr. Guyion's power of persuasion persisted.

"Natasha, call Dr. Palmer and instruct him that I will receive him at 3 PM," Helle said as she reclined on the huge leather sofa overlooking the beautiful view of the lake.

At three sharp, Dr. Palmer arrived carrying a bouquet of flowers and went through the laborious process of even getting to her floor at the hotel. Natasha, who was wearing chic business attire, very attractive, about five foot seven, jet black hair with Goth makeup, greeted Dr. Palmer at the door and led him into the huge suite.

"Hello, lover. Just give the flowers to Natasha and come over here and sit beside me." Helle never rose from the couch. She wore a sheer covering over her.

Dr. Palmer was astounded at her beauty. Helle was in her forties and looked like she was twenty. She had never aged, not a wrinkle on her face.

"Still a little lagged from the trip, Helle?" was all that Eric Palmer could think of to say, still smitten with her.

"Not at all. I've been looking forward to seeing you again." As she raised herself from the couch, the sheer cover fell to the floor.

"I'm a nudist now, Eric. Hope you don't mind."

"Uh, mind? No, no, I don't mind at all. Uh, uh, you're as beautiful as ever Helle. You haven't aged a day…"

"Don't stare, Eric. You'd make me feel uncomfortable in my own skin," she said with a flirtatious giggle.

"Sorry, Helle, you caught me a little off guard. Nice tattoos."

Helle's thighs, upper arms, neck, abdomen, groin area and back were covered with brightly colored tattoos that were obviously done by skilled artists. As she turned and walked away, Eric saw the large crafted inverted pentagram on her back with a perfectly drawn goat head in the center. Several areas of her body were covered by differently colored "666" impressions. "Satan" was tattooed just under her large breasts.

"Are you shocked, Eric?"

"Helle, nothing you do would ever shock me. You've always been unique and charming…"

"You're too kind, Eric. Can I have Natasha get you a drink? You look like you need one."

"No, no. I'm fine."

Helle waved at Natasha to leave the room and reached over and pulled Eric close to her. Without much resistance on Palmer's part, Helle showered him with tender, passionate kisses.

"Now you're fine, Eric. Feel free to touch. I don't mind."

By this time Eric had almost forgotten why he was here. Gathering his wits about him, he said, "Would you like to catch up and tell me what's been going on in your life all these years…"

Helle cut him off in mid-sentence.

"Oh Eric, I'm sure by now you've done enough research on me to know what I've been doing, and I know your history since we last met. Let's just be honest and enjoy each other's company for a while. Relax."

Dr. Palmer could not take his eyes off of her shapely naked body and tried to get control of his own thoughts again.

"Okay, uh, let's talk about Betwixt if you don't mind."

"I do mind, lover. Let's begin with you telling me about your clients who claim they have been there. That piques my interest. But first, I am a bit tense from the long flight. Let's just have a drink of some wonderful Russian vodka I brought. Then think about how you can help *me* relax…"

Liz Gabriel put in a call to Hank to talk about their date later that night.

"Hi, Cowboy! Lot's stirring around the old Hilton today. Do you know of anyone really important who's supposed to be arriving today?"

"Just me, Liz. Is seven too late?"

"Seven is great. Where we going so I'll know what to wear?"

"I thought I would take you on a romantic boat ride on an old paddle boat here on Clear Lake called *The Spirit of Texas* that's been converted to a restaurant. Great food. Sound interesting? So what's the excitement at the hotel?"

"I like your plans. Dinner on Clear Lake is great. As for the excitement, someone, actually an entire entourage arrived this afternoon with all kinds of security. I mean black limos, a bus load of people—looked like they were European. What was strange is this albino woman who seemed to be the center of attention. I saw her in the lobby. Everyone was catering to her every wish and command. Like she was someone real important."

"Albino, huh? No, can't say I know any important albino women, Liz. You're the apple of my eye, but you already know that, don't you?"

"I suspected as much. So I can dress up for you tonight?"

"Sweet Thang, you can dress up, dress down, anything you want to wear. You just keep smiling my way and we're good. See ya at seven."

Several hours later, Liz was coming down the hotel elevator to meet Hank. As the doors to her elevator opened, the adjacent elevator doors opened at the same time. Dr. Guyion, Natasha Patski and two security guards literally bumped into Liz as they quickly exited their elevator.

"I'm so sorry," Liz said to Helle. "Are you okay?"

"I'm always okay, Ms…?"

"I'm Liz Gabriel, and you are?"

"Dr. Helle Guyion. I just arrived in town." Helle could see that Liz looked like a woman of means. "Could you recommend a restaurant with a great menu and atmosphere?" Helle never apologized for almost knocking Liz to her knees as Helle quickly recovered from the brief encounter.

"Nice to meet you, Dr. Guyion. I'm actually going out with a local business owner who knows the area well. We're going to dine on a paddle boat, *The Spirit of Texas*. It's a great view of the lake. If you'd like, you can follow us. Do you have transportation?"

The two women immediately gave each other the once over, determining whether either threatened the other. Helle was wearing a beautiful long gown, lots of bling and it was more than obvious she was sans bra. No tattoos were visible but she was certainly showing off her voluptuous trim figure.

"Of course. My limo is waiting outside. How kind of you…uh, Ms. Gabriel."

Hank walked into the hotel lobby and saw Liz talking with a beautiful albino woman and figured Liz wanted to know who she was and what all the earlier commotion was about.

"Hank, meet Dr. Guyion and her friends…uh?"

"My assistant's name is Natasha Patski. Pleased to meet you, Hank, is it?"

"Yes m'am," he said removing his cowboy hat, "everyone around the lake just calls me Hank. A pleasure to meet all of you."

"Hank, Dr. Guyion and her staff just got here today and asked if I would recommend a restaurant for them and I told them they could follow us. Do they need reservations?"

"I'll get them seating, Liz. Y'all just follow me. I'm in the silver pick-up. What are you driving Dr. Guyion? I'll make sure I don't lose you."

"The black limo outside."

Hank walked Liz to his truck, tenderly grasping her hand. "You're an eye-full, Sweet Thang. You look wonderful. But who the hel…, sorry, who the heck is that crazy smug woman friend of yours?"

"Just met her, Hank. I have no idea who she is. I just told her about the restaurant."

"Did you see that woman's eyes? I mean they're like bluish pink. And her skin is white as a daisy…"

"She's albino, Hank, or she's from one of those countries in Scandinavia. Haven't you ever been around an albino person?"

"Only saw one or two in my whole life, Liz, like the Johnny and Edgar Winter Group. Remember them? That Dr. Guyion speaks perfect English. Did you see those two goons with her? I'm guessing they were some kind of body guards; she never introduced them."

"Oh, you noticed her goons and not her almost see-through dress?"

"Uh, no, I guess I didn't notice that…"

"Get real Hank. I saw you staring at her chest. You just keep your smile on me and we'll be good," Liz said clutching Hank's arm.

"I sincerely didn't mean to stare, Liz. It was kinda hard not to notice and I am a man. Not a perfect man, but I do the best I can." Hank squeezed Liz's hand and smiled back at her.

"Hank, that's what's so interesting about this NASA community. People from all over the world come here."

"Liz, all I know is she isn't from Texas. She may speak good English but she hasn't got that Texas drawl."

"Neither do I, Sweet Stuff. If you're going to call me Sweet Thang, I'll call you Sweet Stuff and be a little more of a transplanted Texan for you. How will that do?"

"Works for me, but I hope you didn't invite them to sit with us, Liz. I kind of wanted you all to myself tonight."

As the small convoy of vehicles arrived at the wharf, Hank accompanied Liz onto *The Spirit of Texas* and made seating arrangements for Helle, Natasha and the two security guards. The maitre d' placed Helle's party next to the windows, back-to-back with Hank and Liz. As the paddle wheel began to turn and the boat left the wharf, there was the usual hustle and bustle of waiters taking orders, clinking of glasses and a buzz of conversation that made it a little difficult for Hank to hear Liz.

"Sorry Liz, I didn't catch that…"

"I just said that I wished you could have found our new friends a table on the other end of this boat. I know I only just met them and I'm not supposed to judge but…that woman, Dr. Guyion, gives me a feeling that she is evil. I can't explain it, just a woman's intuition."

"Don't let them spoil our time together, Liz. You make all my worries go away when I'm with you."

As the night passed, Liz excused herself to go to the ladies' room. Immediately, Dr. Guyion leaned back to speak to Hank. She had files on every acquaintance she had ever made and wanted to know more about Hank and Liz.

"Lovely lady you're with, Hank. Are you married?"

"No, Dr. Guyion, Liz and I are great friends…at this point. She *is* lovely, isn't she?"

"Liz told me that you are a business owner. What is your line of work, Hank? Incidentally, I don't even know your last name."

"Sorry, I'm Hank Hawkins. I own the club Tequilaville next to the Bay Hilton, along with my daughter and her new husband, Wayne Tyler. You and your staff should drop in some night, great food, great music and a good time."

At the sound of Wayne's name, Helle zeroed in with her probing questions, knowing that Wayne Tyler was the center of the DNA tests and their investigation.

"I certainly will drop in, Mr. Hawkins. Do we get a discount for being friends of the owners?" Helle was practically whispering into Hank's ear. A little too close for comfort for Hank.

"Of course, Dr. Guyion. What brings you to Clear Lake?"

"As a matter of fact, I'm here because of your son-in-law. I'm sure you know Dr. Eric Palmer over at NASA. He and I are colleagues, both parapsychologists. He asked me to come over from Belgium and confer with him on Mr. Tyler's investigation into the unknown. I'm sure we'll be seeing more of each other."

Hank didn't respond and began to get the same eerie feeling that Liz had mentioned.

"Mr. Hawkins, I'm indebted to you for getting our reservations on such short notice. I'm going to pick up your tab for dinner tonight."

"Thanks just the same, Dr. Guyion. I'd prefer to pay it myself."

Helle got up from her table, looked Hank in the eyes and said unpleasantly , "I insist!"

For a moment, Hank had no response, like his tongue wouldn't form words. Helle sat back down and waved for the waiter to bring her the bill. When Liz returned, she and Hank walked off the boat as soon as it landed at the wharf. There were no 'good-byes' exchanged between the two groups.

Once in Hank's truck, Liz could sense that he was upset over something.

"Hank, is there anything wrong? You were a little rude to Dr. Guyion and her group. No good-byes? Nice to meet you? What gives?"

"When you left the table, Dr. Guyion wanted to know who we are, what we do and offered to pay our tab."

"So? Why would that upset you?"

"When I politely told her I would take care of my own tab, she got in my face and said, 'I insist!' I couldn't even speak. It was like she had some kind of spell on me. I don't like that woman. And there's more. She's a parapsychologist from Belgium and said that Dr. Palmer has asked her to get involved in Wayne's investigation. What's your take on all of this, Liz?"

"My take is that we should enjoy our time together and not worry. I'm sure Dr. Palmer has his reasons. As for Dr. Guyion and the investigation, we shouldn't judge a book by its cover. I'll pray about this. Let's take another long walk down the beach. I want you to whisper some 'sweet nothins' in my ear, Cowboy."

The next morning, Dr. Palmer walked into his office, instructing Belinda to come in and shut the door. She could hear the intensity in his voice.

"I blew it with Helle, Belinda. I didn't last ten minutes with her."

"That could be taken in several ways," Belinda shot back, trying to suppress complete laughter. "Do you want to give me some details? Are you talking about professionally or sexually?"

"T.M.I., Belinda. I mean, uh, I mean I've always been attracted to her, even after all the grief she caused me when I was younger. She completely seduced me yesterday, and I was completely helpless to resist her."

"Details, Dr. Palmer."

"Belinda, why am I discussing my sex life with you?"

"Uh, because you brought it up?"

"No more. I made a mistake and it won't happen again. I was weak, now I'm strong again."

"So you had a night. So what?"

"Belinda, the problem is…I can't wait to see her again. I'm still smitten with her beauty. How can I work with her professionally if we are having sex?"

"Be strong, Dr. Palmer. Just say 'no.' When do I get to meet this woman with all that power over my boss?"

"Soon. Start lining up new sessions with Wayne Tyler and Lieutenant Stark. Helle's assistant is Natasha Patski. When the sessions are scheduled, tell Natasha. I think I'm going to take the rest of the day off, go over to Tequilaville and get snockered."

"Perfect plan, Dr. Palmer. You deserve a day off. I'll make the appointments and see you tomorrow." Belinda didn't know whether to laugh, quit or take the day off herself. She made the calls and set up the sessions, then went home, chuckling about seeing her very professional boss absolutely losing it. She could hardly wait to meet Dr. Guyion.

Without thinking about his professional reputation, Dr. Palmer drove over to Tequilaville and knocked on the front door. It was too early for the club to be open. T-Bone opened the door.

"Hi, Dr. Palmer. We're not open yet."

"T-Bone, I'm having a bad day. Mind if I duck in for a couple of drinks? I don't normally do this and I don't want anyone to know."

T-Bone let Palmer enter, locked the door behind him and led him to Hank's corner table in the back of the club.

"Tequila and some lime if you don't mind." It was plain to T-Bone that Palmer needed something. He was stressed to the max.

Mr. Elroy was practicing on stage and knew what was going on with Dr. Palmer. He walked over and introduced himself.

"Howdy do. I's Mr. Elroy. Seems to me that you either got work problems or women problems. Do you mind if I join you? I'm a pretty good listener if I do says so myself."

"Nice meeting you, uh, Mr. Elroy. I'm really not in the mood for any company."

"I's probably gonna be better company than that bottle of tequila you is fightin with. Why don't you tells an ole man all about it, son? Jus mebbe we's can figure this out together."

Eric Palmer had no idea who this old black man was, but since he was at the mercy of T-Bone allowing him into the club before opening he used partial judgment to talk to Mr. Elroy, whom he considered having no education but possibly someone who could pass on some wisdom to him and not create a scene to get him kicked out. Eric began to talk.

"Women, Mr. Elroy. You nailed it. It's like she has a hold on me. I can't resist her. So what advice do you have about that?"

"Well sir, you must be talking about that albino woman, Dr. Guyion."

"How could you know about her?"

"Oh, Mr. Hank told me that you and her would be working together on Mr. Wayne's case. I must say so myself, that's some pretty interesting stuff, huh?"

"Mr. Elroy, how long have you known Wayne Tyler?"

"Oh, since he was a youngin. I taught him to play guitar. How long you know him?"

"Not as long as you. So what do I do about my 'woman' problems, Mr. Elroy? I'm open for advice for the first time in my life."

"Well, let's see here Mr. Eric, can I call you dat?" Without waiting for a response, Mr. Elroy went on. "Ya see, womens are wonderful creatures, but they ain't like men. The Almighty gave them diffrent traits and emoshuns than us men. We just have to be patient with 'em, appreciate their differences and try out best to understand them women folk. Most of all we's got to respect 'em and somehows we got to get them to respect us men. Now dats da hard part. Just takes a lot of time, patience and understanding. We's first got to know ourselves and our limitations befo we go judging them and theirs. Does this make any sense to ya, Mr. Eric?"

"So, Mr. Elroy, you're saying this is all my fault that I have all these problems?"

"Naw, sir. I'm saying that you should furst get to know yoself and establish your own boundaries befo you go judging someone else."

"And just how do I do that, Mr. Elroy?"

"Well, I knows you's smart with all your book learning but jus mebbe you've been readin the wrong books. I'd suggest you read the Good Book, in Proverbs where it sez to guard your emoshuns above all things, for emoshuns determine everythin else you do in life. Yessir, dat's where I'd start."

"Not very religious, Mr. Elroy, but thanks for the advice. One of these days I may look into all that."

"Here's something else you's can think on, Mr. Eric. You can't find love in someone else's heart unless you gots love in yours first. Some girls have it, some don't—just like men. You just got to find one that do. Life's pretty meaningless without love, Mr. Eric."

"Never really had time for love in my profession. I'm a scientist. I believe in facts."

"Fact is, Mr. Eric, love lasts forever. Science don't. I sho thinks you should consider it. In the meantime, why don't you run on home and sleep it off. You'll feel better in the morning caus joy comes in da morning."

9

LOOK INTO MY EYES
KEYS TO THE MIND

Wayne arrived at Tequilaville shortly after Dr. Palmer left. Mr. Elroy was still up on the bandstand playing his guitar, singing, grinning from ear-to-ear as he swayed his head around like Stevie Wonder at his piano. His happy nature added an extra measure of light to the songs he was singing and it was contagious.

"Mr. Elroy, I still can't believe that you've come back into my life," Wayne said reaching out to shake hands. Mr. Elroy waved off the handshake and gave Wayne a gentle hug.

"I loves seeing you again, Mr. Wayne. Hey, you wants me to learn you some of my songs? I's been working on some new material."

"I was just listening to you play and sing. It's like blues music, but it's different. What do you call it?"

"I's calls it *happy blues*, Mr. Wayne. It's got the same guitar runs as blues songs but with happy words. Not crying in your beer and tellin about all the bad in dis ole world. The words are uplifting, joyful. They helps us count our blessings and gets our minds off all the bad stuff going on. Do you wants me to learn you a few of my new songs, Mr. Wayne?"

"I can't wait, Mr. Elroy. You start and I'll try to learn as we go."

As the two played together, Wayne heard a different sound coming from his guitar. Yeah, it was blues runs okay but even the guitars seemed to exude a spirit of joy in their tunes. As the two musicians got deeper into their jam session, Wayne began to smile, laugh and move his head around keeping time with the music. The music got louder, the runs became natural and the words began to flow. They were writing new songs that had never been heard before. Wayne was completely in the music as he began to regain his passion for singing and playing again.

"Ya see, Mr. Wayne, I knows lots of songs. Like Ray Charles singing *Born to Lose, I've lived my life in vain*. Lookin' back on the past and all our bad memories and hurts. But then I think of my ole departed friend, Zig Ziglar who wrote a great book entitled *Born to Win*. It's all in the way you looks at life. We can decide every morning whether to be sad and see all our problems or we can look forward to being happy. It's a choice and a vision we all have. To be happy or sad. Ya getting' my meaning here, Mr. Wayne?

"Bye the way, you look happy today Mr. Wayne. Yo voice is back, yous playing like never befo. Does Abby have somethin to do with dat?"

"She's got everything to do with it and the fact that I'm saved. I know what love is. I'm a new man. No worries anymore. I'm completely happy, fulfilled and now this new music is the icing on the cake. Wow, *Happy Blues*! I may have a few new songs left in me yet, Mr. Elroy. Let's write some together and share the joy."

Helle, Natasha and two body guards arrived at Dr. Palmer's office suite a full half hour early for their first appointment with Coast Guard Chaplin Lieutenant Stan Stark. Much to Eric's relief, Dr. Guyion was wearing appropriate business attire. Natasha Patski carried a file containing more information on the Lieutenant than Dr. Palmer had. Palmer made the introductions.

"Dr. Guyion, Natasha, this is my assistant, Belinda Sealy. We'll all be working together." Turning to Helle's body guards, Palmer pointed to the door. "If you two men would like to remain outside in the lobby, I can assure you that you are in safe surroundings."

Belinda extended her hand to Dr. Guyion. "I've heard a lot about you, Dr. Guyion. Looking forward to our time together. Natasha, pleased to meet you. We're sort of counterparts, I'm guessing."

In a condescending manner, Helle offered her hand to Belinda and said nothing. Natasha did the same. Their arrogance wasn't a great ice-breaker for the first meeting and Dr. Palmer could see an air of tension beginning to form with this team of women.

"Eric, lover, I do hope the Lieutenant arrives early. I can't wait to dive into my questions for him."

Dr. Palmer was obviously miffed about the *lover* comment but professionally pushed pass the jab.

"Dr. Guyion," Palmer was trying to put their meeting on a professional plateau from the beginning and establish his authority, "we must be clear that these clients are *my* clients. You are here to assist."

"Eric, skip your authoritarian speech—which I'm guessing is for the benefit of your assistant. I thought we were sharing these interviews like we shared my Russian vodka the other night. We must do that again soon. Ms. Sealy, your boss is a great lover. Did he ever mention that to you?"

Eric was livid, embarrassed, as he took a deep breath and turned away, looking at the stone-like expression on Belinda's face.

"Dr. Guyion, my boss usually keeps his private life private, as do I." Turning to face Dr. Palmer, she said, "Lieutenant Stark is here. Shall I show him in?"

"Please do, Belinda."

Stan Stark was wearing his dress uniform, clearly showing his rank and Chaplin's insignia. After talking with Belinda about the meeting with Dr. Guyion, the Lieutenant wanted to look his best.

"Oh, aren't you a handsome one, Lieutenant?" Helle said offering her hand to Stark.

"Uh, thank you, Dr. Guyion. I've been looking forward to meeting you, too. I've got another meeting today so could we get started?"

Dr. Palmer opened his file on the Lieutenant and began going over their previous session to bring Dr. Guyion up to speed while Stark was present.

"If you don't mind, Eric, I'll begin with some of my questions for the Lieutenant. Can I call you Stan? You can call me Helle.

"I've read your description of Betwixt—I prefer to call it Second Heaven—it's a magical place isn't it, Stan? Give me the ten-thousand-foot view of what it looked like to you."

"You seem to know a lot about Betwixt, Dr. Guyion. Have you been there?" Stark asked, getting an uneasy first impression of the lady across the table from him.

"Oh yes. Many times."

"So…where's the distinct white streak of hair over your right ear, Doctor?" the Lieutenant asked Dr. Guyion.

"Stan, all my hair is white. I'm an albino as if you couldn't tell. Could you answer my question, Lieutenant?"

"Parts of Betwixt, or Second Heaven as you call it, were beautiful, depending on the setting caused by the demons who were present. Parts were like hell itself, very scary. I saw flowers and rainbows at some points in my experience and I saw the Lake of Fire in others. When I was a spectator at

Wayne's ordeal, I saw beautiful, godly people on one side of the huge, Roman coliseum, and I saw terrible ghoulish-looking look-alikes on the other side of the stone bleachers."

Helle never took her eyes off the Lieutenant knowing that Natasha was writing down every word, as was Belinda. Stark felt uneasy looking into Dr. Guyion's eyes, like she was trying to look into his very soul.

"So, Lieutenant, being a man of the cloth, do you believe in demons and supernatural dimensions?"

"The Bible says there are demons, so yes, I believe there are demons living in this world and in other dimensions that you choose to call a second heaven."

"I prefer to call them angels, Lieutenant. Powerful angels!"

"They're fallen angels, Dr. Guyion…"

"Fallen, schmallin, Stan. Angels are angels. They all answer to a higher power and follow orders from their god. These *fallen angels* as you call them, answer to Satan who is the Prince of this Earth—that's written in your Bible—and ruler over the second heaven. The only difference between them and the other so-called holy angels is that they made the choice to serve a different master, wouldn't you agree, Stan?"

"I would agree that they have made their choice to serve Satan. I wouldn't agree with his agenda to steal, kill and destroy or that he is a god. Satan brought sin into the world. Remember the Garden of Eden…"

"Of course, I know the Garden of Eden, Stan, but Satan didn't bring sin into the world, mankind did. He brought the freedom to choose what kind of life Adam and Eve wanted to live…"

Lieutenant Stark immediately cut Dr. Guyion short. "Yeah and look what happened to them. They endured isolation from God, they had to work hard to scratch out a living when the Almighty provided everything for them. Eve endured the pain of child birth and both, who were created to be immortal, eventually died. What kind of choice was that, Dr. Guyion?"

"It was a choice to live their lives the way they wanted to, Stan. Just like you and I do. Let's face it, being good all the time is absolutely no fun. There's little pleasure in being good. On the other hand, who says having fun and pleasure is not good? Who says that, your God?"

"And who's your god, Dr. Guyion?" Stan shot back.

"Settle down, Stan. I'm not your adversary here. I'm trying to understand your views and your experiences. We're not here to talk about me but to understand your two trips to an unknown dimension. Can we just agree on that?

"I'm trying to help you see this experience from a different perspective, Lieutenant, so that you will have a better recollection and understanding of the gaps in your experiences. We want those lost visions to become more clear to you so that you remember more of what happened. We want you to recall those pieces of the puzzle you have buried deep within your mind." Helle was very relaxed in her interrogations, subtly suggesting that Stark may not be correct in his beliefs, planting little seeds of doubt in his mind.

For the next half hour, Dr. Guyion, in her exaggerated, untactful European style, began hammering the Lieutenant with question after question. She often cut him off in mid-sentence as if she knew the answer already. Dr. Palmer had to break in more than once to keep the atmosphere of the meeting friendly. He could see a tension building up between Stark and Helle.

"Dr. Guyion, you said you, too, had been to Betwixt *many* times. Why don't you tell me what you saw? I can't wait to hear this, if you've ever been there at all and I'm not convinced that you have." The Lieutenant was firing back at Dr. Guyion as he sensed an evilness about her.

"Of course, Lieutenant, if it will put your mind to rest…I've seen a great god sitting on an ebony and gold throne. Angels all around serving him. I've seen the power he has and exerts over the world. He is worthy to be praised…"

"Dr. Guyion, do you believe in Jehovah God, the creator of all heaven and earth?"

"Lieutenant, of course I believe that Jehovah exists. But I do not believe he reigns supreme and I certainly don't believe he is the creator nor will he be victorious over my god, Satan."

"So you're a devil worshipper, huh, Dr. Guyion?"

"I worship Satan. You call him the devil, but I call him master. I'm also a scientist. I don't believe in divine creation because I was not there when the heavens and the earth were created. Who says that Jehovah created everything, Lieutenant?"

"He does! In his Holy Word, The Bible, and I believe everything in His book. He said, 'Let there be light and there was light!'"

"Lieutenant, you're going on blind faith. I go on scientific knowledge and what I've seen with my own eyes. Have you seen Jehovah with your own eyes?"

"Dr. Guyion, the very definition of faith is believing in what you can't see. Have you ever seen Satan?"

"Well, Lieutenant, no one can see Satan's face and live. I have been to Betwixt, the second heaven, and I have seen his feet. The rest of his image was clouded by a smoky mist to protect me. This I have seen with my own eyes so therefore I believe in him. And by your own admission you say that you have seen demons that I call angels of Satan…"

"And I saw God's Holy angels there, too, Dr. Guyion. I saw the mighty archangel, Michael, and the messenger angel, Gabriel. I also saw Michael banish all of the fallen angels who were at Wayne Tyler's trials. They obeyed the Word of the Almighty. How do you explain that, Dr. Guyion?"

"Lieutenant, we're getting off topic. I want you to trust me so that I can help you put the missing pieces of your experiences together. With your permission, I would like to put you under hypnosis and probe that handsome mind of yours. Is that okay with you?"

Lieutenant Stark had a thousand questions on his mind. He felt uncomfortable around Dr. Guyion, especially after she professed to be a devil worshipper.

"Dr. Guyion, Dr. Palmer, I'm more interested in what the DNA results showed about Wayne Tyler and myself. Do you have the results?"

"Yes, Lieutenant, we do and that's why Dr. Guyion and I must probe deeper into this. Right now, you're and Wayne's DNA are a scientific impossibility. By that I mean, the samples we took of your normal hair, and it was the same for Wayne, showed the normal twenty-three chromosomes that everyone has. The samples of the white streaks showed twenty-three and a half chromosomes. Chromosomes always come in pairs. Therefore, we in the scientific community have a huge mystery to solve. Would you help us solve it? It could be the missing link in the 'God Particle' discovered in 2012. Lieutenant, you have no idea how important this is to science."

Lieutenant Stan Stark heard everything Dr. Palmer said and he knew about the Super Collider in Bern, Switzerland, and the 'God Particle.' After weighing his thoughts and saying a quick, silent prayer, the Lieutenant turned to Dr. Palmer.

"Doc, this is your science, not mine. I don't need an explanation of the God particle, you do. As for going under hypnosis, I choose not to. I'll put the missing pieces together when and if God puts them in my mind. They were my experiences and I'm not so sure that I need to share them with either of you. I'm done. Don't call me back for any more interviews…"

Lieutenant Stark got up and walked out the door.

"Eric, I'm getting bored with the defiance of your clients. I thought they wanted to know what happened at Betwixt. When do Wayne and Abby Tyler come in and where is the nearest ladies' spa in the area? I need pampering."

"I'll have Belinda give Natasha the info on the spa. Wayne and Abby will be in tomorrow at ten. See you then, Dr. Guyion. Maybe we'll have better luck with them. I'd ask you not to be so direct in your questioning. People around here need to trust you before they open up to you, Helle. Telling everyone you're a devil worshipper isn't helping. You may want to keep that to yourself. Now tell me about when you're going to take me to Betwixt…"

When Lieutenant Stark left his session with Dr. Palmer and Dr. Guyion, he dropped by Tequilaville on his way back to the Coast Guard Station. He had something on his mind of great importance, but he just couldn't put his finger on how he felt after the session with a woman he considered evil. He knew that Wayne and Abby were scheduled for an interview the next morning and wanted to talk to them.

As he entered the club, he saw Wayne and Abby sitting at a table talking, seemingly very happy. Abby was smiling, as she went over some new songs that Wayne had written. Mr. Elroy was sitting with Hank in his back corner table. It looked like they were having a deep conversation, oblivious to anything else going on in the club which was stirring in preparation to open a few hours later.

"How's the new married couple getting along?" Stark asked.

"Couldn't be better, Stan," Wayne said, squeezing Abby's hand. "Marrying this wonderful lady was one of the few good decisions I've ever made. We're better than good, we're great together. We've just been talking about another dream that both of us had, but it's kinda private if you know what I mean."

Stan had no idea what Wayne was talking about and it wasn't important to him at the moment.

"Wayne, Abby, I just finished my session with Dr. Palmer and Dr. Guyion. I, uh, can't quite put it into words but I have a concern and wanted to talk to you both about it."

"What kind of concern, Stan?" Abby asked.

"Well," Stan was fumbling with his thoughts, "Dr. Guyion certainly has the credentials of a parapsychologist but she is also a high priestess in Satanical worship. I sense a real evil about that woman and just wanted to warn you both about what you reveal to her in your session tomorrow."

"But, Stan, I thought we were to reveal everything we remembered about our little trip to another dimension so they could add clarity to our gaps in memory. Are you saying not to tell her what we do remember?" Wayne said with a puzzled expression.

"I'm not sure what I'm trying to say. It's just a bad feeling, hard to explain. Just keep your guard up and DO NOT let her hypnotize you!" Stan was adamant in his tone.

Wayne laughed without a care in the world and told Stan he should just chill out a bit. "We'll be fine tomorrow, Stan. But thanks for the warning."

Back at the corner table, Mr. Elroy heard every word that Stan spoke to Abby and Wayne while he continued his conversation with Hank.

"Mr. Hank, you're a natural born warrior with a warrior spirit. I can sees this in ya. Da Good Lord can use a man like you! Have you ever thought of giving your life to Him?" Mr. Elroy spoke in such a gentle tone that everyone liked speaking with him.

"I don't know about giving my life to Him, Mr. Elroy, but I do think about Him a lot, especially since I've met Liz and her close relationship with Christianity. How do I do that? How do I get closer to The Lord?"

"Mr. Hank, you just talk to Him. Some people calls dat prayin, but I just call it talkin. Just like you and me are talkin right now. He'll hear you and He'll talk back to you if you just be still and listen. I'm thinkin He's got a purpose for your life. Maybe even somethin big! I's just getting that feelin all a sudden. Now if you'll scuse me, Mr. Hank, I's gots an appointment I need to be at." Mr. Elroy shook Hank's hand and walked slowly out of the club, unassisted.

10

Divine Warning Leave My Chillins Alone!

Wayne and Abby walked back to Hank's table for a quick talk and to inform him of what Lieutenant Stark had told them after his rather brief meeting with the two doctors. Abby could tell that Daddy Hank was in deep thought about something and wanted to touch base.

"Is everything okay between you and Liz, Pop?"

"Oh, yeah. We're good. I'm taking her to dinner tonight."

"I know you too well, Dad. Something's on your mind. You want to tell your daughter and son-in-law all about it? We're all ears."

Hank looked haggard and began slicking back his long gray hair into a tighter pony tail. It seemed as though he was searching for words to describe what was on his mind. He'd never kept any secrets from Abby and they had always had a very open relationship about what was going on in their lives. Somehow it seemed different now that Abby was with Wayne.

"Oh, just wrestling with a couple of things. I didn't sleep too well last night. Can't put my finger on it."

"Pop, you won't believe what Stan just told us about his session with Dr. Guyion…"

"The albino lady from god knows where?"

"Yep. Stan doesn't like her. Said she seems evil and warned Wayne and me not to let her hypnotize us. What's your take on her, Pop?"

"She's a looker and almost got me in trouble with Liz. And I tell you, Ms. Liz Gabriel said the same thing about the European doctor. She got an eerie feeling about her. If Stan said not to let her put you under hypnosis, I think I'd follow his lead on that one, Sweetie Pie. What're your thoughts, Wayne?"

"All my thoughts are wonderful, Hank. Abby and I are happy, I'm all healed up, ready to sing, I don't have a care in the world."

"Stay that way, my boy. That doesn't happen too often in life. Don't worry about me. I'm thinking seriously about cancelling any more appointments with Dr. Palmer. As far as I'm concerned, it's none of his business anymore, but I will talk to Robbie about it later this afternoon and get her take on it before I make up my mind. Maybe we should all just remember what we remember about that place, that dream, and let the rest go. I don't like living in the past or dredging up bad memories. If you two are happy, I'm happy. Plus, I think my future happiness will depend on my relationship with Liz. I really like that lady!"

"We couldn't help but notice, Dad. She makes you happy like no one I've ever seen. Wayne and I like her, too. You have your daughter's permission to pursue her. I haven't called anyone *Mom* in a long time…"

"Don't get ahead of me, Abby. I really like her, heck, I may even love her, but I still can't tell how she feels about me. I haven't had my heart broken in a long time and it took me a while to get over the loss of your mom…"

"I knew you loved her, Dad! How exciting to hear you say those words to anyone but me." Abby cherished the fact that her dad was in love again after all the years of being alone.

"Go for it, Hank! You'll be glad you did. Marriage is great with the right woman in your life," Wayne said, taking a swig of bottled water.

He'd sworn off tequila thanks to his out-of-this-world ordeal and the nurturing, grounding steadfast love of Abby. She was his soul mate and he almost missed figuring that out. It took seven demons, three angels and a group of friends to pound this into his head. Love didn't come easy for Wayne Tyler.

Wayne and Abby arrived at Dr. Palmer's office right on time. They were apprehensive and somewhat intrigued at meeting with the albino doctor from Europe. As they entered the conference room, Belinda Sealy made the introductions of Dr. Guyion and her assistant, Natasha Patski. The atmosphere was icy.

"Wayne, we have the results of the DNA testing, and Dr. Guyion and I would like to go over them with you…"

"Lieutenant Stark has already filled us in, Dr. Palmer. So we're a genetic wonder, huh?" Wayne was trying to be cordial as Abby sat beside him with a stone face, starring at Dr. Guyion's rather low-cut, see-through blouse that left absolutely nothing to the imagination. She was bearing all.

"Yes, Wayne, you and the Lieutenant could be a huge breakthrough for science. The test results are unexplainable." Dr. Palmer was trying to be professional and quickly noticed Abby glaring at Dr. Guyion.

"Wayne, you are a very handsome man! It is my pleasure to meet you," Helle said, almost ignoring Abby. "And, uh, a pleasure to meet you, too, Abby."

"Please call me Mrs. Tyler if you don't mind, Dr. Guyion!"

"Of course…Wayne, tell me how you got into music. I must drop by the club and hear you play sometimes." Dr. Guyion continued her flirtatious advances, not caring what Abby thought.

"Long story, Dr. Guyion. Why don't we talk about all the missing links in this adventure we've all had? I understand you're very good at filling in the missing pieces." Wayne also noticed Dr. Guyion's sexy innuendos and didn't want Abby to go ballistic on her.

"I love to fill in missing links and pieces, Wayne, dearest. Where shall we begin?" Helle reached across the conference table and gave Wayne's hand a little squeeze.

"You tell me, Dr. Guyion. You're the doctor."

"Let's begin with Ishtar. She tried to seduce you, huh? That must have been an experience. How did you like that, Mr. Rock Star?"

"He resisted her, Dr. Guyion, because of his love for me! He said 'no' and remembers little past that point. Let's start somewhere else." Abby stood her ground in front of the deceiving parapsychologist. She wasn't about to allow this unprofessional flirt-fest to go any farther.

"Mrs. Tyler, are you uncomfortable in your relationship with your husband, Wayne?" Helle glared at Abby, not allowing her to respond to the question. "I believe that hypnosis is the best way to get to the depths of your experiences. Would you look into my eyes?"

"I am comfortable with my marriage, Dr. Guyion, and there's no way I'm going to look into your eyes and allow you to hypnotize either one of us. Dr. Palmer, the atmosphere of professionalism is completely shattered due to the dress of Dr. Guyion. The only thing anyone is looking into in this room is her boobs. And that's going to end right now. We know all we need to know about our little trip to the unknown and as for your scientific breakthrough, you'll need to find another path. We're outta here!"

"Wayne, your wife seems to be displaying some jealously here. Not a good trait for a healthy, long-term marriage. Maybe you could drop by my hotel room for a private session with me…" Helle let nothing stand in her way to gain what she wanted.

"Kiss my ass, you Satanical witch!" Abby shouted.

"Ooh, how exciting! I'd love to kiss your ass, Mrs. Tyler. Wayne bring your wife with you. We can have a threesome." Helle broke out into a banshee laugh as Wayne and Abby stood up from their chairs.

Wayne looked at Dr. Palmer and Dr. Guyion with a weak smile on his face and pointed at Abby. "She's the boss, Doctors. I'd say we're just about done."

Dr. Palmer looked over at Belinda and just shook his head. The list of interviewees was dwindling quickly. He had his big scientific break-through paper to consider about the missing link to the God Particle, his status in the psychology community and Helle was quickly destroying that opportunity.

"Could I speak privately to you, Helle?" Their two assistants left the room.

"Don't you know how important this investigation is to me, Helle? This could be the final one percent of confirming the God Particle. It could launch both of us into the *Who's Who* of the scientific world. Don't you understand that? You're being completely unprofessional and provoking our patients to absolutely clam up. Without them, we have no case."

"Oh, Eric, you look so sad." Helle laughed. "I have my ways and you have yours. Can I change that? Why don't you come by my room tonight? I'll cheer you up. I'm in the mood, lover. See you at seven? Besides, I'm looking forward to meeting Bella tomorrow. Tell me about her…"

As Wayne and Abby were driving back to Tequilaville, preparing for the evening guests, Abby was still silent and said nothing. She was livid.

"Baby, please don't be jealous of that woman." Wayne was trying to calm her. "I made a vow to you to be faithful and love you for the rest of my life and I intend to make good on those sacred words."

"The audacity of that albino freak! That sorry bit…!" Abby blurted out.

"Don't say it, Abby. Remember about the nails in our coffins every time we use expletives in anger?"

"What are you talking about, Wayne?"

"I have no idea, Abby. I think I just remembered something new from my time at Between. Can't really explain it. But I do know that you're my soul mate, my only love song. I'm all in for you, baby. You're the love of my life."

"Well, I'm not exactly feeling loved right now, Wayne. Maybe we can stop by the house on the way to the club and you can show me what you're really feeling…"

Before beginning his day at the club, Hank walked down the hall to Robbie's condo and knocked on her door.

"Come in, Hank," Robbie greeted him. "Can I get you a cup of coffee?"

"Sure thing. I need a cup, got some things on my mind I'd like to toss around with you if you have time."

For the next hour, Hank brought Robbie up to date on his relationship with Liz and how she was stand-offish about his advances. He needed a woman's opinion on what was going on and Robbie was his go-to confidant.

"Robbie, Liz said that I was a good man. I know she likes me but she won't even let me kiss her. I haven't kissed a woman in years."

"Hank, Liz cares for you, but I think there's something standing in the way."

"What?"

"She wants to marry a Christian man. You haven't accepted Christ as your savior yet."

"That's it, Robbie?"

"Yep, Hank, that's it. You need to walk your talk. You need to prove to her that you two are on the same page. She's not going to marry an unbeliever."

"Robbie, that's a big step for me. I mean, I remember the good and the bad that we experienced at that place called Betwixt. I sure don't want the bad, but I really don't deserve the good either. Know what I mean?"

"None of us deserves the good; that's the grace and the mercy of God, Hank. That's why He sent His Son to die on the cross for us. All you have to do is accept Jesus as your Lord and Savior and confess your sins to him. Your sins are removed, you get a blank slate, your name is recorded in the Lamb's Book of Life and you go from there. You have to surrender to Him, Hank."

"Surrender isn't exactly in my vocabulary, Robbie. I'm a warrior. I only know how to fight for what I want and need."

"Then surrender and be a warrior for Him, Hank…"

"That's exactly what Mr. Elroy told me, Robbie. How ironic that you would say that."

"Hank, no one can do that for you. You have to take thirty seconds and personally ask Jesus to be Lord of your life. Just ask Him, just talk to Him. He'll do the rest."

"I'll think on this, Robbie. Thank you for your wisdom and insight. My gosh, I just can't figure women out. You guys are so complicated!"

Later that evening, Hank picked Liz up at the Bay Hilton hotel for their dinner date. Liz was glowing as usual and made Hank tingle every time he was with her. He was falling deeper and deeper in love with this lady who made him feel so special and was past the point of risking being hurt.

At dinner, they had the normal chit-chat, 'how was your day,' while Hank tried to figure out how he could get closer to Liz.

"How're things going at the Cowboy Church?"

"Great! We're building a roping arena for the kids and will have barrel racing inside the arena for the girls. Pastor Randy and his wife, Pat, are thrilled about it. Even the bikers are donating to the funds. God is good!" Liz was all smiles.

After dinner on the Kemah Boardwalk, Hank found a private bench that overlooked the bay. "Could we talk, Liz? I've got some things on my mind."

"Sure. What's the subject?"

"Uh, you and me?" Hank had no idea what he was going to say or how to say it. He just wanted to know where their relationship was going.

"I had a long talk with Robbie today. It's been so long for me that I decided that I really don't understand women and asked for her advice. And quite frankly I don't know what I'm feeling for you, either. Does that make sense?"

"It does, Hank. Love takes patience and understanding. It takes time to be real."

"Are we real, Liz?"

"Time will tell, Hank. I pray about it."

"What do you pray for, Liz? I'd really like to know."

"I pray for a sign, Hank. In the Bible, many of the prophets and warriors asked for signs of confirmation from God. He even made time stand still as a sign and moved a sun dial backwards."

"He made time stand still? How'd He do that, Liz?"

"You should read your Bible more often, Hank. I'm not asking for time to stand still, but I am asking for confirmation about our relationship."

"Liz, you made my world stand still the first time I laid eyes on you. Did I tell you that? Does that count as a sign?"

"Hank, you did tell me that, but that was your sign, not mine."

"So where do we go from here, Liz? You know how I feel about you."

"Hank, don't you dare go riding off into the sunset on me. We are real. I care for you a lot, but time will tell. Please don't push me away and don't you doubt my feelings for you. Can you handle that?"

"I'm trying, baby. I'm trying. Patience! I've got to re-learn patience."

"While you're at it, Hank, re-learn trust. It's what relationships are built on, along with love."

"Do you love me, Liz? And please don't tell me that I'm a good man. I've already heard that."

"Yes, I do, Hank. And you *are* a good man."

Mr. Elroy was singing to himself as he slowly walked out of the Tequilaville parking lot and up to the Bay Hilton lot next to the club. Still in his raggedy old clothes, he went inside and approached the front desk.

"Could you kindly put me in contact with Dr. Guyion? I needs to talk with her. I's Mr. Elroy."

The front desk attendant put in a call to Dr. Guyion's room and informed her of her visitor.

"Sure, send the old black man up!" Helle said condescendingly.

"Mr. Elroy, Dr. Guyion is in room number…"

"I knows where she is. Thank ya. I'll just be on my way."

Mr. Elroy walked over to the elevator, took a quick look around to see if anyone was looking and immediately appeared at Helle's door and knocked. Helle opened the door. She was completely nude.

"My my, Dr. Guyion, you gonna catch yo death of cold. Ain't you got no clothes?"

"What can I do for you, Mr. Elroy? Don't you work over at Tequilaville?"

"Yessem, I do. I plays some blues and sings a bit."

"So to what do I owe the honor of meeting such an old, stinky, uneducated black man?" Helle couldn't stand the sight of the old man and wondered why she was wasting her time talking to him.

"What a way to start off a conversation, Dr. Guyion. I's is old, sometimes I get a bit stinky, it's plain to see that I'm black but I's not completely uneducated. In my years on this earth, life has taught me a lot about people. Even people that tries to make me feel lesser than they are."

"Mr. Elroy, I'm very plain spoken. I call a spade a spade."

"Yes m'am, I may be a spade but I'm the ace of spades when it comes to you. Don't you forget dat." Mr. Elroy chuckled.

"You make me laugh, old man. Now why are you here? I have better things to do than exchange insults with you."

"I comes here to talk to you about my chillin."

"Your what? What's a chillin? I speak many different languages but I have never heard the word *chillin* in any of them. What the hell is a chillin?"

"It's my family that you been talking to, Dr. Guyion. They's my chillin, like my offspring. You know, little chillin."

"You are so uneducated that you can't even speak English correctly. And these *chillin* of yours that I've been interviewing are all white. Now just how could you be related to any of them, Elroy?"

"We's all brothers and sisters, Dr. Guyion. Don't you ever read the Bible about Adam and Eve or Noah and the flood. Everyone came from them, so you's all brothers and sisters no matter the color of your skin."

"So now you're going to tell me that you are believing all those lies written in some book that you call the bible. I knew you were uneducated, completely stupid and without scientific proof…"

"You ever seen a rose grow? Who do you think gave it it's fragrance, some amoeba? Some scientific phenomena that you can't explain? Tell me that, child. Just tells me that!"

"I'm not your child, Elroy, boy! Quite frankly I'm surprised that you have a word like *phenomena* in your limited vocabulary." Helle was getting more and more disenchanted with the conversation. She felt she was matching wits with an illiterate.

"You know, Dr. Guyion, at my age to be called a *boy* is a compliment, I thanks ya for that. But I know you meant it as a racial slur, so I'm just gonna forgive you for that intended comment and get on with why I came to talk to you today."

"By all means, *boy*. Do tell me what's on your feeble old black mind!""Oh, Dr. Guyion, I's going to tells ya alright. But I'm not sure you're listening to me. Maybe I can get your attention a different way…"

Mr. Elroy immediately turned into Gordon, Wayne's angel, a guardian angel with tremendous power from the Almighty. He filled the room with light so brilliant that Helle had to turn away and shield her eyes.

"Have I got your attention now, Helle?"

For the first time in her life, Helle momentarily felt shame for her nakedness. She crawled behind the couch in the room as she tried to escape the blinding light and regain her sense of reasoning.

"Please! Stop that! The light is killing me. I'm an albino and can't take the light. Who the hell are you anyway?" Helle said defiantly.

"I am called Gordon by the Almighty. I'm a holy angel, a guardian angel of the Kingdom of Jehovah God, the Creator of all the heavens and the earth. The One who places every star in the sky and calls it by name. The Giver and Taker of all breath, of all life. Nothing or no one lives without His consent. He has sent me here today to give you and your false god a warning. Listen carefully to His message!"

Still crouched behind the couch, Helle prayed to Satan for power. She emerged from her fetal position with new strength and caused the room to be filled with an icy fog mixed with fire. With her new power, she raised herself off the floor and hovered before Gordon, still shielding her eyes from his brilliance.

"I am commanded by my prince, the prince of darkness. I listen to no other commands!" she said defiantly.

"Helle, you have been deceived! Does a prince rule over the King of Kings and the Lord of Lords? Can darkness walk with light? You display weak powers of fog and fire. I come to you with light and hope which you cannot overcome but can receive. You, too, can be saved from doom as all mortals can…"

"I choose to serve who I serve, Gordon! You cannot change my mind. I do have the freedom of free choice and free will." Helle glared at Gordon. Her eyes shown like red lasers.

Undaunted, Gordon waved his bronze-like hand and the fire and fog disappeared. Helle fell to the floor with a thud and crawled back behind the couch, trying to avoid the mighty angel's commanding power.

"Helle, when you believe in a lie, which is Satan, the father of all lies, you reject the truth. The Son of Man is the way, the truth and the life. Satan leads to eternal damnation. It is not too late for you, with all your sins, to receive salvation."

"My salvation is in Satan, my master. I have made my choices and will not turn from them! Your trickery cannot sway me!" Helle said as she peeked timidly over the top of the couch. She could not look directly at Gordon for fear of death. Even in her defiance, she was scared.

"I rebuke you, lowly guardian! I will not speak to you again. Leave me, please, just leave me!"

Gordon stood before Helle for what seemed to be an eternity. His patience had no end. The longer he stood silently before her, the more frightened she became, wondering why her master had not removed the mighty angel from her presence. She was out of tricks. She had displayed all her powers and nothing worked. Gordon stoically stood before her and peered down upon her. She felt like his eyes were piercing her soul. She could not escape and felt trapped and helpless.

"Where is your master's power now, Helle? Is he able to move mountains? I think not. He can't even remove me from your presence. I act on the strength that The Almighty gives to me. I will deliver His message and you will remember it." Gordon's voice was still, soft and commanding.

"Those children that The Almighty has given His Son can never be snatched away…by you or your prince of darkness. Their names are written indelibly in the Lamb's Book of Life. Stay clear of them or wreak the wrath of The Almighty Himself."

"Your consequences be damned, lowly angel! I do not fear you!"

"Then why are you cowered down before me, godless mortal? It's still not too late for you, Helle. But if you don't turn from your blasphemy and evil ways, all the plagues of His book will be showered down upon you and your branch of the tree of life shall be removed. You have been warned!"

"I reject your warnings. I will serve my powerful master to the end of time. I will be obedient to my mission—to draw Wayne and Abby Tyler to submission. I will make them and all their friends and family renounce their faith. I will destroy their livelihood and reduce them to mere beggars. I will deceive them with the powers given to me. The Almighty may choose to let them live, but they will live in agony. I'll make sure of that."

"Helle, pride caused Lucifer, the son of the morning, to be renamed Satan. Pride caused one-third of the holy angels to fall from heaven. Pride caused mankind to lose a perfect immortal life in the Garden of Eden. And today, your pride will take you down a dark road to judgment if you do not change your ways."

"I fight with my pride, angel! I will not change my mind, today or ever."

"Never say never, Helle. The Almighty loves all mortals of every color, every race, every nation with no matter of their sin. Does Satan love you?"

"I choose lust over love," Helle screamed. "Love hurts; lust pleases and brings me pleasure and power."

"And leaves you empty, wanting for more doesn't it, Helle? Lust is like a narcotic that you can't get enough of. Love and only love satisfies the craving…" Gordon said lovingly.

"Take your love and shove it, angel! I don't need or want love. I crave power, riches and for men to worship my beauty," Helle said defiantly.

"You have spoken, Helle. So, I, Gordon, a holy angel from the Son of Man will give you some time to really cogitate on your decisions going forward. By His power I will strike you blind and cover your body with painful boils for three days…"

"No, no! Please restore my sight. I'm blind! I can't see! I'm in great pain. Please help me!" Helle was screaming with fear, groveling on the floor in her room, grasping for her walkie-talkie so she could summon her security team.

"Helle, you can pray to your false god or you can pray to Jehovah Rapha, the God that heals. Free choice and your free will." Gordon watched Helle wallow in pain, hoping she would make the right decision.

In an instant, Gordon became Mr. Elroy again, still in Helle's room. As he moved toward the door, in his familiar voice he spoke to Helle.

"Miss Helle, dis is Mr. Elroy. You won't remember me as being Gordon. I tooks that from yo memory. Be doing some powerful thinkin with the warnings you got delivered to you. And, you can call me *boy* any times you like. You's all chillin of the Almighty, too. Hope you'll join the family some day. I almost forgot, Dr. Guyion, how'd you like dat word *cogitate*? In case you don't quite get the meaning of it from an old uneducated black man, it means to think real hard on something. I'll just bids you adieu fo now…"

11

Quack! Quack! Mene, Mene, Tekel Upharsin!

"Pastor Randy, this is Hank Hawkins. I've made some decisions and wondered if you could baptize me? I want to be saved."

"Praise God, Hank. That's what I do for a living. Where and when?"

Hank was alone in his corner booth at Tequilaville getting ready for the night's guests.

"If it's not too much trouble, I'd like to be baptized in the wading pool here at the club, where my daughter Abby was baptized, say, in the morning about ten."

"All things are possible, Hank. See you then." Pastor Randy was riding his horse at the Cowboy Church when Hank called.

Hank put in a call to the Tequilaville *family* and asked if they could be witnesses to his public profession of faith and baptism. He only wanted close friends to attend. The next morning, Robbie, Bella, Abby, Wayne, Liz, Lieutenant Stark, Mr. Elroy, and the club staff gathered on the patio next to the wading pool long before opening up for the day. Scott Wood and the band arrived just in time for the ceremony.

"You make me very happy, Hank," Liz said as she walked up to Hank and gave him a kiss on the cheek right in front of the entire group. "I hope you're doing this for yourself and not just for me."

"I'm doing this for both of us, Liz. Been having trouble sleeping and

I've even talked to the Man upstairs about it. For some reason this has been on my mind from the moment I met you. This is what I want to do."

Officer Rob LeGrano of the Clear Lake Police Department was cruising his beat when he noticed an unusual number of cars in the Tequilaville parking lot. It was much too early in the day for so many cars so he decided to stop by to see what was going on. When he found the doors locked, he walked around to the back patio and saw the crowd gathered.

Hank was in cut-off blue jean shorts, no cowboy hat and wearing a Tequilaville T-shirt and flip-flops. No one had ever seen him not wearing his boots or his old gray hat. Mr. Elroy was all smiles and stood patiently next to Liz.

Pastor Randy and his wife, Pat, arrived and joined the group. After a quick private conversation with Hank, Randy stepped into the wading pool and motioned for Hank to join him. Hank entered the small pool and crossed his arms across his chest. Abby had tears of joy streaming down her cheeks.

"Hank Hawkins, do you confess your sins to Jesus and ask Him to be your personal savior?" Pastor Randy asked.

"I do!"

"Then by the power of Almighty God and the saving grace of Jesus Christ, I baptize you in the name of The Father and of The Son and of The Holy Spirit." As Hank's knees bent Pastor Randy lowered Hank below the water.

The wading pool began to churn and swirl with brilliant supernatural colors. Everyone but Mr. Elroy began to gasp in wonder at what was happening right before their eyes. A ray of intense light came from above and shown down on Hank. Pastor Randy fell back onto the deck in complete awe.

As Hank emerged from the water completely dry, he was clothed in a white linen robe. His gray hair and beard had turned to brilliant silver, the crown of old age, and his face glowed like a light house beacon in the night. Hank had no idea what was happening to him. He felt the love and power from above completely engulfing every fiber of his being. Liz and Robbie fell to their knees, praising God. Abby and Wayne were petrified and said nothing while Mr. Elroy continued to smile from ear to ear.

"Breathe, every one! Don't you believe in miracles when you see'em?" Mr. Elroy said as he began to clap his hands. "I told ya, Mr. Hank, that the Good Lawd could use a warrior like you. I thinks He's just about ready to do dat."

Hank's brilliance caused every boater on the lake to see the white light streaming down from above and drew them to the docks. Within minutes, over forty boats cruised up to the Tequilaville docks to see what was happening. The entire lake was glowing.

Still in shock, Liz slowly rose to her feet, almost afraid to approach him. She walked over to Hank and kneeled down before him and offered her hand to him. When Hank's hand touched hers, she felt a love go through her that she had never experienced in her entire life.

"Hank Hawkins, I asked God for a sign. This moment He has given me one that goes beyond understanding and I am thankful for my answered prayers. He has made it clear to me. Will you marry me, Hank Hawkins?"

Without speaking, Hank lifted Liz to her feet before him.

"Now you can kiss me, Hank. I've been waiting for your kiss for a long time." Liz closed her eyes as their lips met for the first time.

Hank nodded his head in a positive gesture to accept Liz's proposal of marriage but he never said a word. He, too, was confused as to what was happening to him. His mind was clear and his path to love was so obvious, looking into Liz's eyes. They didn't need any words of confirmation. Their love spoke for them.

Abby walked over and took Liz's and her dad's hands into hers.

"Daddy Hank, you're not only the poet in my heart, you are my heart and it beats with the passion of happiness for you and Liz. I love you both so much."

Abby looked over at Bella and motioned to her to join them. Bella had her hands over her face and peered back at them between her fingers. She was scared to death at what was happening. She had no comprehension of the supernatural even though she had been present at Betwixt. She chose to shove it out of her mind since it caused her anguish with her rather worldly life style.

As more and more boats crowded around the docks of Tequilaville, Officer LeGrano called for backup, not knowing what would happen next. The boaters had yet to approach Hank. They were still in awe seeing what was happening and LeGrano wanted to be prepared for the worst.

Pastor Randy walked around the pool, still dripping wet, to talk to Coast Guard Chaplin, Lieutenant Stark. "Stan, I've baptized a lot of people during my ministry, but I've never seen anything like this. I'm having a hard time believing my own eyes. What do you make of this?"

Stan Stark was just as amazed as everyone else but since his two trips to Betwixt, he seemed to have a greater insight of the supernatural. He scratched the white streak above his right ear and replied to Pastor Randy.

"Pastor, the only thing I can say is that it's pretty clear from all the prophecies that we're near the end times. I'd say that God has a plan for Hank and has divinely singled him out. What that plan is, I have no idea, but I know that Hank has received a special anointing to do God's will, whatever that is…" The Lieutenant turned from Pastor Randy and went over to congratulate the betrothed couple, almost afraid to shake Hank's hand or to look him in the eyes.

Natasha Patski was trying her best to soothe the pain of her employer, Helle Guyion. Helle shrieked with pain from the boils and was helplessly blind to even get out of bed. From their hotel suite, Natasha could see the commotion down below them at the Tequilaville docks but decided not to say anything to Dr. Guyion about it.

"Natasha! Call Dr. Palmer and put off our appointment with Bella Cantrell. Tell him I'll let him know when to reschedule it. Bring me another bottle of my vodka. I'm in such pain, I can't stand it. Why can't my doctors help me with this pain? No matter what they give me, it doesn't work."

"Dr. Guyion, the doctors have already given you more morphine than they should have. Any more could kill you." Natasha was stressed to the max but she wasn't a physician.

"I want to die, Natasha! Do something!"

A fifty-foot Marauder Cigarette boat came blasting into Clear Lake from Galveston Bay and didn't obey the "No Wake" signs which caused many of the docked fishing boats to start slamming into each other. No one on the lake liked "Ducky" Don DeLozier, the son of billionaire porn producer, Samson DeLozier.

He was nicknamed "Ducky" Don because the name on his $500,000 boat was "Quack Quack" with two rubber ducks painted on each side of the stern of the racing boat. Ducky Don was employed by his rich dad to go into Indonesia and other points of the world where there was sex slave trafficking. He bought and kidnapped young girls and flew them back to the U.S. in his private jet and forced them into the porn industry. The DeLozier label of porn was known for its full contact movies. Nothing was too graphic for their films.

Upon seeing the excitement at Tequilaville, Ducky Don turned to his buddy, "Ink," a sloppy, overweight tattoo artist and told him to head for Tequilaville. Down below in the cabin of the boat was Don's latest trophy from

Vietnam, My Lai. She was a sixteen-year-old beauty who had recently been abducted from her home country. Don and Ink had spent the night at Red Fish Island, tattooing My Lai from head to foot and having their way with her.

The *Quack Quack* pulled up to the dock and Don and Ink stepped off the boat, pushing their way past the crowd of other boaters to see what all the commotion was about. They saw Hank, still glowing and thought it was some kind of weird advertisement gimmick to bring people into the club. Still down below in the cabin, My Lai was shaking, trying to recover from her night of pure hell at the hands of the two men.

"What a way cool ad gimmick! How'd you do that, Hank? I've got to get me some of that body wash you're using. Hey man, you're glowing, did you know that?" Don began his vulgar laugh and elbowed Ink in the ribs to get him to laugh along with him. As Ink laughed, he spit out a mouth full of left over taco he'd been having for breakfast.

No one said a word to these two detestable men. Everyone knew what they did for a living and it wasn't welcomed. Deep down, the people wished that someone in law enforcement would put them behind bars. No charges had ever been filed on them. People just looked the other way since they had no proof of what Don and Ink were doing. But everyone knew.

As their own laughter subsided, they could hear My Lai's moaning coming from their boat.

"Hey Ink! Go get the girl. It's about time she started earning her keep around here," Don said, oblivious to Officer LeGrano mixed into the crowd. The backup officers hadn't yet arrived.

Ink went down into the cabin and put a string bikini on My Lai. She was still shaking as Ink brought her over to Don. When she emerged from the cabin it was plain to see how swelled up her fragile body was from the tattoos and she reeked from the night of abuse at Red Fish Island.

"I want to take this opportunity to introduce DeLozier Films latest star, a Vietnamese beauty named My Lai. She's for rent by the hour or the day. Now who wants to start the bidding?" Ducky Don lived down to his hedonistic reputation, always looking to make a quick buck.

Gathering her courage, modestly trying to cover her almost naked body, My Lai began screaming in broken English…"I kidnapped, they paint my body, I so ashamed…I raped all night. I Christian woman! Help me! Please help me!"

Ducky Don just laughed and said, "Yep, men, she's a feisty one all right. Now's who's going to have a go with her?"

My Lai was desperate. She looked over at Hank, who was still glowing, and said, "I want baptized. Save me! Please save me!" as she tried to break away from the grasp of Ink.

Mr. Elroy looked over at Hank to see what he would do, if anything. Maybe this was Hank's purpose that day.

Hank released his grip on Liz, who was just as livid as everyone else present, seeing the audacity of this terrible piece of humanity, Ducky Don and his partner in crime, Ink.

"Come to me, child." Hank spoke the first words he had spoken after his miracle baptism just moments before. "I will baptize you!"

Hank then turned to Ink and told him to release his grip on this young girl. For the first time, Ink noticed Hank's glowing appearance and looked over at Don for directions.

"Now, Ink!" Hank's voice seemed to boom with a commanding velocity that caused Ink to let go of My Lai instantly. She ran over to Hank and cowered down at his feet, looking back to see if Don was going to grab her again.

"Touch that girl, Hank, and it's a thousand bucks an hour. You can pay me in cash or in drinks. Your choice!" Don said with a challenge in his voice.

Hank pointed his finger at Don as the light going through him from above traveled into Hank's finger and straight at Don's mouth.

"Be silent! Close your mouth. Speak not another word or it will be your last," Hank said to Don.

Officer LeGrano pushed his way through the crowd and drew his pistol, pointing at Don and Ink.

Hank assisted My Lai into the water of the wading pool as she shivered even more. As she entered the pool a peace and calm came over her and she looked up at Hank. T-Bone moved in front of them as if to protect them from any objectors. His six-foot-seven, 285-pound body was daunting and no one dared to intercede.

"My Lai, you are a child of God. Do you put your faith in His hands?" Hank's voice continued to boom to the point it could be heard all across the lake.

"I put faith in Him! I Christian girl, Yes!"

Hank lowered My Lai's frail, swollen, abused body into the water. As he lifted her up, she too was clothed in a white linen robe. Her tattoos had disappeared, her swelling was gone and she had the fragrance of a rose.

"How'd the hell did you do that? Are you some kind of a magician?" Ink shouted to Hank.

"Don DeLozier, you and your buddy Ink are both under arrest for rape of a minor and kidnapping. Put your hands in the air!" LeGrano said, pointing his pistol at them.

My Lai stepped out of the pool. She was warm, she was radiant, she was healed of all the atrocities that had been inflicted upon her, physically and mentally. Pastor Randy's wife, Pat, went over to her and led her away from Hank, comforting her and telling her that they would take care of her.

Before Officer LeGrano could get his handcuffs out of his duty belt, the lake became dark. The sun disappeared as a huge black cloud formed over the entire group standing on the patio of Tequilaville. It was eerie and it was instant. Daylight had left, darkness arrived.

Scott Wood leaned over and whispered in Mr. Elroy's ear. "Sir, I think I should be doing something, but I don't know what to do!"

"Just stand there and watch, Mr. Scott. Mr. Hank don't need our help. Yous about to see somethin to remember for the rest of yo life." Mr. Elroy put his arm around Scott to calm him down.

The party atmosphere that Don and Ink had tried to create soon gave way to hushed anticipation. This was not only a day of miracles, it was a day of continued miracles, one after the next. The crowd was trying to deal with what they saw before them. To some, even trusting their own eyes was difficult. How could a man glow with brilliance so bright that most could not look upon him? How could a fully tattooed woman lose her ink by simply being immersed in water? How could a bright shiny day turn to darkness so soon? Nothing made sense, it wasn't logical and it was very hard to believe. Yet the people were there experiencing the miracles happening before them.

The clouded sky caused the winds off the bay to become colder and colder. Those in bathing suits and bikinis began to get goose bumps on top of the goose bumps they already had from the events. A chill went over the crowd as they wrapped their arms around themselves and huddled together. No one was about to leave.

Ducky Don's mouth was sealed and Ink moved away from his evil friend as did the others present, leaving Don in a small area of the patio all alone. In an instant, the wind ceased to blow, the lake became like glass and the eerie atmosphere became more intense. From the massive dark cloud above the lake came a booming voice.

"MENE! MENE! TEKEL! UPHARSIN!"

Everyone on the deck cowered down to their hands and knees at the sound of the voice from the cloud, all except Mr. Elroy and Hank. They stood firm.

Bella was at her wits' end, scared to death. Way too much supernatural for her. "What the hell is that? Who's talking? What does it all mean? Mom, I'm scared!"

Abby wrapped both of her arms around Wayne while they were crouched down. Robbie and Liz were trying to pray for protection but their prayers were mixed with fear and anxiety. Pastor Randy huddled with Pat and My Lai, trying to comfort them and telling them to just look down and not look at the cloud above. Lieutenant Stark crawled over to Bella trying to be her rock during this intense phenomenon.

Mr. Elroy began to sing softly, "Nobody knows da trouble I's seen…" as he slowly shuffled toward Don, who was face to the planks with both hands covering his face.

There were NASA astrophysicists, engineers, and meteorologists present, taking a much needed rest on the lake from their duties. Some were agnostics, others atheists, some just looking for a sign to believe in a higher power. Their minds raced with equations trying to figure out what was happening mathematically. One meteorologist looked across the street at the NASA facilities only to see that it was bathed in sunlight from the beautiful day and secretly wished they were back there at work. Anywhere but where they were and what they were experiencing. They, too, were frightened.

As Mr. Elroy approached Ducky Don, he reached down, grabbed Don's hand and told him to stand.

"Mr. Don, these words are for you! They are a heavenly language spoken in heaven. Let me explain their meaning. 'Mene' means dat the Almighty has numbered yo kingdom. Yo daddy's empire in porn is about to fall and you with it. Since the Almighty has repeated this word twice, well, Mr. Don, dat means it will happen today with no delay.

"As for 'tekel,' dat means you have been weighed in the balances and found wanting. Or, 'you had yo chance to turn yo life around and hadn't done it in time.' I can't lie to you, Mr. Don. It don't look too good for ya. Uh, you may want to brace yoself for what's about to happen to ya. May the Good Lawd have mercy on your soul."

Officer LaGrano began crawling backward away from Don, hearing what Mr. Elroy was saying. LeGrano was just as terrified as anyone else.

As Mr. Elroy stepped back from the now standing Don DeLozier, everyone could feel electricity in the air. The hair on their arms began to rise. When everyone with the exception of Mr. Elroy and Hank had hidden their eyes from looking upon Don out of sheer fright, a lightning bolt came down from the cloud and struck Don DeLozier squarely on his head and continued until his body had completely vaporized.

The smell of burning flesh covered the deck of Tequilaville. The bolt was so bright that it forced everyone to cover their eyes for fear of blindness setting in. People could hear the loud boom from the cloud, the buzzing of the electricity and the entire deck seemingly being ripped from its sunken pillars. Don had no time to scream, his mouth had been sealed forever.

Then it was over. The cloud disappeared into sunlight. The wind blew in from the bay. There were ripples on the lake. All as if nothing had happened. As everyone began to see the light and feel the breeze, one by one they shakily began to rise to their feet. The only thing left of Don DeLozier was his deck shoes, melted into the planks of the patio, still smoldering…and the stench of burning flesh piercing through the nostrils of the crowd.

People literally ran to get back into their boats and leave the docks of Tequilaville. They ran from absolute fear of what they had just seen. Some were crying, some were tripping over themselves but none were talking.

Officer LeGrano gathered his wits as three Clear Lake Police Department officers arrived. He pointed to Ink and told them to put the cuffs on him and take him in. Ink was just as stunned as everyone else and offered no resistance to his arrest.

Hank's brilliance had subsided and apart from his bright silver hair and beard, he appeared normal, standing stoically, looking down on the melted deck shoes that had just a moment ago been Ducky Don DeLozier. Hank's robe was gone, and he was back in his cut-offs and flip flops.

Pastor Randy put a jacket around My Lai. Her robe was also gone and she was back in her skimpy bikini. She kept looking at her body where the tattoos had been. Her skin was smooth, there was no pain or swelling since the water of her baptism had removed all the markings and pain that Ink had inflicted upon her.

LeGrano asked one of the officers with him to rope off the area for their investigation and reports. A life had been taken. But who or what took it? Was it an act of nature? An accident? The answer was clear but there was no proof, only believing what they saw and what they didn't see. LeGrano began taking statements from the few who remained, still stunned and unable to leave on their own.

"Mr. Hawkins, we're going to have to seal off your patio and dock area for a couple of days until the forensic guys have done their thing. We'll try do make it as fast as possible," Officer LeGrano said apologetically. "We won't shut down the club inside, you can open as usual, but just don't let anyone out on the patio."

Hank thanked him and just looked around the lake at all of the boats speeding away.

"Would you take me home, Stan?" Bella said to Lieutenant Stark. "I don't want to be alone. I'm trembling. I need to talk to you about this. I don't understand what I just experienced…again!"

Bella waved at her mom, Robbie. "I'll call you, Mom! I just don't know what to say right now. I gotta get out of here."

Scott Wood, standing up beside Mr. Elroy with his band all huddled around, said, "Mr. Elroy, how did you know what was going to happen? You knew, didn't you?"

"Well, Mr. Scott, as a man gets older and experiences a lot of life, sometimes we's just gets that notion dat somethins bad about to happen. Can't explain it.

Just comes and goes. What don't you grab Mr. Wayne and the band and we can go in and practice a bit befo opening up tonight. How's dat sound? Whew! What a bad smell we's got out here. Are you guys okay?"

Abby was also trembling as she and Wayne stood looking out over the lake. She took Wayne's hand and began walking over to her dad.

"Pop, are you okay?"

"I'm good, baby. You?"

"Daddy Hank, what just happened?"

"What do you mean, Abby?"

"Pop, look at you! Your hair and beard are bright silver...A light streamed down on you. You were wearing a white robe. Don't you remember any of this? A man was struck by lightning right in front of us!"

"Baby, all I remember is a small voice telling me I was here for a reason. Uh, my hair is silver?"

"Oh, Dad. You don't remember any of this, do you?" Abby grabbed Hank and hugged him close to her.

Hank looked over at Liz and motioned her over to him. Robbie came over also needing a little comforting from what had taken place.

"Liz, did you ask me to marry you? Am I dreaming this, too?"

"Not a dream, Hank. Yes, I did propose to you and you said, 'Yes!' Do you want to take it back?"

Hank pulled Liz close to him and kissed her. "No way do I want to take it back. You're the love of my life. But I thought I was supposed to do the asking..."

"Hank, in your own way, you did ask me. I knew you loved me but I wanted a sign that you were the man for me. When I got that sign—wow and what a sign it was—I asked you, right then and there. You really don't remember much of this, do you?"

"Not much...So when's this wedding taking place? Do I have time to shower and clean up?" Hank said, beginning to laugh.

"Soon, Mr. Hawkins. Soon! Robbie, want to help me plan the wedding? I really want to make it simple and small, just a few close friends."

"I'm so happy for you both." Robbie started hugging everyone. "Who do you want to perform the ceremony? Pastor Randy?"

"He would be my choice, Robbie, but I want to talk to Hank about it first. Are you okay?"

"Shaken but not stirred, Liz. I'll be just fine. Let's start planning a wedding." Robbie was overjoyed that Hank had found his soul mate.

Liz put her arm through Hank's arm and led him back into the club. "Tell me more about this voice that you heard that said 'You're here for a reason.' What do you think that meant?"

"No clue, darling. Maybe it meant that I'm getting to marry the most wonderful woman in the world. Maybe that's the reason. By the way, where's Bella? She's really been on my mind lately."

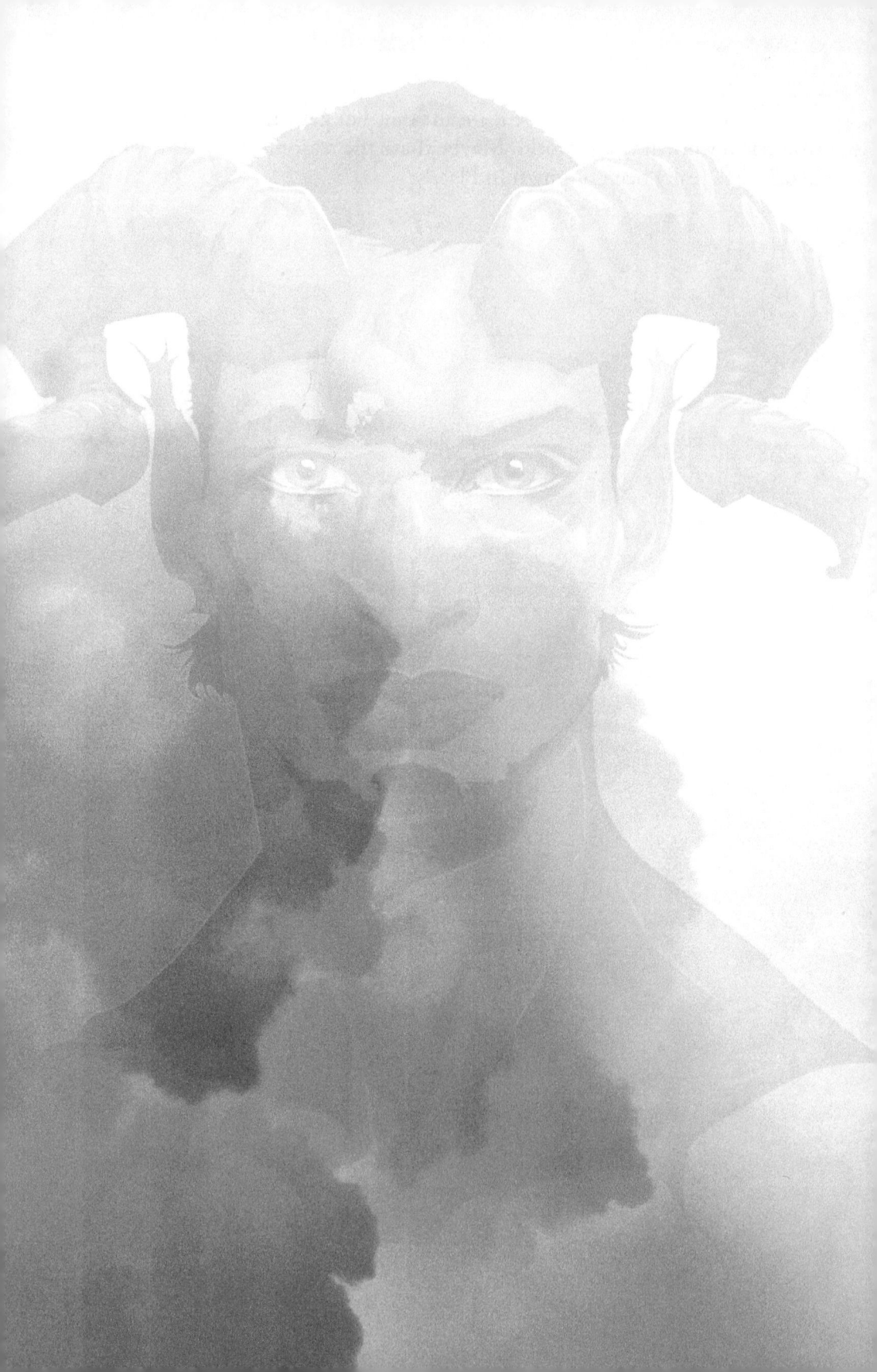

12

Mount Zaphon The Aspired Throne of Satan

Lieutenant Stark drove Bella home and escorted her into her house. It appeared that her yard hadn't been mowed in weeks, Bella's flower beds were full of weeds and upon entering, he could tell that she wasn't the best house keeper in the world.

"Please don't mind the mess, Stan. My life has been so hectic lately. Been so busy with work…"

Stan just laughed it off and sat down on Bella's huge sectional couch and looked around her living room. She had a large sound system, big screen TV, many souvenir shot glasses from New Orleans and from practically every club around the lake. Various articles of clothing left on the floors showed a path to her bedroom. The sink in the kitchen was full of dirty dishes and empty pizza boxes and Chinese food containers ranged over the counter tops.

"Can I get you something to drink, Stan? A beer or a soda?" Bella was still nervous about what she had just experienced at Tequilaville.

"Water will be fine, Bella. You're shaking. Why don't you just sit here with me and let's talk about what we've just seen," Stan said in a comforting voice.

"Stan, what's going on around here! Strange things are happening to my friends, to me and I've just got an eerie feeling that things are going to get worse. Am I crazy? You've seen it too, Stan. Can you explain all of this to me because it's scaring me and I can't sleep for fear of dreaming about all this. I mean, my dreams are horrid. I haven't had a good night's sleep in weeks."

Stan took a deep breath, "Bella, these experiences that we've all witnessed are truly supernatural events. I thought we could confide in Dr. Palmer to help us have some clarity but since Dr. Guyion has joined in our sessions, well, I've got a bad feeling about her and I don't think we can depend on either of them to help put the pieces together. We're going to have to do this on our own."

"I'm still going to my session, Stan." Bella blurted out. "I'm not giving up on either one of them. Besides, I haven't met this mystery albino woman and can't wait to see her. They're smart people. They'll help us out, I know it."

"Be careful who you trust, Bella. They're scientists. Yeah, they're smart, but do they have your best interest in mind?"

"What do you mean by that, Stan? Of course they have my best interest in mind. I'm about the only one left who will talk to them for some strange reason and that means I'm the key to their research at the present." Bella had stopped shaking and was finding her comfort zone in her own home.

"Bella, you're an amazing woman. You like being in the center of attention, don't you?" Stan was smiling and glad to see Bella was returning to her own flamboyant self.

"Of course, Stan, that's my place and thank you for saying I am amazing. I thought you didn't notice." Bella started to flirt a little, rolling her eyes and giving Stan the once over. "But let's get back to all this supernatural stuff. You're a chaplain, can't you tell me what's going on and if I should be scared about it?"

"Bella, no one should live their life in fear. We need to be aware of what's happening and pray for understanding. Do you ever pray?"

"Not much. I just Google anything I don't understand. Right now, I just don't know what to type in. That's why I want you to explain things to me, Stan."

The Lieutenant knew he didn't have clear answers for Bella's questions. Explanations could range from the sublime to the ridiculous and to begin explaining Bible prophecy to Bella was something that he believed was above her ability to understand or believe in a single explanation.

"Bella, let me put it this way…" Stan was trying to find the words. "I believe we're experiencing these events because God is working in the lives of people, not just here in Clear Lake but all over the world. He's been working in your life and my life to tell us something is coming."

"That's what I want to know, Stan, what's coming and will it hurt me?"

"Bella, do you even know what faith and salvation is?" Stan was looking her right in the eyes.

"If you want the truth, not really. Why don't you tell me?"

"Bella, faith is what kept Wayne from falling into the lake of fire. You do remember that part, don't you?"

"I don't want to remember it, Stan. That's what scares me. I don't want to think about that place or even consider that it was more than some wild and crazy dream I've had and I don't want to go there anymore." Bella shivered.

"It was much more than a dream. It was an experience that we were all very fortunate to have had. We got to see into the future, Bella. We had the rare honor to see God's love, healing, and presence, how He stays by our side in the midst of trials and tribulations. Why would you not want to remember that?"

"Quite frankly, Stan, because it scares the hell out of me. I'm not going there ever again. It was a bad dream and that's that! Can't you come up with something that I can and want to think about?"

"Okay, how about this. If God were going to end the world…"

"Stop right there, Stan! I don't want to hear all this end times stuff either. That scares me more than anything."

"Why does it scare you, Bella?"

"Because I'm not ready for the world to end. I'm having fun, doing what I want to do and people have been talking about the end of the world for centuries…and it hasn't happened yet, has it?"

"It's going to happen, Bella. And my guess is that it'll happen sooner rather than later. I'm trying to talk to you, Bella, but I don't think you want to listen…"

"You're right. I don't want to hear where you're going, Stan. I thought you could give me some simple explanation and obviously you can't. Thanks for the ride home. Maybe we can meet another time for drinks…"

Three days had passed since Gordon struck Helle with boils and blindness. Her pain was gone, her sight now restored, and now she was livid with anger and wanted retaliation, revenge against the supernatural authorities that had caused her helplessness. She was off schedule and wanted to fight back. Since Mr. Elroy had taken her memory of the event from her mind, Helle was at odds who to punish with her supernatural powers. But, someone had to pay.

"Natasha! Put in a call to Dr. Palmer. Tell him to get over here right away. I want to see him." Helle was powerfully insistent. Natasha wasted no time in making the call.

When Eric Palmer knocked on Helle's hotel room door, Natasha escorted him into the huge room. Helle was decked out to the nines in a southwest Indian motif dress, a turquoise squash blossom necklace that had to be worth thousands of dollars, cowboy boots with fringe hanging from the tops and a feather in her hair with feather and diamond earrings.

Eric noticed that Helle looked paler than normal. Nonetheless, she looked like a woman on a mission despite her peaked condition.

"Helle, are you all right? You look like you've lost some weight," Palmer said. "Otherwise, you look beautiful. Are we going to a rodeo or something?"

"Oh Eric, my love, I've had a touch of the flu but it's gone now. I'm ready to take Hank Hawkins up on his invitation to visit Tequilaville and you're going to escort me."

"Have you forgotten about taking me to Betwixt, Helle? I'm going to hold you to that."

"We'll go there later tonight, Eric, trust me. But first, we're going to have some fun. Ask me no more questions. You will experience Betwixt at midnight." Helle was looking for vengeance and needed a victim.

As they entered the club on the lake, Mr. Elroy, Wayne Tyler, Scott Wood and the band were singing some happy blues songs. The crowd was light since the experience on the docks that killed "Ducky" Don. Word had spread around the lake community and people were avoiding Tequilaville in droves.

Hank, Liz, Robbie and Bella were sitting in Hank's corner booth while Abby was in her office trying to figure out how to pay the bills. Business had not been good for the past few days.

Eric and Helle chose a table on the other side of the club, off to themselves. Helle looked over at Hank's corner table to let them know she had finally arrived to accept Hank's invitation. Hank tipped his hat at them but didn't get up. Mr. Elroy saw them enter but didn't acknowledge their presence. There was an icy atmosphere that Helle was determined to overcome.

A waitress asked Helle and Eric Palmer for their order.

"Bring us a bottle of your most expensive tequila!" Helle never settled for less than the best. "Also a bowl of salt and another bowl of sliced limes."

The waitress seemed a little confused. "M'am, I can't bring you a whole bottle. Against house rules…"

"Whose rules? Just bring what I ask and set the bottle on the floor beside me. No one will notice. Here's a huge tip. Now can you just do what I ask?" Helle put some cash in the hands of the waitress.

"M'am, we don't accept Russian Rubles."

Helle, a bit disgruntled, reached into her purse and pulled out a wad of U.S. one hundred dollar bills that could choke a horse and peeled off five of them, folded them and handed them to the waitress.

"Will that cover it?" Helle always tempted people beyond their ability to resist. Five hundred dollars was more than the waitress could make in several nights at the club.

"Sure, ma'am. I'll be right back with your order." The young waitress looked over at Hank's corner table to see if they were watching. She needed the money really badly.

"Mr. Hank, is that the albino doctor from Europe with Eric?" Bella never missed anything going on around her. "I've been wanting to meet her. Will you excuse me?" Bella slid out of the booth and walked across the room, not waiting for an answer to her question.

"You be careful of that woman, Bella!" Robbie didn't like Dr. Guyion after conversations with Hank and Liz and didn't want her to be a bad influence on her daughter.

"Eric, this must be Dr. Guyion that I've heard so much about. Could you introduce us?" Bella was beaming.

"Please join us, Bella," Palmer said. "Meet Dr. Helle Guyion. Helle, this is Bella Cantrell. We're going to schedule a session with her in the next few days."

Helle reached out her hand to Bella. "The pleasure is mine, Ms. Cantrell, I've heard so much about you. You are beautiful and your smile could launch a thousand ships."

Bella instantly took a liking to Dr. Guyion. "You're beautiful, doctor. I can't wait to talk to you and Eric about my experiences. I've still got pieces missing and I know you will fill in the blanks for me. So when do we meet?"

"Soon, child. Soon." Helle knew that the way to Bella's trust was through lavishing her with compliments. Bella was self-centered and craved the attention. "Tell me more about you, Bella. Here, let me pour you a shot. It's the best tequila in the house."

Very little escaped T-Bone's watchful eye in the club. Especially on a slow night. He walked over to the waitress who was serving Dr. Palmer's table and spoke to the waitress in Spanish.

"Lupe, I saw you take that bottle of tequila to Dr. Palmer's table. You know that is against the rules."

Replying in Spanish, Lupe said, "T-Bone, please don't fire me. I have tuition coming up and she tipped me big. I'm sorry. Please don't fire me."

"Keep the money, Lupe. I'm not going to fire you. But don't let it happen again. Rules are rules." T-Bone walked over to Dr. Palmer's table.

"Welcome to Tequilaville." T-Bone was anything but pleasant in his tone of voice.

"T-Bone, do you know Dr. Guyion? She's working with Stan," Bella said.

"Yes, we've met. Dr. Guyion I'm going to have to take your bottle back to the bar. Your tab's been paid, but we have rules. Feel free to order your drinks, you will not be billed any further."

T-Bone reached down beside Dr. Guyion to pick up the bottle. As he did, Dr. Guyion touched T-Bone's hand, discreetly. He felt a jolt go through his huge frame that resembled a taser shot and temporarily rendered him helpless to move. Dr. Guyion began talking to him telepathically.

"Leave us, T-Bone. Yes, I know you. I know all about you. You have an unfulfilled contract on the life of Wayne Tyler. Complete it! Then your dreams of failure will go away."

T-Bone's temporary trance left him. He stood in front of the table confused. He smiled at Dr. Palmer, Bella and Dr. Guyion and walked back to the waitress station.

Speaking in Spanish, Lupe said, "T-Bone, what about the rules? Aren't you going to get their bottle and bring it back to the bartender?"

Answering in English, T-Bone looked at Lupe and said, "What bottle? What are you talking about?"

As the night grew later, Dr. Guyion continued her manipulation of Bella. Helle had found her target—Wayne Tyler. She was determined to use T-Bone to carry out her dastardly muse.

"So you want to write a book, Bella? What would the title be?" Helle was enjoying her time and conversation.

"I want to call it, *The Life and Loves of a Beautiful Woman*. How's that for a tell-all title, Dr. Guyion?" Bella filled her shot glass again. She had gulped down lots of tequila and was feeling no pain.

"You should write it, Bella. I have friends in the publishing industry in the U.S. and all over Europe and Asia. You could make millions. I'll help you." Helle continued her pursuit of Bella's trust.

"Millions? I could make millions?" Bella also loved money.

"You start writing the book, Bella. I'll do the rest. A pretty lady like you needs to be independent financially. Being rich is fun."

Dr, Palmer had said practically nothing to add to the conversation of the two women at his table. He watched Helle draw Bella in and wondered what her motives were. The two of them had become instant friends, lavishing compliments on each other all evening.

When the bottle was empty and both Eric and Bella were more than just a little tipsy, Helle ended the evening asking Dr. Palmer to escort her back to her hotel room. Bella staggered over to the corner table where her mother was taking it all in.

"Baby girl, momma's going to drive you home tonight. I think you've been over-served…again." Robbie gently seated Bella down at their table and ordered coffee. Her dislike for Dr. Guyion escalated.

As Palmer and Dr. Guyion headed for the exit, Helle stopped in front of T-Bone.

"Remember what I told you T-Bone. Do not disobey me…" Helle was annoyed that no one but Bella and Eric had complimented her on her lavish attire. She was growing bored with this bunch of red-necks with little couth. It was time to make things happen.

Helle and Eric stopped in front of the door to her room at the hotel. She motioned to one of her security guards standing on each end of the floor.

"Come here! I am going to be in conference until further notice. I will receive no guests or phone calls. Keep everyone away. Is that clear?" Helle was being Helle again, barking commands and expecting them to be carried out without question.

"Perfectly clear, Dr. Guyion. No interruptions until further notice," the guard replied.

Helle went in to her room where Natasha was making them some herbal tea for the evening.

"Leave us, Natasha!" Helle grabbed her heavy squash blossom turquoise necklace and hurled it into the big screen TV, breaking it into a million pieces of glass. "I'll call you when I need you. Stay away from me until then."

Natasha had seen Dr. Guyion's rage in the past and knew better than to say anything. She left hastily. Dr. Palmer just stood in the room waiting to see what Helle would do next.

Helle began stripping off all of her clothes, slinging them around the room until she was fully nude. She instructed Eric to do the same. He complied immediately, folding his clothes over a dining room chair. He didn't know if Helle was in an amorous mood or this was one of the requirements for the journey. Either way, he was excited.

"What's making you so angry, Helle? I thought we had a great time tonight. The tequila was exquisite…"

"Be silent, Eric. I am about to make good on that promise to you. We're indeed going to Betwixt tonight but you must listen carefully to what I will tell you. There are rules that you must know. If you break them, you could die a horrible death. Do you understand the risk involved?"

"I'm not sure I do, Helle. Why don't you tell me and, incidentally, do I have a choice?"

"No. You will go to Betwixt with me. You have been summoned. To resist is futile. You know only a few of my powers. Now you will see more. Let's begin…"

Eric was startled, a bit frightened but his professional desire to visit another dimension superseded any fear that would keep him from this unknown experience. He sat down on the couch while Helle began her dissertation of the rules he must follow to avoid his untimely demise.

"I will prepare you for our journey into the unknown. You will be semi-conscious for the trip. That's the reason I filled you with strong drink, to dull your senses. What you will see and experience is beyond your ability to understand or comprehend so you must clear your mind and stay in a constant state of awe.

"We are going to the throne of my master, Satan, located on a high plateau named Mount Zaphon in the center of Betwixt. Silly, herd-mentality Christians call this place the second heaven but I assure you, Eric, there is nothing second-hand about this kingdom. It is beyond anything you could ever imagine. You will see colors you have never seen before. Your senses will be over-loaded. There will be thousands upon thousands of servants flying around the throne constantly exclaiming, 'All power and might belong to the Evil One, our master and commander. Evil is good and good is evil!'

"You will be able to see his mighty throne but you cannot look upon the Evil One's face and live. You will see only his feet, where you will immediately bow down to him. The rest of his image will be clouded in mist to protect you from certain death. Do not look up and try to see more.

"Helle, I…" Palmer had questions.

"I told you silence, Eric! Your very life is at stake here. Now listen as I continue." Suddenly, the tattoos on Helle's body seemed to appear three-dimensional and began to glow, lighting up the room with a ghostly green light, especially the '666' and the inverted pentagram with the goat's head centered within it. The images reflected like holograms on the walls. Eric was already having a hard time comprehending what he was seeing with his own eyes at this very moment.

"Helle, I gotta ask you this. Can I die at Betwixt?"

"Don't worry yourself, Eric. Satan has the power of fire, pestilence, disease, famine and death. Once you enter his presence, think before you act or say anything. As a rule, don't speak unless spoken to. Quickly be obedient to anything he tells you to do. Hesitation can conjure up his wrath in many forms. Be obedient and perform his acts of will quickly."

Eric found himself taking many long breaths, trying to stay calm during the macabre instructions.

"Eric, you will see creatures that are unknown to mankind. Creatures with multiple heads, arms, eyes and may appear to be unthinkable animals or creatures of the sea. Not all creatures of Satan are created in his image. Many push the sense of our imagination. Do not be alarmed. They will not harm you unless Satan instructs them to do so.

"These creatures are former gods of the different nations that have come and gone during the history of the earth. Former gods such as Nebo, Kaiwon, Yam, Nergal, Tartak, Tannin and Marduk. They, too, are very powerful but answer to their master, Satan. He has used them to shape the history of many nations and instantly do the will of their master, as you and I must do."

"But Helle, you told me that you were the high priestess of Satanical worship in Europe and Asia. Satan has given you power. Do you fear going to Betwixt? I mean, will Satan kill you?"

"If I am obedient, my master will shower me with riches and power over many people and nations. If I am disobedient, he could kill me. Nothing could stop him from doing that. I told you earlier, he has the power of death."

"Helle, are you scared of him?" Palmer was concerned for both of them.

"I fear him, Eric, and his power of life and death. I am not afraid of him. There's a difference. It's like risk and reward."

"I don't mean to keep interrupting you, Helle, but so I can understand things better, how do we get to Betwixt? You haven't told me that yet."

"We get to Betwixt by his power, Eric. It's not something to understand like the laws of physics. He defies all laws. When it's time for us to depart, at midnight, we will simply be summoned to his throne. We will arrive through time and space at the base of Mount Zaphon. I can't explain how so don't ask. Just be honored and amazed."

For the next hour or so, Helle continued to explain the do's and don'ts of Betwixt, of coming into the presence of Satan and his mighty forces of evil. Eric listened and at times tried to reason, but like Helle had said earlier, it did no good. For the first time in his professional career of learning, he had to completely abandon logic and reason and just experience what was about to happen. He had no clue how to do that. He was anxious, alarmed, excited and dumbfounded all at once. He wondered how long they would be there but dared not ask.

"It's time, Eric. Lie on the bed. I will lie on top of you. Look into my eyes. They will appear like red lasers but will not harm you. I will hypnotize you and before you know it, we'll be at Betwixt. Now lie back and relax…"

Eric was obedient to Helle and tried to relax his body while staring into her eyes. They began to glow red just as she said they would. The deeper he peered at her, the clearer their path to Betwixt became.

Deeper and deeper into hypnosis, Eric was incapable of noticing that inside Helle's room at the hotel there emerged an icy fog mixed with tongues of fire. The walls, ceilings and floor began icing over inside. There was at least a six inch frozen barrier barring entry from any direction into her room. The room became an igloo.

Their trip to Betwixt began penetrating a path through time and space. Eric could see lighted objects streaking past them. He could see galaxies swirling around their orbits that were unknown to the NASA scientists. They were traveling beyond any point that was known to mankind and the journey had just begun. He was experiencing unknown realms and visions that sent him into newer realms of awe. Eric was breathless.

He felt like he was sitting in the comfort of a planetarium where the constellations were thrust into light speed, whizzing past the Big Dipper and Orion's belt, moving faster and faster, way beyond the speed of light, way beyond imagination. It was breathtaking. There were instances when Eric had to make himself breathe. He was in space where there was no air, yet he was alive and taking it all without feeling cold or hot sensations.

"How could this be?" Eric thought as he clung to Helle who had him in her grasp.

They entered what appeared to be a black hole. Eric had heard from astrophysicists at NASA that anything entering a black hole was completely torn to shreds and reduced to atoms. He was fearful for his life but it was too late. Eric and Helle were sucked into the black hole with such force and staggering sound that Eric thought that he would surely die. To live made no sense as far as scientific knowledge was concerned. Could all mankind be wrong about these pathways to other dimensions?

Suddenly Eric and Helle, still clinging to each other, were catapulted out of the black void into dimensions never seen by mankind or their explorer satellites. Eric was so scared at this point, happy to still be alive, that he dared a peek at what was before them. In the blackness of space, there appeared a huge orangey-red fireball larger than any galaxy. It had a star in the middle of it that emitted white light. There seemed to be a ghoulish-looking face of a man when he looked at the entire dimension from afar. Like the head of Satan or an open precipice into the pit of hell itself. Was this their destination? Was this Betwixt or the second heavenly realm? Was this what hell looked like? Eric was beyond scared; he was numb and unable to figure out what he was seeing. His ability to comprehend and his psyche were shutting down.

The lights streaking past them seemed to slow. The image of this fiery realm hovering in space began to appear more clearly.

There was a huge mountain that came into view as they entered some kind of atmosphere that sustained life. Millions of creatures were flying all around it. Some appeared as dragons, others were completely indescribable. There were just no words since some appeared to be combinations of living creatures and machines, terrible looking creatures of every size and shape. Some had no shape at all and others were the size of entire states back on earth.

As they slowly descended, Eric and Helle found themselves at the base of a tall, smoke obscured mountain. Helle loosened her grip on Eric.

"Prepare yourself, Eric. Wonder is in store for us. Welcome to Mount Zaphon, the throne of Satan!"

13

VOYEUR
I WANT BELLA!

After Tequilaville closed, Hank walked into Abby's office behind his corner booth. She was writing checks to vendors and employees. He could see the concern on her face. Business had fallen off since the tragedy on the dock where "Ducky" Don had been vaporized by the lightning strike. Even after numerous power washes of the deck, the smell of burning flesh had not gone away. The entire atmosphere of the club had gone from a good-times happy place to one of gloom and doom.

The employees were working hard but there were not enough visitors to the club to keep them busy or earn decent tips. Everyone was in fear of losing their jobs.

"How bad is it, Sweetie Pie?" Hank was not oblivious to the downturn in business.

"I really don't want to talk about it, Pop. Somehow we'll get through this. And before you ask, I'm not ready to start laying off employees…yet."

"Abby, before you lay off anyone, I'll give up my salary and catch up on some of my electrical business around the lake. I still have clients that call me. I made a good living for many years doing that and I can do it again."

Abby tried to lighten up the conversation. "Dad, those old clients of yours may not recognize you anymore with your silvery hair and beard! Are you getting used to it yet?"

"I'm still the same old me, Abby. I kind of like the silver hair thing. Liz loves my new look."

"Speaking of Liz, Dad, have you made any honeymoon plans?"

"I've got a few ideas on that. Let me run them past you. Years ago I was on a bit of a search. I drove to Ruidoso, New Mexico and arrived late at night. I checked in to the Inn of the Mountain Gods but it was too dark to see any of the surrounding scenery. Have you ever heard of it?"

"I've heard of it, Pop. Never been there. What were you searching for?"

"Oh, baby, I think I was searching for a path and a purpose. Just one of those confused times in my life. I really think I was searching for me. Who I was and why was I here. After years of hard work and trying my best to be a good Dad to you, I finally got depressed and thought there had to be more of life that I was missing. Looking back, I just didn't realize how blessed I was to have you and Robbie and Bella in my life. Just feeling down if you know what I mean."

"We all get that way sometimes, Pop. So what happened on this journey and what does it have to do with your honeymoon?"

"When I woke up early the next morning, I opened the drapes of my room and the view I saw outside almost took my breath away. It was beautiful, majestic mountains, trees, birds singing and I just stood there in awe. It was one of the most memorable moments I've ever had.

"When I went into the restaurant, I was greeted by one of the young American Indian waitresses who had such an amazing smile and an over-the-top attitude. It made my day. Such happiness was in that young lady. Plus, the food was great."

"So you want to take Liz to the Inn in Ruidoso for the honeymoon?"

"Abby, let me finish my story. The young waitress asked me where I was headed and I told her I didn't really know. I told her I was searching for something."

"Daddy Hank, are we ever going to get to your honeymoon plans? I've still got some things to wrap up here tonight before it gets too late. I don't mean to cut you off..."

"Okay. The waitress said I should go to Albuquerque and find the world's longest tram ride that went up into the Sandia Mountains. She said to go about 4:30 in the afternoon and I would see mountains turn purple as the sun sets. At the top of the mountain, 10,300 feet high, there was a restaurant called High Finance that had the greatest view on earth. She said I may find what I'm searching for there."

"Did you, Pop?"

"I found peace, Abby. I found tranquility. I felt close to a God that I didn't even know. He was all around me. After spending three hours up on that mountain, just looking around, letting the rest of the world pass by, I was so full of joy that I drove back to Clear Lake, to you and Robbie and Bella and worked another fifteen years, counting my blessings and enjoying life. It took those three hours on the mountain to help me realize that I had a great life already."

"So you're going to spend your honeymoon night with Liz at the Inn of the Mountain Gods and then to dinner on top of the Sandias? Maybe spend some time, just the two of you, watching those mountains turn purple again?"

"I've been thinking about it Abby. We'll spend our first night here at the condo or her hotel suite, then get up early and go to Ruidoso. What do you think of that for a honeymoon, baby?"

"I think it sounds just like you, Daddy Hank. I know Liz will love it, too. So romantic! You have my stamp of approval. I won't tell anyone that you two will be in town after the wedding."

"I love you, Sweetie Pie. How are you and Wayne doing?"

"Life is good with us. If we can just get the business going again…But Pop, don't you worry about this. That's my job. I want you to look forward to being with your new lady and future wife. Have fun and find that peace and serenity again. You deserve it. And, I love you, too, Dad."

Wayne, Scott Wood and Mr. Elroy were trying out some new songs before opening later in the night. It was hard to escape the fact that they were playing to sparse crowds. Wayne and Mr. Elroy had been in the business of entertainment for a long time but the small audiences were getting to Scott. He had lost his enthusiasm and his ever-present smile and good nature were waning.

"Could we have a little group meeting?" Scott said to Wayne and Mr. Elroy.

"Sho, Scotty. What's on yo mind?" Mr. Elroy hadn't lost his smile.

"Uh, it's my job to keep Tequilaville filled with customers. I feel like I'm failing. Anyone got any suggestions? I've just about run out of ideas."

Wayne got into the conversation.

"Scott, it's not your fault. I feel I'm the one to blame. I've lost my passion for the music we've been playing, all the impersonations, the rock and the C&W. I can't do that anymore. It's just not in me. As for ideas, I've run out of them myself, but don't blame yourself, Scott."

"Ain't no one to be blaming!" Mr. Elroy stood up from his stool on the bandstand.

"So what do we do, Mr. Elroy?" Scott was becoming frantic.

"Just three thangs, Mr. Scott. You prays, you trusts and you wait."

"With all due respect, Mr. Elroy, I've already done that. Now what? I've got a job to do."

"You just be still and listen, Mr. Scott. The Almighty knows what's happenin' here. He's got dis. Don't fret and don't worry. None of dats going to help you one bit. You and Wayne just show up each night, sing like your heart's in it and let Him do da rest. Ya feel me?"

"I'm trying to Mr. Elroy, but I have to admit, my trust level needs some bolstering." Mr. Elroy's words weren't helping Scott much and it showed in his voice.

"The Good Lawd said, 'In this world you will have many trials and tribulations, but be of good cheer, I have overcome the world.' When things get tough, that's the Almighty hollering in our ears to trust Him. Ain't nothing you can do but to be patient, Mr. Scott. I knows you's young and patience usually comes later in life, but for now, you just do yo thing and watch. The Almighty is testin all of us. Do we take things into our own hands or puts the present situation in His? Dat's what you have to ask yoself. With all's dats been happenin around here, I thinks there may be some changes in the works…"

"What kind of changes, Mr. Elroy?" Wayne asked.

"Big changes, Mr. Wayne. I just got dat feelin somethins big gonna happen…Like it ain't already been happenin if you know what's I mean? Been some miracles goin on, wouldn't ya say?"

"Yeah. Hank's hair turning silver, the light from above shining down on him, the 'Ducky' Don thing." Wayne also had premonitions of things to come.

"Mr. Elroy, how do you know so much? It seems that you have the answers to everything," Scott said. "And, by the way, have you talked to T-Bone lately? He's been really quiet."

"Mr. T-Bone is dealing with some things on his own, Mr. Scott. He'll figure them out, but you might just say a prayer for him. As for knowing lots of things, well, we learns by listening to what's on peoples' minds. We spend times with 'em. You can't learn when you're talking…""Hmmm…another by-the-way, Mr. Elroy. Is Elroy your first or last name? I never asked you before."

"Oh, Mr. Scott, everyone jus calls me Mr. Elroy. I like dat. But to be honest wit ya, 'Elroy' is my last name. My first name is Gordon. Yessir, Gordon Elroy. Dat's me."

Robbie and Liz were meeting for lunch at the Aquarium Restaurant on the Kemah Boardwalk to discuss the plans for the upcoming wedding. The multiple huge tanks of the local species of fish added to the ambiance of a quiet meeting.

"I haven't been to this restaurant, Robbie. I love this place. The fish tanks are so beautiful."

"Yep, Liz, it's the perfect setting to plan your big day. What kind of a wedding are you and Hank thinking about? Fill me in."

Liz confided in Robbie as Hank's best friend. She asked her to be her maid of honor since she had no living family.

"I'd be honored, Liz. Who's going to give you away?"

"I was thinking Mr. Elroy. Do you believe we can get him into some nicer clothes?" That question made both of them laugh.

"I'll do some shopping for him. Now what about your dress and where do you and Hank want the wedding to take place?" Robbie was taking notes.

"Hank completely left that up to me, Robbie, and I want to surprise him. I remember the night that I began to fall in love with him. It was the night that he had asked Mary and Tito to set up a lighted table under a gazebo out on the patio of Tequilaville overlooking the lake. It was so romantic, so right. I want to relive that moment for our wedding. At night, with lights, candles and flowers. I want everything outside in the moonlight. I want that moment again."

"You got it, Liz. I'm going to make this wedding special for you and Hank. Just leave everything to me. How many people are you planning to invite?"

"Mostly the club family. I'm going to ask Pastor Randy to marry us so I need to invite his rather rowdy congregation of bikers and cowboys from the church. Maybe seventy-five people in all. It should be a lot of fun being surrounded by all our best friends, don't you think?"

"Perfect, Liz! I can't wait. Have you got your dress picked out?"

"Would you go with me on that one, Robbie? Uh...I'm struggling with something and need to talk about it. You know Hank better than anyone..."

"I'm listening, girl. What's the problem?"

"Robbie, Hank mentioned that I reminded him of Abigail, Abby's mom. I can't compete with a ghost and I don't want to. But I know how much Hank loved her and pined for her all those years. Hank said that I look like her and if Hank loves me even half as much as he loved Abigail, so be it. I have his total love now. So I was thinking about a simple embroidered white dress, a single string of pearls and a band of white flowers in my hair. As far as something borrowed, I'm going to ask Abby to loan me the flip-flops that she wore to her graduation."

"I love it, Liz. What about something blue?"

"Hank's blue eyes are enough. There will be nothing blue about our big day. We're going to sing in the moonlight and laugh every day of our lives together…"

"Consider it done, Liz. This is a match made under the skies of heaven. I'll get Wayne, Scott and the band to provide the music. Do you have any songs in mind?"

"Leave that to Wayne and Mr. Elroy. I love surprises, too. Let's splurge; what kind of dessert do you want, Robbie. I'm buying!"

As they were finishing off dessert and having coffee, Bella and one of her real estate clients walked into the restaurant. She spotted her mom and Liz and made a beeline to their table.

"I'm guessing this is the big wedding planning meeting you two are having. What part am I playing in your big day, Liz?"

"Bella, your part is to show up, looking beautiful as usual and bring that fantastic personality of yours. My wedding would not be complete without you."

"Hmmm. I guess I can do that. Mom, do you need any help with all the planning stuff? I can at least do that." Bella was miffed about her 'attendee' role in the wedding.

"Baby, I've got lots of things you can help me with. Are you available tomorrow?"

"I'll check my calendar and let you know, Mom. I've got clients I need to get back to. Tootles!"

"I hear that Bella is going to continue her sessions with Dr. Palmer and Dr. Guyion," Liz said. "I know you care and love her deeply, Robbie, but tell her to be careful around those two."

"I can't talk her out of it, Liz. Bella travels to the beat of her own drums if you know what I mean. She pushes every envelope of life and I can't slow her down. All I can do is pray for her and hope that God Himself watches over her. There's no telling how she will end up. I just have to be there when she falls to pick her up. That's all a mother can do."

Helle and Eric Palmer descended towards the foot of Mount Zaphon. There were smelly gases that reminded Eric of an expedition on earth he had taken to an active volcano, almost un-breathable, but life sustaining. Both Eric and Helle were covered by clouds as they made their way downward. Eric's fear level was fifty on a scale of one to ten. Finally, an opening appeared to them and they could see a huge open-air throne.

The throne was made of ebony, gold, and silver inlaid with priceless jewels of every kind. Before the throne was a black, luxurious marble foyer. The base of the throne could be seen but a gray mist covered most of the rest. Eric saw two huge gnarly-looking feet at the base and guessed they belonged to Helle's master, Satan. Voices could be heard all around the area, constantly giving praise to Satan. The sound of the voices themselves were shrill and terrible as they blasphemed the Almighty constantly, mimicking the Holy Angels that were in the third heaven around the mighty white Throne of God.

As Eric and Helle felt the marble beneath their feet, they heard the voice of Satan.

"I have summoned you both here for my purposes, to fulfill my plans back on earth, where I am the Prince! I have power over darkness, life and death. I have power over success and failure. If you obey me, I will reward you beyond your wildest expectations. If you disobey me, you will drink from the cup of my wrath. Now worship me!"

Helle bowed low before her master's throne. Eric was quick to follow her lead as dread overcame him. He dared not look up.

There were twelve creatures on smaller thrones surrounding the black throne, all dressed in magnificent apparel. Their faces were hidden by dark robes with hoods. Their eyes were like green lasers that constantly surveyed and criss-crossed the entire realm. No one could approach Satan's throne without their watchful eyes knowing about it. They were given power to kill any unwanted, un-summoned creature, even Satan's other demonic followers.

"Helle, my high priestess, well done, my evil and faithful servant. You will receive some of your just rewards here before me today. What do you have to say?"

Helle looked up towards the throne covered in gray mist.

"I am honored to serve you, master. Your wish is my command. What would you have me do?"

"You and Eric Palmer will bear me a son, a mighty son who will change the course of the future on earth. He will be born in Europe at a place that I will tell you."

Eric, even though he followed no form of religious belief, had read the Bible and saw many similarities of what was going on. He also knew that if Satan himself had sex with a mortal he was endangering himself to judgment, at least that is what he had read. He remained silent and afraid to look up at the booming voice coming from the mist-covered top of the great throne.

"Eric Palmer!"

When Eric heard his name, he began to shake and almost became incontinent.

"Yes, master. What would you have me do?" was all he could say, still with his head facing down on the black marble.

"You will copulate with my high priestess, Helle. There is a bed next to you. Enjoy the pleasures of my rewards and fear not. I will watch and enjoy your lust."

Helle moved onto the huge bed and, without hesitation, summoned Eric to join her. They were both still naked. Eric wasted no time to begin his performance before the watchful eyes of all the demonic deities present. At first, he had trouble getting in the mood, but Helle's beauty quickly began the event. Their sex was wild. Helle screamed and shrieked like a wild hyena from the pit as their bodies intertwined like two serpents in the grass. Eric was literally holding on to her for fear of being thrown across the room. There was nothing loving or sacred about their intercourse. It was morbid, scary, like doing it with a real demon, which was beyond Eric's ability to imagine. He just wanted it to be over, but Helle's insatiable lust continued for what seemed to be hours. Eric was exhausted in Helle's arms that seemed to grow stronger by the second.

"Enough! The deed has been done!" Satan said with a mighty sound.

All through the fiery realm of Betwixt millions of demonic voices could be heard screaming and shouting, "It is done! It is done! All hell to our glorious master, Satan!" The entire dimension shook and rumbled.

By this time, Eric was lying on his back in the bed before the throne, panting for breath, looking up to see such strange creatures flying in circles above him with thousands, if not millions, of eyes gazing down on his nakedness. He heard their mighty shouts. He was feeling so many emotions at the same time, emotions of shame, violation and even modesty, but fear kept him from saying anything.

"Not bad, Eric, my servant. I will allow you to speak with me. Being a scientist, I'm sure you have questions. Speak freely so that I will be amused. You will address me as master!"

A creature of undefined shape approached the ruffled bed and gave both Helle and Eric a cup of swirling liquid to refresh them. Eric drank the liquid and felt better, instantly restored.

"Master, I don't know what to say…" was all that Palmer could utter.

"Oh come now, Eric. You are a learned man as mortals go. Surely you have questions for me. This is a rare event that I will grant you, and I will reward you for obedience. Fear not. What are your questions?"

Eric's mind went immediately to the DNA tests he had gathered from Wayne Tyler and Lieutenant Stan Stark. Tests that would propel him to the forefront of science itself.

"Can you show me the hidden link between the DNA tests that Helle and I are working on so that we can understand how to apply them to the Super Collider in Switzerland to confirm the 'God Particle?'"

"Absolutely not! You will not confirm anything having to do with the belief in or the existence of my enemy! Drop any further investigations on those tests or I will strike you with such pestilence that you will surely die a horrible and painful death. Do you understand?" Satan shouted.

Timidly, Eric responded, "Yes, uh, master. But you said you would reward me. What can I expect? You know that I'm a scientist…"

"Silence! I will reward you in my own way. You will not need the approval of mankind to achieve the success you seek. Never mention the DNA tests ever again!" The tone of Satan's voice alone caused Eric to bow down lower to the throne.

"I have another task for you and my servant, Helle. I want Bella Cantrell! She will replace my concubine, Ishtar, who was cast, without proper judgment I tell you, into the pit. I miss her company, and I will have Bella to be my constant concubine to take her place."

"But master, how do we do that?" Eric asked timidly.

"Oh, you mortals who think you are so smart. It is so simple, you of little faith. I will tempt Bella with my demoness, Chemoth. Then I will bring Bella here to my throne and shower her with luxuries…just like I chose Ishtar. When I return Bella to earth, I will strike her with a terrible disease…"

Satan laughed in delight at his own brilliance, his own plan of deception and lies, as he paused to applaud himself.

"She will die young before accepting any offers of salvation made to her by other immortal beings or deities, even though they tug at her heart. Bella will be judged and immediately sent to me. I will receive her as my queen forever!"

Eric began remembering his study of the Bible years ago. What Satan was saying complied perfectly with what was written: "First comes death, then comes judgment."

"Master, you are truly wise and powerful. Could I ask you… from where does your power come?" Eric asked sheepishly.

Satan's face and upper body could not be seen in the mist that shrouded his image. Eric could tell by the sight of Satan's lower legs that he was beginning to stand upright.

"The question of all questions, Eric! Let me tell you from where my power truly emanates. It comes from the sin of all mankind that began when mankind itself began—in the Garden of Eden. It began with Adam and Eve when they made the choice to be free of all those Thou Shalt Not's.

"The more their descendants chose free will and free choice throughout the ages to enjoy life on earth, the more they explored the erotic freedoms of sex and lust, the more that they depended on their own pride and strength, the more mankind lied, cheated and murdered, the more power I gained. My power is from the people I rule over and it strengthens every second of every day! It strengthens every time people on earth worship false gods. All of the false gods throughout time are here with me in Betwixt. When people on earth worship them, they worship me…It is written!"

Helle praised her master, somewhat disappointed that she had not been chosen as Satan's own concubine.

"I am blessed before all other women of the earth, great and mighty master. I will bear you a son. What greater honor could an earthly woman have? I truly praise you and give thanks to you, mighty Satan."

Satan provided a magical box with a golden key that floated down from the mist. It contained mysteries that would center attention on his power and away from his adversary's attempts to draw people to Him. The box was jeweled with priceless stones, unknown stones that could never be valued in dollars, rubles or yen. The box was about one-foot square with an oval, clear but opaque top. It would baffle science for ages to come.

"This is my reward to you, Eric Palmer. I will give you the key to it. It will make you famous above all scientists who have ever lived," Satan said.

"What is the meaning of this box, uh, master?" Eric asked.

"On earth there are fantasies of Pandora's Box. Contrived by the minds of simple mortals given to fables. It is said that this box contains many mysteries. I give to you the *real Pandora's Box*. You are the only human with the key to it.

"You can attend your simple science conventions and the rest of the world's scientists will be amazed when you unlock the box I have set before you. Mysteries, equations, holograms and voices will emerge from this box when you open it. There is nothing you have to do, Eric. Just open it before the scientific community of earth. What's inside the box that I have prepared for you will do the rest. Tell them it came from me, Satan, and science will be unable to prove otherwise. The great minds of the earth, feeble in my eyes, will be drawn to me for explanation. This is your reward for serving me."

Eric looked at the box. Nothing about it was normal. It appeared heavy but was light as a feather. It floated just above any surface on which it was placed. The materials were indistinguishable. The jewels blazed brilliant. Eric had no conception as to what kind of jewels they were or their origin.

"Thank you, master. I accept your reward. I will present it to my colleagues back on earth so that they can truly be challenged and amazed just as I am standing here before you. Thank you. Thank you."

Eric clutched the box under his arm and held on tightly to it. He bowed once again, holding the treasure that would baffle all mankind.

"Now, my servants, return to earth. Do my bidding. Do not delay and do not disobey my commands," Satan commanded.

Without repeating the unexplainable trip that brought Helle and Eric to Betwixt, in the blink of an eye they were both back in Helle's bedroom at the Bay Hilton Hotel. She looked even more beautiful than Eric had imagined. Helle glanced over at Eric with an air of power and dominance.

"How did you like Betwixt, Eric? I told you it would be exciting. Did I deliver or what, lover?"

Eric immediately turned his gaze to the floor beside the bed. There in front of him, hovering about an inch above the carpet was his own Pandora's Box. He had no idea what was enclosed within it but couldn't wait to present it to the scientific community.

"Do you think I should open it now, Helle? Uh, just to see what's inside?" Eric asked.

"Share the experience with your colleagues, Eric. Remember what my master told you, word for word. To bring up an old cliché, 'the devil is in the details.' He said, 'when you open it before your colleagues.' He didn't say 'any time you open it.' Have faith and be amazed what you will see and follow his instructions to the letter. Besides, I'm famished. Let's have dinner."

Eric looked at his watch. He knew that they had departed to Betwixt at midnight and it seemed like they had been there for days. His digital watch flashed on and off as if they it had experienced a power shortage. But the clock on Helle's wall revealed that it was one minute after midnight. Had time stood still?

As Eric began putting his clothes on to leave the hotel, he noticed deep scratches in his back and arms. No doubt caused by Helle's animalistic love making.

"Do you feel pregnant, Helle? Satan said you would bear him a son…"

"It will be an immaculate conception, Eric. I have been sterile from birth. The world will be in wonder of my son." Helle looked up to the ceiling with raised hands of praise.

"Then Satan must be powerful. There has never been immaculate conception except the fairy tales written in the Bible. I've never really believed in the 'virgin' birth thing. Now I'm having second thoughts on that also." Eric was a scientist who dealt in facts. One unbelievable fact could lead to the authenticity of another.

"Just do the master's bidding, Eric. You will see in his own good time." Helle pushed Eric to believe.

"Your sterility explains to me why you've never gotten pregnant in the past, Helle. If what you claim is true, you've slept with world leaders all around the globe. Are you proud of all your sexual escapades?"

"I do what is necessary to gain power, Eric. My beauty has given me influence over many powerful people. They are at my beck and call. Are you jealous?"

"Not anymore. We had our time and you destroyed it. Helle, I may be under Satan's bidding but he's *not my* master! Free choice and free will. Remember that, Helle?"

"Eric, remember the consequences! How soon you forget what you just experienced."

Bella showed up for her first session with Dr. Palmer and Dr. Guyion dressed in fitting business attire yet revealing just enough to Eric so as not to cause any conflict with Dr. Guyion.

Belinda Sealy and Natasha Patski were present as always to take notes on their laptops. The setting was professional but friendly. Dr. Guyion needed to draw Bella completely into her confidence. As Bella walked into the conference room, before any announcements were made as to her arrival, Helle greeted her at the door with a sincere embrace.

"How's my beautiful client feeling this morning, Bella? You are stunning as usual." Helle pulled Bella close to her.

"Just perfect, Dr. Guyion. I can't wait to get started. Are you going to hypnotize me?" Bella was playing right into Helle's plan.

"It would be my pleasure to help you understand your great experience, Bella. Have you ever been hypnotized before?" Helle asked.

"Never! But I can't wait. This is exciting. Will I remember anything?"

"Who knows, my lovely. If you want, we'll just dive right into it and see what happens." Helle was ecstatic at Bella's eagerness to let her discover what had happened during her first trip to Betwixt.

Bella took a deep breath and sat upright in her chair, relishing every moment of being the center of their attention. Eric began the process by talking to Bella, telling her she was feeling refreshed, no problems to think about, relaxing Bella so that she had the right frame of mind to enter deep hypnosis.

Dr. Guyion motioned for Belinda and Natasha to leave the room as Bella's head began to sag downward during the early stages of going under.

"But Dr. Guyion, I'm here to record everything that Bella says. Dr. Palmer, do you want me to leave?" Belinda had always been present during hypnosis sessions.

Before Palmer could answer, Helle glared at Belinda, fixing a stare on her that could kill.

"Leave now! Never disobey me!" Belinda left the room without further questions as she followed Natasha out of the conference room.

At this point in the hypnosis, Dr. Guyion took over and started her red, laser-like stare into Bella's closed eyes, penetrating her mind to a level of such deep hypnosis that resistance was futile.

"Bella, are you sure you were at a place called Betwixt or was this just a bad dream that you had?" Helle asked the motionless Bella.

Bella began to breathe more quickly, obviously in deep thought, trying to figure out her answer.

"I don't know if it was real or not."

Dr. Guyion continued the questions, one after the next in rapid succession.

"Think, Bella, tell me what you saw during this dream." Helle was planting thoughts of disbelief into Bella's mind.

"Uh, uh…" Bella clenched one of her hands in the other and began to shake.

"What did you see there, Bella? Describe what you remember."

"It scares me! What I remember scares me!" Bella began to fidget in her chair with an obvious expression of fear and pain on her face.

Dr, Guyion looked over at Eric.

"Bella is in denial. Her conscience is bothering her. She's blocking out the experience to Betwixt and that's a good thing. She doesn't want to explore the experience she had any further. She only remembers the bad that happened and can't remember any pleasant thoughts at all."

"That's obvious, Helle," Eric said. "Are you going to push her any further during this first session? We could lose her if you know what I mean."

"Not on this subject, Eric. We'll have to form a gentler approach, even to her subconscious. I'll change the topic and let her settle down. I'm pleased with this so far and have no doubt that she did enter this realm. She is so frightened of her memories. This confirms her experience as far as I'm concerned."

"Where to next, Helle?"

"I want to know about Bella. I'll ask her some questions much easier to answer."

Helle sat there for a few moments until Bella stopped shaking and began to breathe normally again. Then Dr. Guyion began with new questions.

"Bella? What are your dreams and aspirations? What did you always want to become when you were a little girl?"

Bella began a small smile and a pleasantness came over her.

"I wanted to be Cinderella! I wanted my Prince Charming to take me away to a big castle in the sky where there were flowers and unicorns running all around."

"You are Cinderella, Bella. You're beautiful!" Helle was guiding her mind into a world of make-believe.

"Did you ever want to be rich?"

"Oh yes! The richest woman in the world," Bella replied.

"Are you rich now, Bella?"

"No!" Bella shrugged her shoulders as her head hung down in deep hypnosis.

"Do you think you deserve to be rich and successful, Bella?"

"Yes, I do. I work hard being a great…, uh…uh, I can't think of what I do. Am I Cinderella?" Bella was lost in fantasy land and was having a hard time coming back to reality.

"You're a realtor, Bella. You sell houses to very successful people," Eric said.

"Yes, I do. I'm a successful, beautiful, independent woman. I'm a modern day Cinderella."

"Have you found your Prince Charming yet, Bella?" Helle asked.

"No! Men are all alike." Bella began to frown even while she was under deep hypnosis.

"If you found your Prince Charming, Bella, would you be faithful to him always?" Helle continued her questions in a way to allow Bella to speak her real mind and thoughts.

"Maybe."

"Explain, *maybe*, Bella," Eric asked.

"Maybe I would be faithful, maybe I wouldn't. I like men and men like me. Why should I have only one? I get bored easily," Bella replied with complete truth during her hypnotic state.

"Have you had many lovers, Bella?" Helle asked.

"Yes, many lovers."

Helle looked over at Eric with a Cheshire cat smile on her face.

"That's all I want to know at the first session, Eric. Bella will make a great candidate for one of Satan's concubines. Wouldn't you agree?"

"Helle, I thought the purpose of our inquisition about where Bella had gone in her dream was to fill in some gaps of her experience and to learn more about Betwixt and piece all of this together for the entire group. What's changed? That's why I called you into this investigation." Eric Palmer still had his own professional ethics. He also cared about Bella.

"Eric! You've been to Between! Why must you know more? You've seen it firsthand. Besides, our mission has changed. We're here to send Bella to my master or bear the consequences of failure. Who cares what happened to this group of red-necked southern hillbillies?"

"But, Helle, Bella is a human being. Does she deserve this?"

"I'm leaving, Eric. You bring her back out of hypnosis. Be thinking of what failure to the master may mean for you and what can happen. We'll talk later." Helle walked out of the office.

14

BFFs
Return of Mama-Che

Late in the afternoon, Robbie put in a call to Bella. She couldn't wait to hear about her session with Dr. Palmer and Dr. Guyion. She knew her daughter well and was afraid of the influence these two learned parapsychologists might have on her free-spirit life style.

"Bella? It's Mom. How did your interview go this morning with the weirdo, albino doctor?"

"Mom, Dr. Guyion is no weirdo. She's very smart, speaks a ton of languages and is pleasant to be around. I like her." Bella always had her own opinion of people and listened very little to others.

"You didn't let her hypnotize you, did you?"

"Oh, Mom, Dr. Palmer hypnotized me. I feel perfectly comfortable in his presence…"

"What did you say under hypnosis, Bella? Did they tell you afterwards?" Robbie was more concerned than ever.

"All I remember is that it was pleasant, I felt happy and refreshed afterwards and 'No,' they didn't tell me what I said because I have another appointment next week. Eric told me they had to put all the pieces together before they would tell me anything and quite frankly, Mom, that makes sense, wouldn't you agree?"

"Maybe, Bella. I'm just trying to protect you, baby girl. You know how much I love you."

"Mom, I'm a big girl and don't need your protection. I can take care of myself and make my own decisions…"

"Baby, I just want to ask you one question. I know how busy you are." Robbie's main concern was that one day Bella would be saved. "Do you believe in the saving grace of Jesus? Have you asked Him to be your Savior and to forgive you of your sins?"

"Don't want to go there, Mom. We've had this conversation so many times before. Please don't bring this up to me anymore. I've got to go; my phone is ringing." Bella hung up on her mom.

Before she could answer, Bella's call went to voice mail. A few minutes later, after she had gone over a couple of pending contracts, she listened to her missed call.

"This is Irma Chemoth. I've got a two and a half million-dollar home I want to list with you, Bella. I forget who referred me to you, but they said you were a hard worker. I also want to find enough land here in the Clear Lake area to build a custom seven and a half million-dollar home. Could you call me?"

Bella dropped everything she was working on and called the number left on her phone. She was so excited. Selling a $2.5 million dollar home and getting a builder to build a $7.5 million home would mean a huge six-figure payday. Multi-million dollar deals like this were few and far between in Bella's experience. This made her day.

"Ms. Chemoth, this is Bella Cantrell, your realtor. Sorry I missed your call…"

"Thanks for responding so quickly, child. I heard so many great things about you." Ms. Chemoth spoke in a real southern drawl. "I didn't even shop for a realtor, honey, you're my girl. When can we talk in more detail? I want to get moving on this. That little house I have now is kinda cramping my style and I need a little more elbow room. And, please, Bella, just call me Irma.

"I've got a real busy schedule, writer and publisher conferences to attend, so I want you to deal with my administrative assistant, Trikki Sanders. I'll text you her contact info, baby. She handles my checkbook if you know what I mean."

Bella got some basic information; where the existing house was located and began pulling up comps on other houses in the neighborhood to give her a better idea of a realistic selling price. She wanted to list the house as soon as possible. She could see those dollar signs flooding her bank account.

The next morning Bella placed a call to Trikki Sanders. Trikki spoke with a heavy middle eastern accent. Bella set up a meeting for them to meet at Irma Chemoth's present home, not far from Bella's office.

When Bella pulled up into the gated driveway, she put her realtor's face on and quickly began viewing the property. The grounds were immaculate, well-kept and manicured. The house was two-storied with large white columns at the entry of huge double doors leading into the foyer of the home. There was a circular drive way in the front. After making notes, Bella rang the doorbell excitedly, awaiting her meeting with Trikki.

"Ms. Sanders, I'm Bella Cantrell," she said with a big smile on her face.

"Please call me Trikki, Bella. Pleased to meet you. Aren't you a beauty!"

Bella's hunch on Trikki's accent was confirmed. Trikki had olive skin, big brown eyes and dark hair. She was slim and dressed lavishly. Trikki's nature was very laid back but professional. Bella could tell that she was highly educated from her aura of confidence that filled the room of the huge entry way.

As Trikki led Bella into the living room, Bella noticed a distinct combination of African and middle eastern décor. The mantle of the fireplace was lined with thick inlaid gold trim. A carved brass grill covered the opening of the fire pit area. The spiral stair railings were made of pure ivory, no doubt taken from the tusks of many a fallen elephant. Overall, the inside of the house was more breathtaking than the outside. Huge cathedral windows opened up onto the back grounds where Bella noticed a cascading waterfall that filtered water into the lavish swimming pool, surrounded by plush cabanas. There was a patio area that contained a huge cooking area complete with custom barbeque pits and ceiling fans. A huge well-stocked bar with electric ice-freezers behind it offered guests any type of drink they could imagine.

Two and a half million seemed like a steal and Bella knew she would have no trouble up-selling this house. She just had to find a buyer with big bucks.

"What a beautiful, well maintained property, Trikki. I'll have no problem selling this house. Uh, can you tell me what Irma has in mind for her new home?" Bella was awestruck by the house she was selling. She couldn't imagine anyone wanting anything more.

"Do you know anything about Feng Shui, Bella?" Trikki and Bella were sitting outside on the patio around the pool area.

"Feng Shui? I've heard of it. I have to admit I'm not up to speed, but I can be. Why don't you give me some details?" Bella was caught off guard.

Trikki began her eloquent portrayal of ancient Chinese astrological charts and how they foretold future events and channeled energy and good will from the universe equally into every room of the new home.

"The new house has to have a feeling of welcome and comfort to all who enter. I'm already working with an architect skilled in Feng Shui design so you don't have to worry about that, Bella. Have you ever studied New Age religions?"

"I've dabbled in it, Trikki. I've had a couple of 'beyond explanation' experiences recently, and I'm working with Dr. Eric Palmer at NASA and a world-renowned parapsychologist, Dr. Helle Guyion of Europe to put some of the pieces together. Have you heard of them?"

"No, not really. I'd like to hear more of your experiences at a later date. Maybe I can add meaning, also." Trikki was lying through her teeth.

She was part of the conspiracy to bring Bella to Betwixt for Satan's approval. Helle Guyion had chosen Trikki to be the organizer of a future U.S. headquarters for Satanical worship in the Houston, Texas, area. Right in the middle of the Bible belt.

"Just to give you an idea of how the new house will be laid out, Bella, let me explain basic Feng Shui to you as it pertains to the home that I will oversee the building of for Irma."

"Please do, Trikki. This is exciting. I want to learn more." Bella was not about to blow her big opportunity for big bucks. She sat attentively across from Trikki.

"Feng Shui is based on a combination of ancient Buddhist philosophies, Shamanism and emotional intelligence. Everything in the universe emits energy of one kind or another. Every inanimate object has its own energy. Some positive and some negative. We concentrate on positive energy nourishment which is called 'Che' and channel it throughout the home.

"For instance, we never have the front entrance and the back entrance of the home in alignment. And we don't put staircases in the center of the home. This allows energy from the universe to quickly escape and not filter into the rest of the house. Another example is that we never build a bedroom over a garage. This unsettles the energy of the bedroom which is for perfect union and love making. Are you following me, Bella?"

"I'm trying to, Trikki. I know the importance of energy in the bedroom if that's what you're asking." Both of them giggled and gave each other a high five. Bella was feeling more at ease with her new friend.

"I'll have to come over to your house one of these days, Bella, and 'Feng Shui' your bedroom. You won't believe the fun you'll have in there when I'm finished."

Trikki went into the massive kitchen and got a bottle of wine and two glasses and brought them out to the patio. She had Bella where she wanted her and was going to go a couple of steps farther in sucking her into the big conspiracy.

"What religion are you, Bella, if you don't mind me asking?"

"To tell you the truth, I really don't have one. My mom is a Christian and is always trying to get me to go to church. I'm not sure I'm ready for all that stuff." Bella wanted closer ties to her new client and was willing to listen to anything Trikki told her.

"That's what New Age is all about, Bella. It is taking all the good of the universe and putting it together so we can experience so much more than any one religion offers. Do you want to hear more?"

"Of course. This is like expanding my thinking, huh, Trikki?"

"Bella, you, yourself can create miracles when you hear what I'm about to tell you."

"I can? Me? Create miracles?" Bella was all in to hearing Trikki's instruction.

Trikki and Bella sat together for another three hours, getting a bit tipsy as Bella hung on every word her new friend was telling her. Trikki explained to Bella about the power of positive thinking. How she, too, could channel the massive energy of the universe to accomplish all of her dreams and wishes.

"Bella, you have to make something happen in your life by saying to yourself, 'I will make this dream come true.' You have to be in harmony with your dreams and the power of the universe to make them happen. Call it what you want, call it a source, god or spirit. There is so much more going on all around you than you can imagine. But you need to expand your mind and really link your imagination to your dreams. This is how you can use this energy. It's called linking and channeling. Linking your dreams to energy by positive thinking. That's when your dreams begin to form and come true. Do you understand?"

"I'm getting there, Trikki. Give me an example of how to do this. Excuse my ignorance, but I haven't a clue where to begin."

"Bella, Mama-Che was my mentor in New Age thinking. That's what I call her, Mama-Che, because she's like a mother to me. She began teaching me when neither of us had two pennies to rub together. We were both poor even though well-educated. I left my low paying job to sit at her feet and learn. Those were tough times.

"As Mama-Che developed my dreams and aspirations, I channeled what I had learned into helping her build a huge publishing business. We publish New Age material for a world that is crying out for something better than most of the world religions have to offer. People all around the globe are starving, oppressed and abused by their governments and their poverty, and have no hope.

"We gave billions of people the path to success and our book sales went through the roof. We have such a following I couldn't count them all. Young adults are some of our most loyal book buyers since they haven't experienced enough of life to know how to make their dreams come true, but they hold the dreams of the future."

"That is so true, Trikki! Most of us young people just fight the daily grind. We don't have time to figure out what to do. We just survive in our own little worlds to pay the bills and put food on the table."

"What are your dreams, Bella? Do you aspire to be a huge real estate developer?"

"I just try my best to sell real estate. I don't have the backing to become another Donald Trump. Even if I did, I really don't know how to do that."

"Then switch gears, Bella. Dream a dream of success. What would that dream be?"

Bella took another sip of wine, let out a huge sigh as she remembered something that Dr. Guyion had mentioned.

"My parapsychologist said that I should write a book and maybe, through some of her influential friends, I could even get a large advance against royalties."

"Now you're speaking my language, Bella. What would your book be about?"

"Oh, the life and loves of a beautiful woman, or something like that."

Trikki frowned a little, showing her disapproval of the title.

"Bella, the number one genre in the book world is how to be successful with proven results. How about I teach you and mentor you into making those dreams of being a successful author come true. People want proven success, not just roads to success.

"I can spot a best seller from a mile off. How do you think Mama-Che and I built such a huge empire? I'll begin to show you how to channel the energy, you see how it changes your life and then we'll write a book about all of the events and miracles that come to you. If it's good, I personally will write that advance check of at least seven figures. You'll have instant success and be in demand for speaking engagements all over the world. I'll even be your publicist and book the engagements with some of our influential clients and companies that we train. How's that?"

"Oh, Trikki, can we really do that? What about me doing miracles, how do we do that?"

"Given your present income bracket, Bella, and I'm not trying to get into your personal finances, if you were to become a millionaire author with high paying speaking engagements all over the world, I'd call that a miracle, wouldn't you? Plus, your satisfaction or miracles, would be seeing the success of others. Bona fide miracles, making slum dog millionaires of poverty stricken people all over the world. You, too, will become a teacher of New Age success with proof positive of how to attain it. We'll do a story of your own road, the ups and the downs to success. You will be the example. But we will have to work closely on this, Bella. Do you have the desire and the discipline for me to mentor you?"

"When do we start, Trikki?"

"We already have. How do you think you got involved in a multi-million- dollar real estate deal with me and Mama-Che? I prayed to the universe for someone just like you to come into our lives and here you are.

That's the power of positive thinking and praying to the stored up energy that is all around us…"

Eric Palmer placed a call to Helle Guyion. His mind was swirling as he thought about his trip to Betwixt, being watched by a powerful voyeur of unknown strength, the thought of fathering a baby who would change the history of all mankind, and about the Pandora Box that was now in his possession.

How could he write a scientific paper on an object when he had no idea what it contained? Could he trust Satan, a fallen angel who was called 'the father of all lies?' Did he have the faith and confidence not to open the box until he could present it to his world colleagues? He needed reassurance.

"Helle? Eric. Are you feeling pregnant yet? Having any morning sickness?" Eric said facetiously.

"Hardly. What do you want?" Helle was not at her best.

"I need your advice. As far as I can figure out, there is no way of presenting this Pandora's Box to the scientific community. I can't write a paper on it, I don't know what's in it and I can't just set up a meeting and tell our colleagues that I have something out-of-this-world to show them. I'm in a box, myself, Helle. Got any ideas? This box is driving me crazy!"

"Where is the box now, Eric?"

"It's here, in my bedroom at home. I was thinking of taking it to my safe at the office at NASA but, depending on what's inside of it, it could set off all kinds of alarms if I try to enter with it. I'm thinking of having a vault installed in my home for safe keeping…"

"Don't waste your money, lover. There is a curse on that box conjured up by Satan, himself. No one but you or I can lay hands on it before the grand presentation lest they die. It is safe where it is. Don't take it to NASA!"

"Okay, that's reassuring. So how do I arrange for a presentation of its world-changing contents? Tell me that."

"Check your calendar, Eric. Give me a date and I'll do the rest. I can contact a couple of hundred of the world's best scientists in all fields and arrange a private meeting in one of the hotels I own in Europe. Probably in Paris. I'll even fly you over in my own plane so we don't have to worry about baggage checks with normal airline procedures. Anything else?"

"How do you do this, Helle?"

"You already know how I do this, lover." Helle laughed and hung up the phone.

15

Vengeance! Pandora's Box

"Eric, my lover, this is your common law wife. Good morning."
"My what? Helle, what are you talking about? I'm not your common law anything."
"We're having a baby together. Have you forgotten?"
"I've been doing some thinking on that, Helle. How are you going to have a baby if you're sterile?"
"I told you, Eric, immaculate conception. Do you doubt our master? You heard all the followers of Satan cry out 'It is done, it is done!' Do you not believe?"
"I'll believe it when I see it, Helle. I'm a scientist, you know that. When did you stop being one?"
"As you wish, lover. Hey, I'm feeling wonderful. Take me to Tequilaville tonight for dinner. It's going to be a very special night for me."
"What's so special about tonight, Helle? What's the occasion?"
"You'll see, lover. You'll see. Pick me up at 8:30."

The alarm went off next to their comfy bed as Wayne and Abby snuggled in the covers. It was going to be a beautiful day. The sun was shining bright, not a cloud in the sky as their bedroom lit up to welcome in the day.

"Wake up, Cowboy! I love you." Abby kissed Wayne on the cheek to get his day started as she had done every morning since they were married.

Wayne was not a morning person and it usually took him time to wake up and get into his day.

"Baby, why are you waking me up in the middle of the night? What time is it?"

"You are so funny, Wayne. It's almost nine in the morning. Open your eyes, baby, and enjoy the sunlight."

Wayne rubbed his eyes over and over.

"Abby, help me to the bathroom."

"What's wrong, Wayne?"

"I don't know. Just having a little problem getting into the day. Please, just guide me into the bathroom."

Abby helped Wayne out of bed. He was more logger-headed than usual and appeared to be confused and disoriented. He held out his hands in front of him as Abby led him into the bathroom. Wayne grasped for the water faucet, missing it a couple of times. Finally, he put his hand on the faucet and turned on the water. He cupped his hands under the water flow and began splashing it into his eyes. They were wide open.

"What's wrong, Wayne?" Abby was now concerned.

He continued to splash water on his face and eyes at a frantic pace.

"I can't see, Abby! I'm blind as a bat."

Abby wiped his face with a towel and helped him back into bed. She was a strong woman and didn't want to panic in front of Wayne.

"I'll call an ophthalmologist, Wayne. I'm sure this is just temporary. Maybe an after-effect of the bacterial meningitis. Just rest. I'll get you some coffee."

Two hours later, Abby and Wayne were waiting in the patient area for the doctor to give them the results of his eye tests.

"Mr. Tyler, after looking at my preliminary tests, I find absolutely nothing wrong with the internal areas of your eyes. So far, there are no medical reasons for your blindness. It could be the recurrence of the bacterial meningitis that you mentioned, but we'll have to wait for the results of some of the tests I have done. That's all I can tell you right now. I'll let you know when we have more to go on."

Abby took Wayne home and immediately put in a call to her dad.

"Sweetie Pie! How's my favorite daughter doing this morning?"

"Pop, Wayne woke up blind this morning. We've already been to the doctor and he said there's no reason for the blindness, but…Wayne can't see his hand in front of his face. He's supposed to play tonight. You're going to have to get Scott Wood and Mr. Elroy to fill in for him."

"Whoa, Abby! Slow down. I'll take care of the club. Don't worry about that. What can I do to help out? I'm here for you and Wayne."

"Just pray for him, Pop. Could you ask Liz and Robbie to pray for him?"

"Consider it done, baby. Don't worry."

Hank placed the calls to Robbie and Liz for prayer then called Scott Wood and Mr. Elroy and told them what was happening with Wayne. Scott was flabbergasted and promised that he and the band would do their best to fill in. Oddly enough, Mr. Elroy wasn't caught off guard at all. He was being his pleasant self and asked Hank for Wayne's cell phone number.

"Hi there, Mr. Wayne. I understand you is having some trouble with your eyes working right dis morning."

"That's an understatement, Mr. Elroy. I can't see a thing."

"Are you feeling okay otherwise, Mr. Wayne?"

"Yeah. My eyes seem to be the only thing not working. Otherwise, I feel fine. Thanks for asking."

"Then let me axed you a question, Mr. Wayne. Do you needs yo eyes to sing?"

"Uh, I guess I don't."

"Do you needs yo eyes to spank the plank on your guitar?"

"No, Mr. Elroy, you taught me well. I've always played by sound. I rarely ever look at the guitar."

"Then come on down to the club and let's rehearse. This too will pass, Mr. Wayne."

When Mr. Elroy said this, Wayne's mind quickly remembered that Gordon, his angel, had said the same words to him during his trials at Betwixt. Those words gave Wayne confidence just as they had months before.

"Abby, take me to the club. I'm going to perform tonight. Mr. Elroy is going to assist. Help me get dressed…"

Bella couldn't contain herself with all the good fortune happening to her and had to share it with her mom.

"Hi, baby girl. What's going on?" Robbie asked, surprised that Bella was calling her after their last conversation.

"Mom, I'm about to be rich! Irma Chemoth and Trikki Sanders are selling a two and a half million-dollar house and building a seven and a half million- dollar home and I'm their realtor! But that isn't all, Mom. Irma is the largest publisher in the world of New Age books. She's rich and Trikki's going to make a success story out of me and give me a seven-figure check for the book she's going to help me write. I'll be doing speaking engagements all over the world. That's what's going on with me, Mom!"

When Robbie heard Bella mention *New Age*, it made her blood boil.

"Baby, do you know what New Age teaches? It's not Christian."

"Mom, do you know what Feng Shui is? It's Chinese." Bella shot back.

"You need to slow down, baby, and think about what you're about to get into. This is cult stuff; you don't want to go there."

"Mom, I'm definitely going there. What an opportunity. I knew you were going to get all negative on me."

"I love you, Bella…"

"Well, Mom, it doesn't seem like it. Just think, with all that money, you wouldn't even have to work anymore. I could build you a big house and take good care of you. I love you, too, Mom, but don't stand in my way on this."

"Okay, baby. One more question. Where are you going to find enough land around here to build such a huge house? And who are Irma Chemoth and Trikki Sanders? Have you done your homework? This sounds too good to be true. Remember that?"

"Mom, I've done all the homework I need to do. I'm a very confident realtor as you well know. When have I ever asked you for anything?" Bella was being her defiant self again.

"As for the land, Irma wants to build on Taylor Lake across the lake from Eric's house."

"But Bella, there are already huge houses built all along the water front on the other side of Taylor Lake. There is no land to be had there. Have you thought of that?"

"Mom, all I know is that Trikki said that she and Irma will buy all the houses on the other side of the lake, making the home owners offers they can't refuse. I'm handling those sales, too. More money for me. Then Irma and Trikki will demolish the existing properties, scrape the sites and build their new mansion. Is that enough information for you, my doubting mom? I'm bringing Trikki to Tequilaville tonight. If you're there, I'll introduce you to her. Got to go, Mom, tootles…" Bella hung up.

Officer LeGrano was directing traffic outside of Tequilaville. Cars were lined up on NASA Road One in both directions trying to get into the parking lot.

Many of the drivers ignored his signals and almost side swiped him as they poured in. It was unexpected chaos.

Helle and Eric arrived and found a table center stage of the dance floor in front of the bandstand. Hank was sitting in his corner table watching the club fill up with people he'd never seen before. There were no families coming into the club, rather a bunch of rowdies, from where he had no idea. The business would be good for the club, but Hank had a feeling it was going to be a wild night.

T-Bone stood at the doorway into the club checking IDs. He, too, got the feeling he'd be very busy tonight. Most of the newcomers entering the club had tattoos, lots of bling and some were already partly bombed as they arrived. The club needed the business so T-Bone let the rowdy hordes in hoping they wouldn't cause problems.

As the unknown crowd began to enter, the Tequila Rita waitresses, smiled and seated them. Each of the newcomers began arguing over where they were seated and began causing problems from the get-go.

When they ordered drinks and food, the newcomers began arguing with the young waitresses telling them the drinks were not what they ordered, found problems with the food and began a night of chaos that no one at the club had ever seen before. Hank called Officer LeGrano and told him not to let any more cars into the parking lot. The club, inside and outside, was at capacity.

Master Tito was behind the bar, taking back perfectly prepared drinks and making the necessary credits to the crowds' bills. The waitresses were already stressing out, dreading waiting on their next customers. Hank went up to the microphone, seeing the bad atmosphere that was beginning to take shape.

"Welcome to Tequilaville, ladies and gentlemen. The entertainment is about to start, featuring Wayne Tyler. I hope you enjoy the show. So, in the meantime, let's just have a great night and be happy. I'm the co-owner of the club and if anyone has any kind of problem, just glance over at me in the corner table and I'll be honored to assist you."

Hank's commanding voice temporarily calmed the club clients down a bit. They began laughing and toasting him with their tequila shots raised high.

Bella arrived shortly after Hank's little speech. T-Bone had held a table for her on the left side of the dance floor. Robbie and Liz were sitting at Hank's corner table and both saw Bella enter with her new friend. Abby was in her office trying to work with Tito on the contested bills that had already begun to pile up.

As Bella and Trikki were seated, Trikki looked over at Helle, who had arrived at the club earlier and gave her an unnoticed wink just to let her know that she had sent out the mass emails to many of the followers of their cult in and around the Clear Lake area. Their plan was in place. This would be a night to remember. Helle was having her vengeance.

As Wayne was escorted up to the stage, he and Mr. Elroy began to play and sing along with the rest of the band. Scott Wood was handling sound and had to continuously turn it up to overcome the loud noise in the club.

Without doing any of his old 'shaky-hip' moves, the ladies in the crowd started howling at Wayne.

"Shake it, guitar man! Move your ass! What're you doing after the show?" They began flipping panties at the stage. The men were laughing right along with the women. The dance floor was stacked with panties and bras.

Abby heard all the commotion and came out of her office looking stressed. After seeing all the ladies' undergarments on the floor, she tried to whisper into Daddy Hank's ear, leaning across Robbie.

"We've got to stop this, Pop! Wayne has no idea what is happening. He can't see, and this is getting out of hand."

Again Hank walked up to the stage, took the microphone. He was trying to be diplomatic, but his anger was rising.

"Hey, everyone, you're missing some great songs here. We appreciate your passion for the music, but let's keep our clothes on. Officer LeGrano from the Clear Lake PD is standing over there, and we wouldn't want anyone to get hauled in for indecent exposure. Now just enjoy the show."

Helle was loving this. What she was not understanding is how Wayne was playing and singing flawlessly. She knew that she had struck him with blindness and yet he was performing like nothing was wrong.

For the next three hours, the money began pouring in as liquor sales went through the roof. But the crowd was becoming more and more belligerent. Helle and Trikki were loving every second of this planned chaos.

Finally, Hank spoke to Officer LeGrano who interrupted the music and took the microphone.

"Unfortunately, ladies and gentlemen, I have been instructed by the Fire Marshall to temporarily close the club. It is over the permissible occupancy level and I'm going to ask you to clear your tabs and go home. If you think you are over the permissible alcohol level, please use a designated driver or we will call a cab for you. I have officers stationed on each side of NASA Road One who will pull over anyone thought to be drunk. You have been warned."

That's when the drunken barroom brawl began. People were throwing shot glasses at the stage, grabbing the waitresses and fighting against each other, breaking chairs, destroying the bottles behind the bar, throwing tables across the room.

Hank pushed Liz, Robbie and Abby back into Abby's office and then got into the middle of the brawl. Hank was trying to separate the brawlers, both men and women, while T-Bone actually began knocking out some of the fighters with a single punch. He'd had enough and was defending the young waitresses from being groped.

Master Tito gathered all the wait staff, bartenders and bar backs behind the heavy bar, then jumped over it in front of the bar and began defending his staff against any who tried to harm them. He went wild with his karate kicks, breaking legs, punching people out with complete disregard for his own safety or thinking about being sued. Many of the men and women in the crowd were determined to take the karate master to the ground. Instead, there was an area of moaning bodies lying around him.

Officer LeGrano pulled out his service revolver and fired shots into the ceiling of the club.

"Everyone freeze! You're all under arrest! I'll shoot the next person that throws a punch!" LeGrano was on his radio calling for back up and ambulances. There was blood all over the dance floor. People cut with glass, others completely unconscious and people with broken bones.

T-Bone pulled out his 9mm Glock to back up Officer LeGrano as Hank went to Abby's office and came out with a sawed-off shot gun. The violence was going to end, one way or the other. The club was a complete disaster. When the violence began, Mr. Elroy led Wayne off of the stage as the band crowded around them to protect them from all the flying glass.

Bella was apologizing to the max to Trikki for all the violence and hoped that her money trail would not dry up with Trikki. During all of the brawl, Eric and Helle sat quietly and watched. Helle was smiling during the entire event. As they left, Helle walked over to Wayne and whispered in his ear.

"Great performance Wayne. I'll be *seeing* you soon." Eric escorted Helle from the club.

Officer LeGrano walked over to Dr. Palmer and Dr. Guyion and told them they were free to go since they had not participated in any way in the violence. He said the same to Bella and her friend Trikki as ambulances and paddy wagons flooded into the parking lot.

"Helle, did you have anything to do with this tonight? You acted as though you enjoyed it!"

"I did enjoy it, Eric. Isn't life exciting? Let's go back to the hotel. I've scheduled your event to present Pandora's Box to our colleagues. It's going to be your fifteen minutes of fame. Aren't you excited about that?"

T-Bone had been watching Dr. Guyion throughout the entire brawl and noticed her smug smiles. He noticed that she had not been hit with a single piece of glass, not a drop of blood or alcohol had splashed on her. It was as though she were protected from the chaos. Deep down, the huge, fierce bouncer believed that she had orchestrated the entire event. His hatred for her was almost uncontainable.

As Helle and Eric walked past T-Bone, leaving the club, Helle looked up at T-Bone.

"Remember what I told you, T-Bone. You have unfinished business with Wayne Tyler." T-Bone was momentarily stunned, moved to the side and let them pass.

He wanted to tell Dr. Guyion to never come to Tequilaville again…but the words would not form in his mouth.

The last person standing between Dr. Guyion and Eric as they left was Mr. Elroy. Helle tried her best to avoid him, but the old black musician stood in her path. During the entire mêlée, he had shown no emotions at all. As Helle hesitated, trying to walk around him, Mr. Elroy spoke to her.

"Dr. Guyion. Remember what I told you, 'leave my chillins alone.' I ain't gonna tells you agin!"

Two days later, Eric Palmer placed a call to Helle. He told her that he had invited some of his colleagues from NASA over to his home to view the box that Satan had given to him to present to the community of scientists in Paris. His associates were comprised of a small group of astro physicists, engineers and mathematicians.

"Helle, I needed some confirmation and affirmation that I would not be laughed off the stage in Paris. I didn't allow anyone to touch the box and explained the penalties for doing so. I hope you don't mind!"

"I don't mind, Eric. What was their reaction?"

"They were intrigued, Helle. I first gave them some idea, as best as I could describe, how we got to Betwixt before I showed them the box. When I mentioned going through a black hole…uh, well, first they laughed. I explained to them that I was under your hypnosis, then showed them the box. They are eager to meet you, Helle."

"Eric, I told you that I would let you make the presentation. It's your moment, your reward from the master for your obedience. What was their reaction to the box? I'm dying to know."

Eric went on to tell Helle that the scientists saw the box hovering an inch or two above its surface, slid paper under it, noticed the unknown jewels that adorned it and were particularly amused at his description of the top of the box—clear but opaque—which they considered an oxymoronic phenomenon, yet accurate. They were perplexed in their own hands-off examination of the vessel.

"Interesting, Eric. Did they give you the confirmation you needed to stand before about two hundred international scientists I have invited to the event next week?"

"Two hundred? Helle, who all did you invite? What languages do they speak? Will I be able to communicate with them? Next week? How can I prepare without a white paper? This is unsettling, Helle! Why so fast?"

"Eric, leave everything to me. Don't you trust me, lover?"

"Yeah, I'm freaking out. Plain to see isn't it, Helle? I risk ruining my reputation, my job at NASA and all out of trust. You know as well as I do, Helle, that scientists only trust proven facts. How am I going to prove our journey through a black hole, no breathing air, no space suits and especially our audience before Satan himself?"

"Simple, Eric. You open the box before our audience and see what comes out. That should be proof enough, wouldn't you agree?"

"I've never trusted in the unknown, Helle. Any scientist worth his salt wouldn't either…"

"The question is, Eric, will they trust their eyes?"

"I hope so! Speaking of eyes, can ten of my colleagues here at NASA accompany us on the trip in your plane to Paris?"

"If that will calm you down, lover, of course. I have plenty of room for them. Incidentally, the conference will be held in the grand ballroom of my Guyion Towers in Paris next Wednesday. I've sent the invitations and first class plane tickets and made accommodations at the hotel for all of our distinguished guests. Be ready; you'll do great, my love."

Abby was in her office at the club. She had insurance adjusters coming in to assess the damage, took video files of the events that had recorded everything and placed calls to the club's lawyers to see how Tequilaville would recoup its damages and discuss the possibility of law suits.

"Abby, I wouldn't worry about law suits. We're going to file them first against everyone present. They were all arrested and taken to jail. I have their arrest records. Most of them have a rap sheet a mile long," stated Micah Jones, Tequilaville's legal counsel. "With Officer LeGrano's statements and the videos of the entire event, there's not a jury in the world that would go against you."

"What about all of the credit cards that were left here at the club, Micah? Can I bill them for the damages?" Abby needed money to remodel and reopen the club.

"Go ahead and bill them equally, Abby. Possession is ten points of the law. If they want to contest it…well, let's just say they don't have a leg to stand on," Jones said. "I'll take care of the rest."

Wayne was up on the bandstand playing some new tunes with Mr. Elroy. The old man calmed him about his sudden blindness and helped him get even better at playing his guitar, by sound, not sight.

Hank walked into Abby's office.

"What a mess, Sweetie Pie! What're we going to do now?"

"Daddy Hank, I'm on it. We'll just hang a big banner in the front of the club stating 'Closed for Remodeling.' We're all taking a few weeks off to get the club back in order and get you and Liz married. Then we'll have another 'Grand Opening.' That's what we're going to do, Pop!"

"Sounds like a plan. How's Wayne?"

"He's blind, Dad. I can only do so much right now. We'll take this one step at a time and pray. For now, that's got to be enough. I can't do anymore." Abby was trying to suppress her anxiety. "Go fishing, Pop. Just go fishing and take Liz with you…"

~~~

On the plane over to Paris, each of the NASA scientists spent time with Eric Palmer and Helle Guyion trying their best to pose questions that would either affirm or condemn their presence at the conference, questions about their unexplained trip to the unknown, what they saw and how they returned. The endless questions were answered only by Palmer and Guyion's replies of "Trust your eyes about what you will see."

The NASA personnel aboard the flight finally settled into the pleasures of the immaculately designed aircraft with practically every creature comfort known to mankind. The flight attendants served them mixed drinks and five star delicacies from the on-board kitchen that would make the trip one to remember. None of them had ever been treated to such royal luxuries.

Upon arriving at Guyion Towers in Paris, Eric requested his own room, apart from Helle, in order to maintain their professional images. He needed time to prepare his opening remarks. After staying up most of the night, the time had arrived for the presentation early the next morning.

Eric emerged from his room wearing his best business suit. Helle was dressed appropriately as she handed papers she had prepared to Natasha Patski to distribute to her invited colleagues. Eric's assistant, Belinda Sealy, shadowed her boss, if nothing else, to lend support. She had no official duties at the conference other than to record everything said on her laptop. She, too, was anxious about the presentation and how it would be received.

The two hundred-plus scientists began filling the ballroom and continuously looked for interpreter earphones which were nowhere to be found. There was murmuring in several languages within the group.

Dr. Helle Guyion walked onto the stage and took her place behind the speaker's podium. As she welcomed her guests, speaking in English, every person in the room understood her perfectly, hearing her in their own language. For the first thirty seconds or so of her introductions, no one noticed. Then, being scientists, they began whispering to each other...

"How is she doing this?" they said to each other.

Eric picked up on it also and remembered the Day of Pentecost events written in the Bible where the disciples, overcome by the Holy Spirit, spoke to the crowds of Jerusalem in many tongues. Helle was mimicking this historical event with her Satanical powers.

"In closing, my distinguished friends and colleagues, I remind you to believe your eyes. I present to you someone you all know well, Dr. Eric Palmer and Pandora's Box!"

Light applause followed Eric's introduction by Helle. The tough crowd of scientists were wearing their "skeptic" faces.

Dr. Palmer began his shortened explanation of their journey, the black hole passage, what he felt on the way and tried his best to describe the images of Mount Zaphon. He told about the throne of Satan and the hordes of spirits that encircled it.

"Some people describe this place as Betwixt, a huge galaxy in another dimension. Others describe this as a second heaven. You can call it whatever you believe it to be..." Eric was leading up to the big moment. His blood pressure was rising off the chart.

Out of respect for Dr. Guyion and the power that many of the attendees knew she possessed, they didn't immediately break into laughter but were secretly thinking that the world famous Dr. Palmer had lost his mind. They weren't buying anything he said to them.

Sensing their disbelief, Palmer said, "Now believe your eyes!" He exited the podium, stage right, and walked over to Dr. Guyion who was standing guard over the box as it hovered on a table next to her.

"The moment of truth, Eric. Enjoy your fame. It is about to begin," Helle said confidently.

Eric grasped the hovering box, walked back to center stage and placed it on a flat presentation table. As he lowered it, the box did not hover above the surface. He quickly looked at Helle for reassurance. She smiled and motioned for him to continue. Eric remembered that Satan was called the Father of all lies and deceit. Had he been tricked?

Taking a deep breath, Eric removed the golden key from his vest pocket and inserted it into the keyhole of the box. Then the box began to hover above the table. The scientists were amused and wondered if this was some sick act of worthless magic Dr. Palmer was trying to display. They had come to see scientific wonders, not magic.

The box lid opened by itself, slowly. The room was silent in anticipation. For what seemed like minutes, nothing emerged from the odd-looking box. Then, one-by-one, three frogs jumped out of the box and sat in front of it on the table. They began to croak…Ribbit! Ribbit! Ribbit!

The crowd broke into uncontrollable laughter, slapping their knees and elbowing each other. Some of the world scholars began getting up and heading for the exits, feeling they had been the victims of a con job.

Palmer just stood there in disbelief. He was humiliated and anger rose up within him. Again he looked over at Helle. She had not changed her expression. He was completely dumbfounded over what to do or what to say in his own defense.

Suddenly, before any of the scientists had made it out the door, the entire ballroom began to shake as if there were an earthquake. The priceless chandeliers began to sway back and forth above them and pieces of the ceiling began to powder down on top of the group. An explosion of light burst upwards from Pandora's Box. It was so dazzling that everyone began to shield their eyes with their arms. No one could look directly at the box. It knocked Dr. Palmer backwards off his feet and he lay looking straight up.

The light subsided somewhat as the shaking of the room continued. Roars and strange sounds could be heard coming from deep within the object on the table. They sounded like ghoulish shrieks and screams that chilled the very souls of everyone in the ballroom. The scientists were crouching down behind the chairs in front of them for fear of being struck. By what, they did not know.

The horrific display continued as barely visible spirits emerged from the box and flew around the room, passing in and out of the walls and right through the bodies of the scientists with ease. Many of the scientists present had gathered their wits enough to turn on the videos on their smart phones to record what they thought they were seeing and experiencing. More and more of sometimes shapeless visions emerged from the box. Fear filled the room of unbelieving scientists. There was no doubt that the unknown was present.

After dodging the spirits passing through their bodies, the scientists began seeing strange equations appearing like holograms on the walls that made $E=MC^2$ look like ancient history. They saw "ones" and "zeros" scrolled out in massive forms like computer programs that had never been written.

Some of the scientists reached for their pens and paper to try and write some of the astonishing equations into their notebooks, fearing that their smart phones might not record what they were seeing. Feverishly, they wrote and wrote, flipping pages in their notebooks, trying to write down as much information as they could gather. The scientists had no idea how long these visions would last, but they could tell that the world of scientific knowledge had never seen such startling formulas.

Next came snippets of visions—hundreds of horrific visions—depicting scenes of nuclear wars, seas turning to blood, asteroids falling and impacting the earth's surface. Then more pleasant visions of a messiah-like savior emerging from Europe who calmed the fears of the earth and promised peace. There were depictions of huge crops growing in desert regions, happy hordes of people worshipping in a new Solomon's temple in Jerusalem.

Finally, as the shaking of the room subsided, there was a complete vision of the trip Dr. Guyion and Dr. Palmer had tried to describe to their audience amid their pent-up laughter. Every phase of the journey came into view, the expanse of space, entering the black hole and the thunderous noise that was present within it. Even the throne of Satan could be seen with his face covered by a smoky mist. Nothing was left out. Just as Dr. Palmer had described it.

The scientists were trying their best to catch their breaths amid spectacles that had never been seen by mankind. Two of the scientists were clutching their chests as if they were experiencing heart attacks. But the visions continued, unrelenting, over-lapped, one after the other. It was almost too much for the human psyche to absorb. The experience was beyond reason, beyond logic, but the scientific community was seeing it with their own eyes.

The sounds, the brilliant light, the visions, released spirits, and equations finally began dialing back to stillness. The room stopped shaking and silence filled the room.

As the group began standing up from their crouched positions, their focus was once again on Pandora's Box which was now hovering silently above the display table with the three frogs in front of it. There was a hush in the room.

One by one, the three frogs jumped back into the box. With the lid still open, the box vaporized into nothingness right before the eyes of the world's greatest minds. The only thing that remained was the golden key Dr. Palmer still clutched in his right hand.

Helle walked out onto the stage, helped Dr. Palmer to his feet and addressed the entourage of scientists. Her eyes blazoned with red laser-like streams of light as she took the time to look each scientist in the eye. She had each one under her spell as she had many times before.

"Thank you all for joining us here today. I hope you believe what you just saw. Wasn't it astounding?" she asked.

The crowd of scientists, somewhat mesmerized, began to applaud slowly.

"Dr. Palmer and I apologize for not having white papers written for this event. Rather, we would like this community of the world's greatest minds to write your own white papers on what you have witnessed here today. We eagerly await what you will tell the world." Helle paused for a moment, then spoke again.

"Thank you again for your participation. My assistant, Natasha Patski will have all of your return plane tickets in the foyer and will give them to you as you leave. Your hotel bills are complimentary. Have a safe trip home. And, if you have questions, just email Dr. Palmer at NASA. I have provided all of you contact information in the sheets that I handed out earlier. "

Belinda Sealy, who had been standing just off stage, ran up to Dr. Palmer.

"Are you okay, boss?"

"I guess I am. How are you, Belinda?"

"I'm scared to death and just want to get home and away from Dr. Guyion. I can't help it, Dr. Palmer, she scares the hell out of me!"

As they walked out of the ballroom, Helle came over to Eric and hooked her arm in his.

"I told you not to worry, lover. How do you think it went?"

"Where's the box, Helle? What happened to Pandora's box?"

"Who knows, my love. As the stories go, Pandora's Box, once opened, can never be closed. What do we need with an empty box? You've still got the golden key as a souvenir. Isn't that enough?"

16

Segue Temptations

Flying back to Houston from Paris on Helle's luxurious plane, the scientists sat in almost complete silence. The ten NASA scientists appeared to be in a dazed state as they contemplated what they had just experienced hours before. Some of them were working on their laptops, inputting some of the formulas and programs they had copied into their notes from the holograms they had seen on the walls of the ballroom.

Dr. Palmer and Dr. Guyion were sitting in her private quarters aboard the aircraft. Helle was feeling quite pleased with her part in the presentation.

"I've got to admit, Helle, asking your colleagues at the event to write the white papers was a stroke of genius. You let me off the hook!" Eric said with a sigh.

"Of course, lover. Why would I want to hurt you? It will be interesting to see what our wise and talented group will write. At least they are supported by the others present. With so many attending, it will be hard for any of the other leading world scientists not present to refute what they will write." Helle smiled and reached for her vodka martini.

"Do you believe in my master's power now, my love?" Helle said, moving closer to Eric on the huge bed where they were lounging during the return flight.

"To be honest, Helle, my beliefs are pretty well scrambled at this point. Whatever spirits, formulas and equations that were released during the presentation are still…uh, out there. What do they mean? What will happen as a result of this new knowledge?

"Will these atheistic scientists believe in the power of Satan when they begin to figure out the meanings of the formulas? Will the information reveal new and terrible weapons? Will the experience benefit mankind or harm it? There are so many unanswered questions, Helle! I'm not certain at this point that I want my name to be associated with giving these formulas to mankind when we don't know what they mean yet. And what was with the three frogs? Was that supposed to mean something?"

"Eric, you aren't the one who presented this to the scientific community. You will receive no credit. Satan was the giver and presenter of the formulas, equations and holograms. He will receive the praise and glory for this. Don't forget it, Eric? As for the three frogs, lover, I thought you said you studied the Bible and all religions of the world. I think you skipped over a few things…"

In the midst of all the real estate deals going on between Bella, Trikki Sanders and Irma Chemoth—whom Belle had never met in person—Bella's plate and mind had become a bit overwhelmed. She continued to meet with Trikki privately to learn the New Age power of Positive Thinking every single morning, five days a week. The promise of riches, fame and becoming a wealthy best-selling author and speaker drove her.

"Trikki, how did you get the last name of 'Sanders' if you're from Persia?" Bella was trying to fill in some blanks of her own.

"I married a very rich and powerful man from the U.S. and took his last name. He died many years ago."

"That's the way to do it, Trikki! Marry rich! Way to go sister!" Bella said giving Trikki a high five.

"Another question: Did you learn everything about this New Age era while you were in China or did you have another mentor besides Mama-Che? Just curious, Trikki." Bella continued her own little investigation into the background of her new friend.

"I did have another mentor, Bella. So perceptive of you to ask. My other mentor is a very intelligent woman originally from Norway named Dr. Helle Guyion. Have you ever heard of her?"

"Heard of her, Trikki, I know her! How ironic! She's here in Clear Lake working with one of my boyfriends, Dr. Eric Palmer at NASA. She's my psychiatrist! What a small world."

"Where is she staying, Bella? This is amazing! We must all have lunch together," Trikki said, sealing the conspiracy to get Bella to Betwixt.

"Over at the Bay Hilton. Here's her cell number, Trikki. I just love this. Dr. Guyion is so smart, so charming, so beautiful. But I think I have a bit of an edge over her in the beauty department. I'm younger!" Bella would never yield to another woman's beauty over her own.

"I'll arrange our lunch, Bella. Now, are you ready to get started? You've got so much to learn."

"Trikki, I'll do the best I can, but I have to admit that there's so much that I don't understand and I'm having a hard time dealing with it."

"Like what, Bella?"

"Like praying to the universe. I mean, uh, who exactly am I praying to? Buddha, Mohammed, God? Most people pray to someone specific, don't they Trikki?"

"Bella, that's the power of praying to the universe. You pray to all of them. Who knows who is the highest god? Who knows who really created mankind or the galaxies, or has the universe as we know it always just been there? Who knows if there are many paths to paradise? We're covering all the bases! That's the power of the universe." Trikki was filling Bella's mind with more than she could comprehend.

"You're completely blowing my mind, Trikki. Isn't there a better way for me to understand all of this?"

"Yes, there is, Bella. I can hypnotize you and implant this knowledge in your mind way quicker than you can comprehend it on your own. Want to give it a try?"

"Let me think about that, Trikki. It's not that I don't trust you; I just have to do some thinking about it. Can I tell you in a day or two?"

"Sure. Till then, girlfriend. I'll leave you with some homework from some of the many books we've published on New Age." Trikki had a stack of ten to twelve books that she shoved over to Bella, knowing it would be too much for Bella to read all of them. She knew that Bella was not much of a reader and had hated homework ever since she was in the first grade.

"How's my cowboy this morning?" Abby asked Wayne as he was waking up.

"Blind as a bat and unable to see my beautiful wife. How're you doing?" Wayne had a smile on his face.

"I'm coping, Wayne. That's all I can say right now. You know I love you, don't you?" Wayne couldn't see the distraught expression on Abby's face, but he could hear it in her voice.

"And I love you, too, my bride. We'll get past this together. Keep your chin up, Abby. The doctor said there was nothing medically wrong with my eyesight. Maybe it's just a test of our faith and love for one another. Till death do us part! Remember we said that in our wedding vows, pretty girl? I may be blind, but I'm not near dead. We've got a lifetime before us."

No matter their differences of belief, when Bella felt overwhelmed and had decisions to make, she always turned to the one person who truly loved her, her mom, Robbie. She placed a call to her and asked if she could come over and spend the night, have a great meal and just have some mother/daughter talk. Robbie was delighted but had no idea what was going in Bella's life. She was so independent.

Bella arrived at Robbie's condo with an overnight bag slung over her shoulder. She put her stuff in the guest bedroom then walked into the kitchen and poured two glasses of Zinfandel. Sipping it slowly, Robbie waited for Bella to tell her what was going on.

Before long, Bella flipped back her long black hair, folded her legs on the couch and started talking. She told her mom about where she was with the real estate deals with Irma Chemoth, how she was enjoying her new friend, Trikki Sanders, and what Trikki was teaching her about New Age.

Robbie tried her best to hold back at the sound of *New Age* and just let Bella get whatever was bothering her off her chest without interrupting. She could see the concern on Bella's face and figured that was a good thing. At least her daughter was not just diving into this without some thought.

"What's so ironic about this, Mom, is that Dr. Guyion was Trikki's mentor. They studied together in China," Bella said.

"So what's eating you, baby girl?" Robbie asked.

"Well, Mom, what Trikki is promising me—fame, fortune, best-selling books, traveling the world—all sounds good, but it's not going to be easy like I thought it would."

"Nothing in life is easy, Bella. So what's the problem?"

"Trikki is giving me all these books to read. Mom, you know I'm not a reader. And, quite frankly, praying to the universe sounds kind of silly to me. But Trikki makes it sound so easy. It's not. I'm just not that smart, Mom."

"You're smarter than you think you are, Bella. The fact that you're here discussing this with me shows that. Don't sell yourself short, baby girl. All you need to read is one book, the Bible. It's got more wisdom and insight in it than all the New Age books ever printed. Tell me more…"

Bella and Robbie stayed up late into the night. Robbie knew better than to tell Bella what to do. Bella would reject it. Robbie listened to everything Bella told her, taking a special note of the fact that Trikki Sanders said she could hypnotize Bella and implant all this information in her mind. It seemed that all roads led back to Dr. Guyion. Robbie hadn't liked her from the first time she'd met her. Her feeling hadn't changed and her anger for the albino woman was growing.

"Baby, you've got a great mind. Don't let anyone get in there and plant thoughts that aren't your own."

Bella seemed to pass off that bit of motherly advice and changed the subject. "Mom, I forgot to tell you about my new friends," Bella said.

"What new friends?"

"I call them my wallflower friends, Mom. They're shadows on my walls at home. At first, they freaked me out because shadows don't move across the wall without something else moving. But they seem harmless, no threat and they even wave at me. So I call them *friends*. What do you think about that, Mother dearest?"

"Bella, I don't know what these shadows are or if they are real or not. I know you think they are. My best advice to you is that you may be playing with fire, baby girl. Leave a light on at night. Don't look at them. Pray to God to remove them, not the universe, Bella. No good can come of it. Is that why you wanted to come over here tonight?"

"Oh, the shadows don't really bother me, Mom. They're shaped like flowers, bunny rabbits and sometimes just an arm that waves at me. They're really kind of funny, amusing and great company sometimes. I just wanted to come talk to you and chill for a while."

As soon as Bella left the next morning, Robbie placed a frantic call to Liz Gabriel. When Liz answered, Robbie exploded.

"Liz, I've got to ask a huge favor of you." Without waiting for Liz's reply, Robbie kept talking. "That witch, Helle Guyion and her friend, Trikki Sanders, are playing with Bella's mind. I want you to go with me to confront her at her hotel so that I can give her a piece of my mind. I'm mad as hell, Liz; no one messes with my daughter. I'll kick her butt!"

"Whoa, Robbie! Slow down. What's this all about?"

Robbie ranted and raved for another twenty minutes, telling Liz everything Bella had told her. When she finally ran out of steam, Liz replied.

"First off, Robbie, I can understand your concern for your daughter, but there is an old saying, 'If you lose it, you lose,' whether or not you are right or wrong. Calm down. No one will listen to anger talking. I'll be there in twenty minutes and we'll go see Dr. Guyion together. In the meantime, we'll say a prayer for God to speak through us when we confront her…"

Within the hour, Liz and Robbie were at the Bay Hilton. Dr. Guyion told the front desk clerks to send them up to her suite. When Natasha Patski opened the door to let them in, Robbie couldn't hold back. She walked right past the assistant and headed straight over to Helle, who was sitting naked on the couch.

"Cover yourself, you maniacal witch! You have no modesty and your tattoos are offensive to me!" Robbie shouted with Liz right behind her.

Helle was unfazed at Robbie's outburst. "Ms. Cantrell, please lower your voice. I'll be happy to put on a robe. Obviously, you are upset over something." Helle had Natasha bring her a robe which she slowly put on in front of the two women. "Now, why are you so upset?"

"You and this Trikki Sanders are playing with my daughter's mind, and it's going to stop right now. You got that?" Robbie blurted out, unable to control her anger.

"I haven't seen your daughter in a couple of weeks, Ms. Cantrell. And I have no idea what you are talking about. Could I have Natasha get you something to drink…?"

"No!" Robbie cut Dr. Guyion off. "Now you listen to me. If you even get close to my daughter again, I'll…"

Helle had had enough of Robbie's ranting and accusations.

"You'll do what, Ms. Cantrell? You have no idea who you're talking to or the power that I possess. Let me show you!"

Helle's eyes became red lasers, piercing, as she looked simultaneously into the eyes of Robbie and Liz.

Liz grabbed Robbie's arm to stop her forward advance toward Dr. Guyion. Robbie, in defense of her daughter, would tangle with the devil himself with no regards for her own life.

"You're obviously possessed by demons, Dr. Guyion. Now we know from where your powers come. You cannot harm us. We are children of God," Liz said in a calm voice.

Helle interrupted Liz, "Yes, I can see that by the sealed mark on your foreheads. But you have no power over me, either."

Robbie interrupted Helle. "We'll see about that! In the Holy Name of Jesus, demons, come out of this woman!"

Helle just laughed. They were at a stand-off. Neither had power over the other.

"Robbie, we cannot exorcise the demons from someone who will not agree to be free of her demons. God gave us free choice and free will. Dr. Guyion has made her choice." Liz remained calm. "Dr. Guyion, what Ms. Cantrell and I *can* do is to pray to Almighty God that He pours out His cup of wrath on you…"

"Get out! Get out now before I show you who can do what to whom!" Helle was furious. Her eyes blazed. Robbie and Liz had no fear of her, only anger and left the hotel room.

"Do you feel better now, Robbie?" Liz asked, smiling.

"You bet I do, Liz." Robbie was still shaking. "At least we finally know who she is."

"She's a living demoness, Robbie. She worships Satan. We have to pray that God will remove her from our presence, our families and our city. We really have to become prayer warriors since it's perfectly clear who we're up against. Only the Father, The Son and The Holy Spirit can protect us now. We're not fighting against flesh and blood…"

Helle put in an urgent call to Trikki Sanders, her lieutenant in forming the Clear Lake Satanical worship organization.

"Trikki! This is Helle. They know! Robbie Cantrell and Liz Gabriel just left my room at the hotel. They came to confront me about Bella. They're both sealed and I can't do anything to them; my spells will not work. We need to get our 'Shadows' working immediately before Robbie can convince Bella to avoid us. Our master's wrath will be upon both of us if we don't deliver Bella to him. Start the temptations now!" Helle hung up.

After work the next day, Bella returned home, ordered in sushi and watched TV until late into the night. She felt good about her talk with her mom even though she discounted most of the advice that Robbie had given her. Bella just wanted to be heard and understood and her mom was always the best listener.

Just before midnight, Bella went into her well-lit bedroom, trying to avoid her shadow friends, put on one of her favorite night gowns and went to bed. After only a few minutes, she was in a deep sleep.

The shadows on the walls appeared once again in the completely dark room. Slowly, they moved from the walls toward Bella in the forms of dark spider webs. They wrapped themselves around Bella's head and shoulders until she was completely sealed from any noise or distractions. Now dreaming, Bella seemed to awaken in a beautiful desert setting. She was neither hot nor cold but felt the sensation of being very hungry and thirsty.

She paid no attention to where she was or how she got there. Deep down in her mind, Bella knew she was dreaming. In the distance, she saw a figure of a man in white carrying a staff, walking across the sand toward her. He was a beautiful man, glistening in the sunlight.

"I can see you need some nourishment, beautiful lady. Let me help you," the man said.

He touched a stone with his staff and it turned into bread. The bread floated over to Bella. She could smell the fresh hot fragrance and began to eat.

"Thank you, sir. Could I have some water, also?" she asked.

The man touched the sand around them and a pool of fresh, clear water sprang up out of the desert. He produced a drinking ladle, dipped out some of the refreshing water and handed it to Bella. She drank a little and threw the rest across the sand. Everywhere the water from her ladle landed, fresh flowers bloomed in every color. Their fragrance was like fine perfume.

I'm enjoying this dream, Bella thought to herself.

"You're such a handsome man. We haven't been properly introduced. I'm Bella."

"I am here for you, Bella. I'm here to show you the riches and wonders of the world that can all be yours. Come with me now. We're going to fly to and fro across the earth. The first stop is the Cathedral Notre-Dame de Paris which means 'Our Lady of Paris.' Have you ever been there?"

"No, but I've always wanted to see it," Bella said excitedly.

As they flew through the clouds, hand-in-hand, they neared the Gothic loftiness of the cathedral that dominated the River Seine. Bella pointed to the highest spire on the building.

"Take me there, Adonis! I want to get a closer look at this place."

"Adonis? You called me Adonis?"

"Hey, you never told me your name so I'll just give you one. You're 'Adonis' as far as I'm concerned." Bella laughed at her own arrogance, trying to be more personal with such a beautiful man.

"As you wish, Bella."

The man carried her high above the building to the top of the highest spire. They lightly touched down on top of the cross that adorned the world's most famous cathedral. Bella gave no thought to the blasphemy of standing on a cross as she took in the wonderful view of Paris.

"How much do you trust me, Bella?" the man said.

"Trust you? I hardly know you and this is just a great dream. Why should I trust you?" Bella was actually being flirty with this beautiful man.

"Because trust is important. You have been chosen to receive wealth and fame and riches. But first you have to prove that you trust the one who has sent me."

"So who sent you, Adonis? What have I got to do?" Bella asked.

"I'll tell you who sent me after you prove your trust. Just jump off of this spire and trust the one who sent me to save you," the man said.

"Are you kidding me? No way I'm jumping off this spire and splattering myself all over the street below. I'd break my neck!" Bella fired back at the man.

"Bella, haven't you ever had a dream where you were flying or falling?"

"Not recently. I did have a rather weird dream not long ago about going to some old Roman coliseum. Was that a trip, although I don't remember too much about it. But to answer your question, I wasn't the one flying around in that dream, but I saw others who were. We may as well just move on. I'm *not* jumping and that's that!"

The man took Bella's hand in his and began flying her around the world to such places as London where they saw the Crown Jewels of England, then to Russia where they saw the beauty of the spires in Moscow, then on to China where Bella got to see priceless objects of the Ming Dynasty. The man took her to India, along the Yamuna River to see the ivory-white marble mausoleum of the Taj Mahal in the city of Agra.

From there they went to diamond minds in Africa and to the De Beer's vaults to see massive amounts of cut diamonds. Bella even held the world's largest cut diamond, the Golden Jubilee, a 545-carat diamond, in her hands and marveled at its beauty. She couldn't imagine the cost of the huge stone and was overwhelmed at the riches and the wonders of the earth.

Finally, their journey ended on the border between Nepal, Tibet and China on the summit of the 29,000-foot Mount Everest. The view was breathtaking as her senses were overloaded. Again, Bella was thinking that this was the best dream she had ever had.

"Now that's what I call a great dream, Adonis! Thank you. I can't remember when I've had a better time, and believe me when I tell you, *I* have had some great times in my life." Bella was taking in the beauty around her as the wind on top of the mountain blew through her hair and nightgown.

"You're welcome, Bella. It has been my pleasure to be your guide on this journey."

"Okay, let's get to the point. I'm impressed. So what do I have to do to gain favor of this guy who sent you and attract all this wealth and beauty to me?" Bella could sense that she was about to awaken out of the dream and wanted some finality before doing so.

"Bow down to him, Bella! Worship the one who sent me. That's all you have to do," the man said in a kind, authoritative voice.

"You must be joking! I don't bow down to men, they bow down to me!" Bella said arrogantly.

"And that's the reason you have been chosen, Bella. You have such great pride in yourself."

"You got that right! I truly do have pride in myself. Now who's this guy I'm supposed to bow down to and gain all of this wealth and power? If you don't tell me, the deal's off."

"He is Satan, lord and ruler of the universe."

"That does it. I'm out. I don't believe in all this Satan and God stuff. It just scares me and I don't need any of that in my life. But…hmmm, wealth and riches…If I change my mind,—you know every woman likes to have that option—how do I contact you and talk further about this?" Bella remained non-committal.

"Just talk to the shadows on your wall, Bella. They brought you here tonight. They can bring you back. But don't wait too long; this is not an open-ended offer. You must act quickly."

"And just when I was kind of liking my little friends on the wall. Now you're scaring the crap out of me again. I feel like I'm being watched. Hey, I'll let you know. It's time for me to wake up and get started on my day. Tootles!"

Bella yawned as she began waking up from her dream. Next to her on her pillow was a beautiful red ruby. She remembered that during her dream when she and 'Adonis' were in India, she had secretly picked up one of the gems from a vast treasure chest and had put it in her pocket, hoping the man hadn't noticed.

Bella knew she had been dreaming, but she couldn't explain the precious stone lying on her pillow. Had this been a true dream? As the morning sun burst into her bedroom, she quickly glanced at her walls to see if the shadows were still there. They were gone. Maybe she had missed her chance, but time would tell. She was in no rush, but she was scared again.

"Mom, this is Bella. I just had another weird dream, and I'm not sure these little shadow friends are really friends. I think they may be some kind of poltergeists or something. Can I come over and stay at your place for a while?"

17

THE MOMENT
ENJOY IT WHILE YOU CAN...

Abby was just waking up as she slid out of bed trying not to awaken Wayne. She wanted him to rest and not burden him with everything going on at Tequilaville. The club was closed until further notice, but the bills were still piling up. An hour later, she crawled back into bed next to Wayne and whispered in his ear.

"Time to wake up, Cowboy. Tomorrow is a big day for Daddy Hank and Liz. We've got lots of things to do. I'm so glad that Liz came into Pop's life. I didn't think he would ever get over my mom."

Wayne pulled Abby next to him.

"I'm awake. I've been awake for some time."

"So why don't you open your eyes?"

"Abby, it's the weirdest thing…Sometimes being blind isn't such a bad thing. I mean, uh, I guess I always took my sight for granted in the past."

"Baby, how can being blind be a good thing?" Abby snuggled closer to Wayne in bed.

Wayne put both of his hands on Abby's face and pulled her to his lips and kissed her.

"Abby, what I mean is…now that I'm blind, I can actually see you more clearly. I can feel your face. I can caress your skin. It seems as though I can see your heart. Does that make any sense?"

"It makes a lot of sense, Wayne. Tell me what my heart looks like." Abby was snuggling and giggling.

"You have the most beautiful heart, my love. And I know it belongs to me. You have cared for me, supported me. Abby, you are closer to me now than when I could see. It's like our souls have become one...I don't think I could have ever seen this without being blind. I have such a higher sense of touch, I can hear every inflection in your voice. I can feel the anxiety in your shoulders and...I can actually feel the love you have for me inside of you. It's like I can see into your soul, baby, and you have a such a wonderful soul. I can see it even though I am blind."

Abby kissed Wayne softly and firmly.

"Baby, I want you to see again, but I don't want us to ever lose what you just told me." Abby took Wayne's hand in hers and wiped away her tears with it. "I needed to hear that."

Robbie walked into the guest bedroom which used to be Bella's room before she moved out on her own. Bella hadn't said a thing about going back to her house for several days. Robbie was patiently waiting for Bella to tell her what had happened. She knew Bella would tell her in her own time.

"Get up, baby girl. Can you help me with some of the final arrangements for Hank and Liz's wedding tomorrow?"

Bella yawned and stretched out her arms feeling a lot more secure at her mom's condo than in her own house. "Got any coffee, Mom?"

"I've poured you a cup just like you like it. It's on the end table in the living room," Robbie said.

Bella went into the bathroom, washed her face, slid on some house shoes and put on her robe and came into the living room and grabbed the cup of coffee. She was pitching the ruby up and down.

"Wow, Bella! Where did you get that?" Robbie couldn't take her eyes off the beautiful stone.

"A little something I picked up in India during my dream, Mom. Isn't it pretty?"

"Baby, you can't bring things back from a dream. Now where did you get it, really?" Robbie sometimes delighted in Bella's wild imagination.

"I really got it in my dream. I'm telling you the truth, Mom!"

"Impossible, Bella. Now tell me the whole story about this dream of yours."

Bella began telling her mom as much of the dream as she could remember, including meeting this beautiful man that she called 'Adonis.'

After going over every detail that she could remember, she said that while in India, looking at a treasure chest of jewels, she just slipped the ruby into her pocket, as a souvenir.

"So you stole it, huh, Bella?"

"Mom, how can you steal something in a dream. I'm trying to tell you the truth. Now do you believe me?"

"Bella, let me ask you something…Have you been reading the Bible that I gave you?"

"Heck no, Mom! Why would I be doing that? I told you I wasn't convinced about all this God and devil stuff. It just scares me. Why would you even ask me that?"

"Because, Bella, what you described in your three temptations were almost verbatim the three temptations Christ was subjected to shortly after His baptism by John the Baptist. For the next forty days, Jesus was in the desert where Satan tempted Him with the same temptations. Do you find that ironic?"

"I guess *you* find it ironic, Mom. I don't even know or care about all that Bible stuff." Bella was getting defensive again. "I shouldn't have told you about my dream, anyway. I knew you wouldn't believe me."

"I didn't say I didn't believe you, Bella. But if you did bring that ruby back from a dream, there's more going on here than you can imagine."

"Like what? I had a dream and I have a big ruby to prove that it was a true dream. How do you explain that, Ms. Bible Thumper?"

"Bella, there is a lot of symbolism behind rubies. I've studied all about gemstones and birthstones when you were born. You know that the ruby is your birthstone?"

"Of course I do, Mom. That's what makes this such a personal prize to me. It's got to cost lots of money, huh, Mom?"

"It may cost more than you think, Bella. The ruby has long been a symbol of love and passion. It is meant to arouse the senses and stir the imagination…"

"I'm already liking this, Mom. I can't wait to hear the rest…"

"Bella, listen closely to me, little girl. You're playing with fire again. Given as a gift, the ruby is a symbol of friendship and love. But you stole it. Therefore, it means just the opposite now, like being an enemy of love itself. It's now a symbol of fire and death! Psychics use rubies for dream recall and dream work. Are you getting what I'm saying to you, Bella?"

"Oh, Mom, that's just old folklore. I guess you're going to tell me next that I should walk out onto your patio and throw it into Clear Lake. And before you do: It ain't happening, Mom. This is my souvenir from the dream and I'm keeping it."

"Bella, I swear. You sound just like you did when you were five years old. 'It's mine! It's mine! You can't have it!' When are you ever going to grow up and accept responsibility for your life and your beliefs?" Robbie was exasperated once again with her self-centered daughter. Deep down, she feared the direction that Bella was choosing for her life.

"Quit preaching to me, Mom. Let's change the subject; who all is on the guest list for the wedding tomorrow night?" Bella asked with her ever present attitude.

Robbie slid the guest list over to Bella.

"Just as I thought! None of *my* friends are on there, well, no one but Lieutenant Stan. What's the deal here, Mom?"

"The *deal* is, Bella, that this is Mr. Hank and Liz's wedding, not yours. Their wedding, their list."

"Blah, blah, blah. I can tell already that I'm just going to have a blast tomorrow evening," Bella said facetiously. "What time should I be there?"

The weather was perfect around the lake, sunshine and very little wind coming off the Gulf of Mexico. Tito, Mary, T-Bone and the rest of the Tequilaville crew had turned the outside deck into a beautiful setting for an afternoon wedding with huge pots of flowers surrounding a small gazebo with a pulpit under it for Pastor Randy of the Cowboy Church to officiate. Wayne was going to stand up with Hank as his best man and Robbie was Liz's maid of honor.

Hank looked handsome in his tux and black cowboy hat. Abby helped Wayne into his tuxedo and was there to guide him under the trellis at the right time.

As the small group of people gathered outside on the deck, Pastor Randy went over some final instructions with Robbie, Hank and Wayne. Liz was inside the club getting her hair done and, with Robbie's help, got into her wedding dress which had belonged to her grandmother. Scott Wood and *South* began playing some country and western music to lighten the occasion.

Instead of sitting in the front row where family was usually seated, Bella chose to sit alone on the very back row of seats lined up for the wedding. As usual, she was over-dressed for the occasion as most of the other attendees were in simple boots and jeans. Some, like T-Bone, even wore their best starched jeans. Lieutenant Stark wore his white uniform and sat next to Bella. She practically ignored his act of kindness.

Abby knew her Daddy Hank well and could see the anxiety in his nature. Not the anxiety of marrying the love of his life, but the anxiety of just getting the event over with. He wasn't much for pomp and ceremony.

"Are you ready, Pop?" Abby said giving Daddy Hank a kiss on the cheek and trying to calm him down a bit.

"Yes, Sweetie Pie, I'm ready. I've been ready for this woman ever since I found out your Mom was killed. It just took me a long time to find Liz." Hank wiped a little tear from the corner of his eye. "Are you sure you're okay with this, Abby?"

"One hundred percent, Pop. Liz reminds me of Mom, and I look forward to having her in my life."

Inside the club, getting Liz ready for her entrance, Robbie turned to her.

"Something borrowed and something blue, Liz. I'd like you to wear this single string of pearls that belonged to my great grandmother, and I have a blue garter for you if you would accept them."

"Thank you, Robbie. I had completely forgotten. Of course I'd be honored to wear them both. You are so thoughtful." Liz gave Robbie a big hug.

"I'll always be here for you, Liz. I'm so happy for my two BFFs in the whole wide world. God's blessing be upon you and Hank."

Abby led Wayne over next to Hank and asked him to stay close to Wayne so he wouldn't lose his balance.

"Hank, I'm so happy for you and Liz. I know we've had our ups and downs, but I am so honored that you would choose me as your best man," Wayne said extending his hand.

"You're my son-in-law, Wayne. You've won my daughter's heart. Who else would I have chosen to stand with me today?" Hank pulled Wayne into him and gave him a manly hug. "How's your eyes doing, son? I wish you were better today and you could see this with your own eyes..."

"Hey, Hank, just do a video of it and I'll see it later when I get better. And speaking of better, being blind isn't near as bad as I thought it would be. It's actually drawn Abby and me closer together...Now if I can just get your ring out of my pocket at the right time—you may want to give me a little nudge—we'll make this a very memorable and happy day..."

Helle Guyion walked outside of her top-floor suite onto her patio at the hotel next to Tequilaville and peered down on the ceremony beginning on the deck of the club. Angrily, she turned to Natasha Patski.

"Just look down there, Natasha. Looks like we weren't invited to the wedding. I hope it rains..." Helle said.

Mr. Elroy looked up to his right and saw Dr. Guyion staring down on them. He pointed his old feeble finger right at her to remind her of what he had told her earlier. He was watching her.

Helle saw the old man, flipped him the bird and went back into her hotel room.

"They better enjoy this day of celebration. It will be their last for a long time…"

Natasha didn't know what Helle meant.

As Scott Wood and the band began to play the wedding march, Liz emerged from the back of the club with Mr. Elroy leading her down the aisle. Tito's two little ones again acted as flower bearers and sprinkled rose petals in front of the stunning bride. Hank had to gather himself the moment he laid eyes on this beautiful brown-haired lady. She was wearing a band of flowers in her hair and the sight of her almost made Hank Hawkins cry. He hadn't shed a tear in years, but the moment and Liz's simple beauty was almost overwhelming to him.

The crowd stood as Liz made her walk on her special day. Mr. Elroy gave her hand to Hank as they stood before Pastor Randy. The music ended. Hank couldn't take his eyes off of Liz as she placed her soft hands in his.

Pastor Randy began the ceremony. "Ladies and gentlemen, we are gathered here in the presence and sight of Almighty God to join these two godly people in Holy Matrimony…"

Hank and Liz said their tender vows without hesitation. They were truly in love. Finally, Pastor Randy said, "I now pronounce you husband and wife. Let's honor this marriage made in heaven. I present to you Mr. and Mrs. Hank Hawkins."

Hank drew Liz close to him and began a little nose rub before the ceremonial kiss. His mustache tickled Liz's nose and she broke out into the greatest smile Hank had ever seen.

"Now, Mrs. Hawkins, can I kiss you?" Hank asked like a little school boy about to get his first kiss.

"You'd better kiss me you hunka hunka man!" Liz laughed.

The band cranked into high gear playing *The Orange Blossom Special* and the celebration got into full swing. After pictures were taken of the wedding party, the bachelor's and wedding cake, the proverbial stuffing cake into each other's mouth by the bride and groom, the Tequilaville staff began serving the champagne and people began lining up to get barbeque and beans. Hank and Liz were finally one with hugs and kisses all around.

Bella was chugging one glass of champagne after the other. She was determined to have a great time. After the fourth or fifth glass in about the first ten minutes, she grabbed Lieutenant Stark and dragged him onto the outside dance floor.

"Yee haw, ya'll!" Bella said mockingly as she was leading Lieutenant Stark to twirl her round and round the deck.

Then it happened. The champagne started swirling around in Bella's stomach coupled with the constant twirls on the dance floor, and she hurled all over Lieutenant Stark's white uniform.

"Oops. I'm so sorry, Stan. I'm so embarrassed," Bella said standing in the small puddle of stench. "Mom, could you take me back to your place? I'm not feeling too well. Must be cheap champagne."

Robbie was embarrassed that her daughter had made such a fool of herself, but it wasn't the first time and probably wouldn't be the last. Everyone knew Bella.

"T-Bone, could you help me take my drunk daughter home?" Robbie said it loud enough so that Bella would hear her embarrassing question. "We can put her to bed and be back in fifteen minutes. Sorry Stan. If you'd send me the cleaning bill for your uniform, I'd be happy to pay…"

There were a lot of boaters on the lake but none pulled into the Tequilaville docks to check out the obvious wedding going on. People were avoiding the club in droves especially with all the signs, front and back, declaring, 'Closed for remodeling.'

Half an hour later, Robbie and T-Bone returned to join in the festivities. Hank looked proud but exhausted. It had been a long awaited day for him. After several more hours of dancing and gift giving, Hank went over to Abby.

"Baby, Liz and I are going to slip outta here if you don't mind. We've got an afternoon flight to Ruidoso tomorrow and have some last minute packing to do."

"Have a great wedding night and honeymoon, Pop. I've got all the flight and hotel information you left me. And don't worry about a thing here at the club. You two just see the sights and enjoy each other. I'll take care of the rest. See you in a week or two." Abby hugged both of them and led them out of the club without anyone noticing.

Wayne knew that Abby had a thousand things to do so he asked her to walk him over to Mr. Elroy just to get out of her way. Mr. Elroy was sitting in one of the deck chairs near the edge of the sprawling patio.

"Mr. Elroy, would you look after Wayne for a while? I don't want him to walk off the deck and drown." Abby giggled.

"Sho thing, miss Abby. Wayne and I have a few things to talk about. You just do what ya have to. I'll take good care of him." Mr. Elroy was always smiling.

"Thanks for baby-sitting me. So tell me what I missed. I didn't quite *see* it all if you know what I mean." Wayne sat down in a chair next to his old mentor.

"Oh, Mr. Wayne, it was a glorious wedding. Mr. Hank looked happier than I ever seen him befo and that Miss Liz was just beaming. Those two will be in love for a lifetime."

"I could almost see their faces, Mr. Elroy. Even though I can't really see…You know, this blind thing isn't so bad. My other senses seem to fill the gaps of my sight. Kind of like a greater insight. Can you relate to that Mr. Elroy?" Wayne was just staring off in the distance.

"You bet I can, Mr. Wayne. I understand the doctor said there ain't nothing physically wrong with your eyesight. So why don't you see?"

"Don't know. The doc said I'd see when I was ready to see. Sometimes I think that this may be a punishment for all the bad things I've done in the past. What do you think, Mr. Elroy?" Wayne asked.

"The Almighty don't always punish us like that, Mr. Wayne. Sometimes He gives us a little affliction to teach us a lesson or to glorify Himself. He did it to Job. Remember that ole story, Mr. Wayne?"

"Parts of it, Mr. Elroy. Don't remember the whole story. So which do you think my blindness is? Is it punishment or learning a lesson?"

"Well Mr. Wayne, I's got to think on it a bit. Let's see, uh, you said that being blind wasn't so bad, that it put you in closer touch with your senses and drew you closer to Miss Abby, right, Mr. Wayne?"

"Yeah, I can't explain it. Being blind should have freaked me out, but it didn't," Wayne said, rubbing his eyes.

"In dat case, I'm gonna guess that this was a test of yo faith, Mr. Wayne. You accepted your affliction with a great attitude. I thinks it's about time for you to see again. What do you think, Mr. Wayne?"

"Of course, Mr. Elroy. But I can't just open my eyes and see…"

"Mebbe yous just got a plank in yo eye, Mr. Wayne. Let me take a look." Mr. Elroy spread open one of Wayne's eye with one hand and reached down with his other hand and got a handful of dirt.

"Sho nuff, Mr. Wayne. You do have a big ole plank in yo eye. Let me get that bugger outta there." Mr. Elroy spit into his hand holding the dirt and began to rub the mud into Wayne's eyes.

"There you go, Mr. Wayne. Open up your eyes. You ready to see again." Mr. Elroy backed away from Wayne as he slowly opened his eyes.

At first things were hazy, but Wayne could see light for the first time in a while. Slowly, his vision returned.

"I can see, Mr. Elroy! I can see again!" Wayne shouted.

Abby came running over to him when she heard his shouts.

"Baby, I can see again! Mr. Elroy healed me!" Wayne was jubilant.

"Oh, naw sir, Mr. Wayne. Yo faith healed you. Give God Almighty all da praise. He's da One that done healed you. I just pulled that ole plank from your eyes…"

Abby immediately put in a call to her dad and his new bride, hoping not to disturb them. She couldn't hold back.

"Pop! This is Abby, I just had to tell you and Liz that we've experienced a miracle here today on your wedding day…"

"One second, Sweetie Pie," Hank put his phone on speaker so Liz could hear. "Go ahead, baby, tell us about the miracle. Liz and I are all ears. We're just walking into my condo."

"Mr. Elroy rubbed some mud into Wayne's eyes and told him to see, Pop! And Wayne could see! He's got his sight back! It's a miracle!" Abby was jumping up and down, kissing Wayne as she broke the good news.

"Oh, praise God, Abby! I'm so happy for you and Wayne," Liz spoke into Hank's phone. "It's right out of the Bible just like when Jesus healed a blind man in the same way. It truly is a miracle. It made our big day complete." Liz had tears rolling down her cheek. Abby hung up.

"Hank have you read that part in the Bible?" Liz asked, wiping her face with a tissue.

"Guess I missed that part, Mrs. Hawkins. You're going to have to teach me more about all the stories in God's Word."

"Believe me, I will, Mr. Hawkins. I'm so happy right now. I've been looking for you my whole life and now we're married, ready to start our lives together."

As they entered his condo, Hank was obviously a bit nervous about their wedding night. It had been so long since he had been with a woman. Liz was completely calm.

"Hank, my husband, you're going to find out anyway so I'm just coming right out with it. I'm a virgin. I've never done this before in my entire life and I don't even know where to start."

"Let's start by changing clothes, getting into something more comfortable, say a prayer and have a little glass of champagne, Mrs. Hawkins. It's been a long time for me, too."

Shortly thereafter, Liz came out of the bedroom wearing her finest negligee. She was stunning. Hank had to take a deep breath at the sight of her. "You're beautiful, baby. I love you so much…"

To Hank, it was like going back in time. He remembered Abigail, the single night they had spent together and how much Liz looked like her, right down to the band of flowers in her hair. Now Hank had a new memory to replace the past. No more thoughts of Abigail. Liz was the apple of his eye now. He was totally and completely in love with this woman and she with him.

They began to kiss and embrace each other. Laughing, without a care in the world, Hank picked Liz up and carried her into the bedroom. Even though they had a fairly early flight the next morning to Ruidoso, neither looked at the clock. They laughed, they loved, they held each other for most of the night. A few hours before dawn, both began drifting off to sleep, completely fulfilled in every way with joy and peace and love.

"Mrs. Hawkins?" Hank looked into Liz's eyes. "I just hope you'll be here in the morning when I wake up." He couldn't help but remember the night with Abigail when he woke up and she was gone.

"Mr. Hawkins, I'm not going anywhere for the rest of our lives. You just make sure you're here when I wake up. It took way too long for me to find you…" Liz said as they drifted off into a deep sleep in each other's arms.

At three in the morning Dr. Eric Palmer put in a panic call to Dr. Guyion.

"Helle? Eric. All hell's breaking loose here at NASA! I've been here all night. I've got ten very frightened scientists just outside my office. Did you know what those equations were that came out of Pandora's Box at our presentation?" Eric was shouting.

"Slow down Eric, my love. Of course I know what the equations are. I knew from the moment I saw them. You never were very good at physics or you would have known also…"

Eric interrupted. "Helle, our scientists just gave me the information that these equations represent formulas of how to construct weapons of such mass destruction that it's like combining nuclear warheads with hydrogen and neutron warheads and putting them on steroids. This weapon makes everything we have look like mere firecrackers. One bomb could wipe out an continent! And Russian, Chinese, European and Israeli scientists were at the presentation also. They are bound to figure it out!"

"Don't worry, darling. The materials for such weapons are so rare that it will take years to compile them. It's not like this is going to happen tonight. I can't believe you woke me from my sleep to tell me what I already knew," Helle said calmly.

"You don't understand, Helle." Eric was panicked to the max. "The local F.B.I. have been giving each one of us polygraph tests all night. The Vice President of the United States is on his way to NASA in Air Force Two. The head of Homeland Security, the Chairman of the Joint Chiefs of Staff, the Defense Secretary and the Deputy Directors of the C.I.A., F.B.I. and N.S.A. are all on flights to the Space Center…"

"Have your scientists figured out all the ones and zeros that they copied down at the presentation in Paris?"

"They're working on it, Helle. Why don't you give me a little preview of what they're going to find out if you know that, too!"

"They are so slow to be such learned men, Eric. I thought your scientists would have figured that out by now. Do you know if any of the other scientists attending the conference have knowledge of it?"

"No, we haven't heard anything from anyone. This is going to start a global arms race, Helle. It's going to upset the balance of world power. Now tell me what the ones and zeros are? Please, I'm begging you!"

"In time, Eric. We have more important things to do…"

"More important? How can you say that at a time like this, Helle? Didn't you hear what I am telling you? Can't you grasp what is happening around the world right now? We're all in a panic!"

"Stop panicking, Eric, and listen very carefully to what I'm about to tell you. Our first duty is to our master, Satan. It is time for us to deliver Bella to him. Just stay in your office. I'll do the rest. Now settle down and leave it all to him." Helle hung up the phone.

"Helle! Helle! Don't hang up! You've got to tell me about the ones and zeros!"

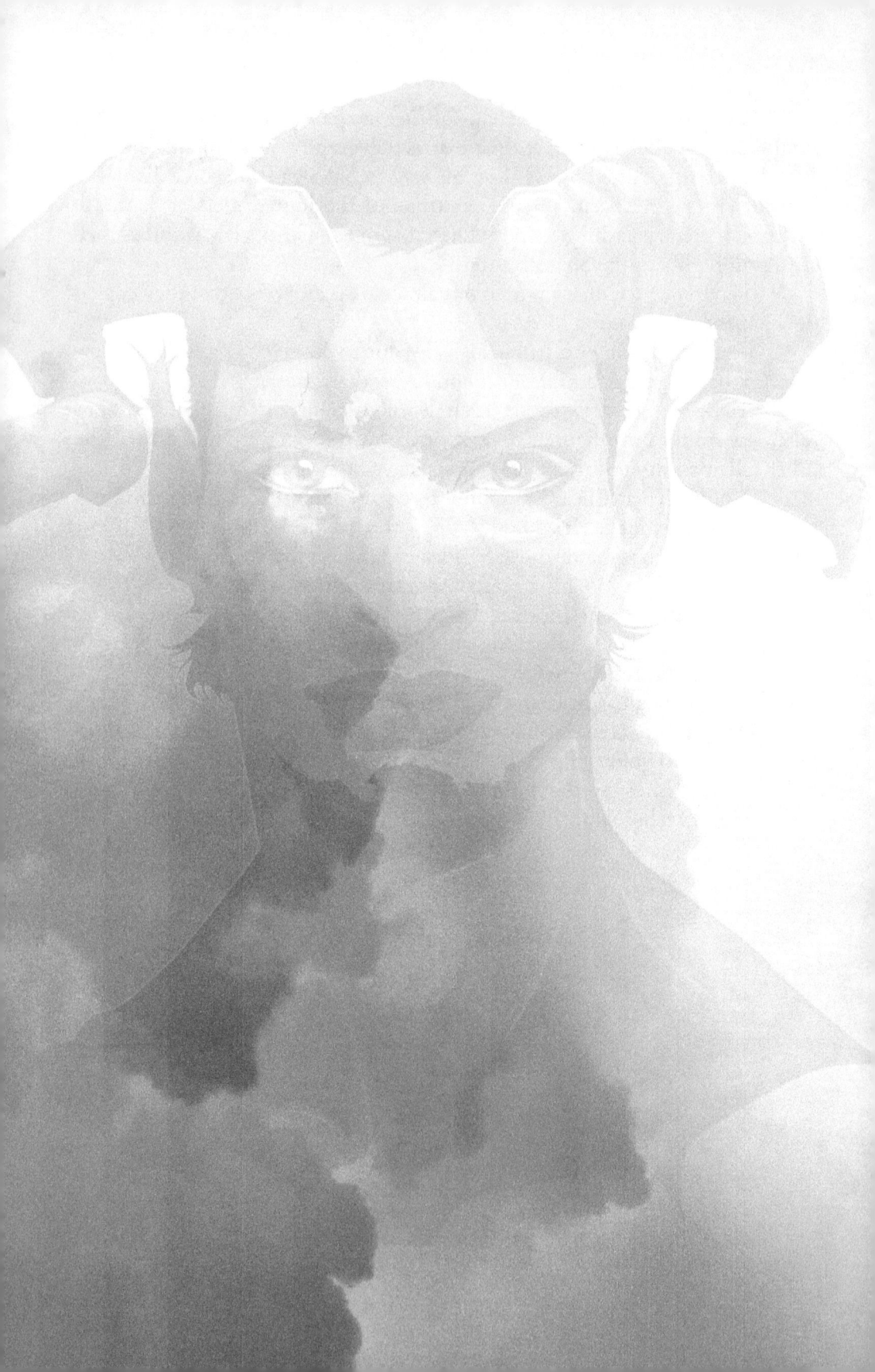

18

Houston: We Have a Problem! Altered States

Thirty minutes after Helle had hung up on Dr. Palmer, he placed another call to her. Her phone rang and rang and she had no voicemail set up here in the States. In desperation, Palmer kept dialing her number. Finally, she answered.

"What is it this time, Eric? You're being very rude," Helle said.

"Helle, NASA is about to go on lock down. No calls in or out, no visitors in or out except for the heads of our government that are en-route. Our super computers here are almost at melt-down trying to solve the codes that were revealed at our presentation…"

"And have your scientists discovered anything new in the last thirty minutes, Eric?" Helle yawned.

"Yes! There is a missing element in the formulas for what our scientists are calling 'The Doomsday Bomb.' The element is not known on any of the charts. We don't know if it exists on this earth or on another heavenly body like the moon or Mars. NASA has already prepared to set up testing labs and have research projects scheduled not only on earth, but we're in preparations for sending probes to the lunar surface, Mars, asteroids near earth just in case the missing element is not on our planet. Helle, this is going to lead to a global arms race for power like has never been seen before…"

"None of the scientists of any nation will find that element, Eric. Do you think our master would leave it up to mankind to rule the earth? Absolutely not! The nation who completes this weapon would rule the earth out of fear of annihilating the rest of the world. What will happen is that many nations will use what knowledge they have to construct as much of this weapon as they can and will wait for this final ingredient before they can complete such a weapon. Our master will bring this element with him when he comes to rule the earth. Eric, I told you not to panic and to stay in your office and I'll take care of the rest."

"Helle, hold on a second. Don't hang up. I'm getting a new report." Eric was hyperventilating.

"Oh my god! Helle, our scientists have just figured out some of the 'ones and zeros.' It's a video. They're playing it for me as we speak."

The video showed Eric and Helle, face-to-face on their trip to Betwixt, into outer space with no protective suits or breathing apparatuses. There were no astral charts, just a two-minute video recording their trip through space, into the black hole and their emergence and landing at Mount Zaphon. Then the video ended. Eric described what he saw to Helle.

"The master has provided proof of our trip, Eric. We should thank him! It was part of the video at the conference. Don't you remember?"

"Thank him? He's put a target on our backs, Helle. The F.B.I. and N.S.A. are going to lock both of us up and throw away the key. We're going to disappear, Helle. You better get ready for a visit from a S.W.A.T team!"

"Eric, must I remind you that I have diplomatic immunity?" Helle said calmly.

"Helle, you don't understand our government. When they feel there is a clear and present danger to our national security, all bets are off. They've already raised the Defense Readiness Condition to DEFCON 3. After the meeting with government heads and the Chief of Staff, there's talk of raising it to DEFCON 2. That hasn't happened since the Cuban missile crisis. They're probably already on their way to your hotel.

"Our lives are in danger, Helle! Not only from my government but from every nation that had scientists at our presentation in Paris. They've connected you and me with this knowledge in that video. They're all coming to get us!"

"Chill out, my lover. Just trust me. No one's going to *get us*." Helle hung up again.

At 6:30 AM, Robbie's phone began to ring, awakening her from a dead sleep. She reached for her cell and noticed it was Liz calling.

"Girlfriend, you're the last person I expected to call this early," Robbie said, yawning, trying to gather her wits. "Is everything okay?"

"Not really, Robbie. You know Hank better than anyone. Is he hard to wake up in the morning?"

"Are you kidding. Hank's a former Marine Force Recon. He can hear a gnat fart at fifty feet and be wide awake. You two must have had a late night or something," Robbie said, laughing.

"We had a wonderful wedding night, Robbie. Better than I could have ever imagined, but we need to get up and get going. We've got an afternoon flight to Ruidoso."

"Did you try hugs and kisses to awake him, Liz, or should I say, Mrs. Hank Hawkins?"

"I tried everything, Robbie. Hugs, kisses, I've shaken him, put a hot cup of coffee under his nose. He just won't wake up. He's tossing and turning like he's having a bad dream or something, and I can't get him out of it. Could you come over and do a little nurse assessment of why he won't wake up?"

"Sure, Liz. Let me throw on a robe and grab my stethoscope and I'll be right down. You must have exhausted him last night," Robbie said trying to lighten the mood.

Within minutes, Robbie was knocking on Hank's door. Liz greeted her and showed her in. Liz was wearing a sheer nightgown, her black hair was in disarray and she had on no makeup. Robbie walked past Liz into Hank's bedroom without saying a word. She could see him tossing and turning, breathing in short breaths, in a deep sleep. She walked over to his bedside and began shaking him gently.

"Hank! Hank! Wake up you ole married man. You're going to miss your honeymoon if you don't get up!" Robbie said, kneeling down and speaking right next to his ear.

Hank continued to toss and turn and gave no notice to Robbie's attempts to wake him. Robbie took out her stethoscope and placed it on Hank's chest. His breathing was rapid like that of a sprinting athlete. She wrapped her blood pressure monitor around Hank's arm. Robbie knew from their long years of friendship that Hank usually had abnormally low blood pressure. At this moment, his BP was very high, approaching heart attack levels. Liz was hovering over Robbie as she conducted the tests.

"Liz, I don't want to alarm you but just to be safe you need to call 911. We need to get him to the emergency room at Clear Lake General and run some EKGs on him. You can always reschedule your flights." Robbie had a concerned look that was very evident to Liz. "I'm going to run back to my condo, put on some clothes, check on Bella, and I'll ride with you to the hospital. Just stay here with Hank until the ambulance arrives and I'll put in a quick call to Wayne and Abby. I'm sure they'll want to be there with us."

Within four minutes, there was a fire truck and an E.M.T. ambulance pulling into the parking lot of the condos. Liz had thrown on some jeans and opened the door for the medics, who had to climb one flight of stairs to get there since the condo was lakeside and elevated above the waterfront property.

"Come in. He's in the bedroom!" Liz said to the medics who were carrying a gurney.

The two E.M.T.s, assisted by two firemen, lifted Hank onto the gurney and began rolling him down the outside hallway, past Robbie's condo to their awaiting unit. As they rolled past Robbie's condo, they could hear her screaming.

"Oh God! Oh God, Bella! Bella!" Robbie shrieked.

As she was leaving, she had taken a quick look to see if her daughter, who had been very drunk the night before, was doing okay. What Robbie saw in her guest bedroom where Bella was staying was her daughter floating three feet above the mattress, covers hanging down, in a semi-comatose state.

Robbie ran out of her door and screamed at the E.M.T.s.

"Please come in here and help my daughter! Oh God! What's happening to her? Please help us!"

Two of the firemen ran into Bella's room and saw her hovering above the bed. At first sight, they were stunned. There was no training manual on people levitating above their beds. They contacted their chief back at the firehouse for instructions of what to do.

"Chief! This is unit 88. We have a situation. There's a 30ish white female woman hovering three feet above her bed in a comatose state. What should we do?"

"Hovering above her bed? Uh, uh, Unit 88, can you get her vital signs?" the chief asked.

The two firemen brought in a step ladder from their truck, stepped up on it and got her blood pressure and pulse while she hovered over the bed. They relayed the information back to their chief. She was breathing and her blood pressure was elevated.

"Can you strap her down to a gurney?" the chief asked.

"We can try, Chief! We can try!" the firemen replied. "Oh yeah, Chief, I forgot to mention. The patient has a glowing red ruby embedded in her forehead. It's turning the whole room red. Should I try and remove it?"

"Just transport the patient. Leave the, uh, ruby where it is. How deep into her forehead is it embedded?"

"Don't know, Chief. We'll leave it in place and try to get the patient to the hospital."

They quickly brought up another gurney from another ambulance and placed the straps over Bella's hovering body to guide her over it. Her floating body moved with ease. As they carefully pulled the straps over her to attempt to tie her down to the gurney, her body wouldn't be lowered onto the gurney. No matter how much pressure they applied, she was still floating above the stretcher. The firemen pulled hard on the straps, but their efforts only pulled the gurney off of the floor up to Bella's height.

"Chief, you're not going to believe this, but we can't lower her body down to the gurney. What now?"

"Stay where you are, men. I'm putting in a call to Clear Lake P.D. to assist. Take the other patient on to Clear Lake General. This is crazy," the chief said over the radio.

"Robbie, we'll figure this out with God's help. Try to stay calm. I'm praying for you and Bella. I'm going on to the hospital with Hank. I'll see you when you and Bella arrive." Liz tried to stay calm but what was happening was neither natural or logical. This was a time for faith.

Two police officers arrived on the scene at Robbie's condo, not believing their own eyes at what they saw. The two firemen figured out that Bella's body would hover three feet above whatever surface was below her. It went no higher than that. They came up with a plan to remove her from the bedroom and attached leg and arm restraints to Bella's body. Then they attached ropes to the restraints.

They began floating her body out of the condo and down the steps without the gurney as the two firemen and two police officers held the ropes to guide her down the stairway to the awaiting unit. Again, with little effort, they slid Bella into the ambulance and raced off to the hospital as she hovered near the inside top of the unit. Robbie had to follow them in her car since there was no room in the ambulance. All four of the rescue officers had to stay in the ambulance and hold the ropes to keep Bella from banging against the walls inside. Since it was early morning, most of the other tenants of the condos were still asleep and no one saw the rescue effort.

The two police officers called in what was happening and asked other units to clear the area around the emergency entrance at the hospital and to alert the medical staff of the situation approaching them. They knew this could cause a panic since it was so unbelievable.

Robbie followed very closely behind the ambulance, praying, crying, and hardly noticing a long convoy of U.S. Army trucks rolling down NASA Road One. Fully armed troops began off-loading in front of the Space Center, eventually forming a perimeter around the entire complex.

Wayne and Abby arrived at the Clear Lake General ER. They had contacted Tito, Mary, T-Bone and Pastor Randy at the Cowboy Church for prayer and support. Upon arriving, they saw Liz at the bedside of Hank who was in one of the cubicles of the ER with all kinds of monitors hooked up to him. Trying to be calm, Liz told them about Bella's situation and that she and Robbie should be arriving shortly.

"She's floating in a comatose state, Liz?" Abby asked thinking that she hadn't completely understood what Liz was telling them.

"Yes! Robbie's freaking out! Everyone is freaking out, Abby. Just try to stay calm and comfort Robbie when she arrives. This is going to be a bit of a mind-blower when you see Bella arrive. We need to stand firm and deal with it. Hank's hooked up to monitors, and we should have some information from the doctors soon. Right now we just need to pray and cope the best we can."

As Bella's ambulance arrived and the two firemen opened the back door of the unit to start floating her out, holding onto the ropes, one of the ER nurses was the first to see their new patient. It was more than her professional, logical mind could handle. She fainted on the spot.

Abby gasped and ran over to her levitating sister.

"Oh Bella! What's happening to you?" Abby broke into tears as Wayne tried to get a grip on his own emotions and hugged Abby close to him. "Why is that ruby embedded in her head? Why is it glowing? Doctor, you've got to help my sister."

The rest of the medical team took the ropes from the four rescuers and floated Bella into another cubicle, attaching more monitoring equipment to her, trying their best to do an assessment. They, too, were fighting their own fears.

As the rest of the group from Tequilaville gathered at Clear Lake General, there was nothing else they could do but wait and pray and comfort each other. Only God knew what would happen next.

T-Bone sat by himself in the ER waiting room. He quickly began to relate what was happening to Dr. Helle Guyion. She was on his mind. His hatred of this woman began to burn in his soul. He was not alone in his thinking.

At the same time that all the craziness was going on at Clear Lake General Hospital, two F.B.I. special tactics teams stormed into the Bay Hilton. Their mission was to secure Dr. Helle Guyion and bring her to the NASA facilities for questioning, giving little or no regard to her diplomatic immunity. One team rode up on the elevator while another climbed the stair well to her floor.

When the elevator opened, Dr. Guyion's head of security was standing in front to the F.B.I. team with his gun drawn. The team shot him dead on the spot. Natasha Patski ran out of her room and down the hall, screaming at the F.B.I. agents.

"We have diplomatic immunity! You can't do this!"

The team handcuffed Natasha without anything else being said then went room-to-room on two floors and took the rest of Dr. Guyion's group into custody. Finally, the two teams stood outside of Dr. Guyion's room.

"This is the F.B.I., Dr. Guyion. Come out with your hands over your head!" There was no response. Again they repeated their command to open up the door.

The F.B.I. team leader tried to look inside the peep hole on Dr. Guyion's door and noticed that it appeared to be frozen over. He called for a battering ram to knock down the door. Two special agents began beating on the door with the heavily weighted iron ram but to no avail. It wouldn't budge. Then they noticed ice began forming all around the door and was creeping out from all four edges.

"Let's get a probe under the door so we can see what's going on inside. And bring the laser," commanded the team leader.

Two of the agents in full body armor began to unzip one of their bags of equipment, pulling out the very powerful hand-held laser while the other agent began to assemble the probe to slip under the door.

As they began trying to melt the ice away from the bottom of the door, it seemed to re-freeze as quickly as they could melt it.

"Turn the setting to high and get me a hole under that door!" ordered the agent in charge. "I've got to get a probe under there."

For just a moment, the agents were able to penetrate the ice with the laser to form a small hole before the ice began to form over it again. They quickly pushed the probe under the door. What they saw inside of Dr. Guyion's room rocked them all back on their heels.

The commander of the team radioed back to his F.B.I. superior, John Bensen, inside the NASA facility. In the famous words of Jim Lovell of the infamous Apollo 13 space craft, the agent in charge at the scene said, "Houston, we have a problem!"

"No time for jokes. Tell me what you see inside of Dr. Guyion's room." Agent Bensen ordered.

"I'm not joking, sir. We have one heck of a problem. There's a two-foot thick barrier of ice inside all the dimensions of the room. It's like we're looking inside of an igloo, Agent Bensen. We can't break through it and the ice is self-generating. When we melt it with the laser, it reforms. Dr. Guyion is in a frozen state, hovering above the room in a crucifix position, arms outstretched, and there seem to be red lasers coming out of her eyes. That's what I see. What are your orders, sir?"

"Hold your position. Post guards at all exits and entrances of the hotel, get some men on the roof and encircle the outer perimeter of the hotel. I'll call the manager to evacuate all the tenants. We're locking that hotel down. Stand by," said Bensen.

Agent-in-Charge Bensen placed a call to Dennis Colley, head of security for the NASA facility.

"Dennis? This is Agent Bensen. Could you bring Dr. Eric Palmer to my office? I need to speak with him immediately."

"Sure thing," Colley said.

Dennis Colley walked down the hallway to Dr. Palmer's office. Belinda Sealy was seated at her desk feverishly typing reports on some of the findings of the scientists who had attended the Paris summit. She didn't know everything that was happening, but she could tell something big was in the works with all the government officials descending on the space complex.

"I need to speak with Dr. Palmer immediately, Belinda. Is he in his office?" Colley said in a very demanding voice.

"He is in, Mr. Colley, but his door is locked. That's nothing unusual. I'll get him for you." Belinda walked to his door and began knocking. "Dr. Palmer? Dr. Palmer? Can you open your door? Mr. Colley is here to see you."

There was no reply from Eric Palmer.

"That's unusual, Mr. Colley," said Belinda. She looked surprised. "I do have a key to his office. Should I use it?"

"Yes, Belinda. Use it now!"

Belinda got her key out of her desk drawer and tried to insert it into the lock on Palmer's door. She began to fidget with the key but it would not go into the lock.

"For some reason, the key won't go in. It's like the lock is frozen shut or something." Belinda looked confused.

"Let me try," Colley said.

As he attempted to insert the key, he looked down at the base of Palmer's door and saw ice began to emerge.

"What the..!" Colley exclaimed. "That's impossible. It can't get that cold in there."

Colley called Bensen and told him what was happening outside of Dr. Palmer's office.

"Colley, stay there at Palmer's office. I'm sending a team to get a probe inside his office." Bensen had a feeling of what he was going to discover.

It was the same scenario. The F.B.I. team repeated the procedure to get a probe under Dr. Palmer's door. They discovered that the entire volume of his office was enclosed by a thick layer of ice and that he was also frozen, levitating just below the ceiling with his arms down to his side. He looked to be lifeless but they couldn't determine whether he was alive, dead or in some kind of suspended state.

Two hours later, the Vice President and all the heads of the various defense agencies were assembled in a large conference room at the NASA facilities for a full briefing on the events taking place. F.B.I. Agent-in-Charge Bensen was chosen to give the briefing as information files on all the people present at the Paris convention were being put into folders.

Belinda Sealy became a central figure in the briefing notes since Dr. Palmer was sealed in his office. Agents interviewed her for several hours, compiling information on the group from Tequilaville that Palmer was privately working with who claimed to have been to this place called Betwixt long before the Paris conference revealed what the equations, ones and zeros were telling them. Belinda did not mention the DNA tests that were conducted on Wayne Tyler or Lieutenant Stark because of her sworn oath of secrecy to Dr. Palmer.

When the name Lieutenant Stan Stark came up, Bensen sent agents to bring him into the NASA briefing since he was military and must follow orders. Bensen was almost overwhelmed at the volumes of information that were continuously flowing in. There seemed to be so many parts of this puzzle and at present, they were just pieces. Somehow, Agent Bensen needed to fit them together for the most important presentation of his career.

He organized many different teams to get as much data on all phases of his presentation as he could in such a short period of time. He hadn't slept since the day before and was running on adrenaline.

"Sir, sorry to bother you but you have a call from Dr. Tom Maley over at Clear Lake General. He says it's very important and that you two are neighbors out in Taylor Crest," Bensen's assistant reported.

"No time to talk to him. Tell him I'll call him back later," Bensen snapped.

"Sir, Dr. Maley sounds pretty shook up. He says you need to send some agents over to his ER. Would you please talk to him for just a second?"

"Sure, uh, put him on," Bensen said. "Tom, this is John Bensen, I'm terribly busy. What's going on?"

"John, I've got a young Anglo woman in her thirties who just checked into my ER. She's hovering three feet above the gurney that we're trying to strap her down to. I'm telling you that she is levitating off the ground. Is this something that you would be interested in?" Dr. Maley asked.

"Very much so. I'll send some suits over to investigate. Is the woman alive?"

"As far as we can determine, John."

"Tom, is she frozen?" Bensen asked.

"Frozen? Why would you ask that, John? No, she isn't frozen."

"Never mind. My men are on the way." Bensen hung up, put his face in his hands and took a deep breath.

What else could go wrong today? he thought to himself.

With the President and his remaining cabinet members convened by a secure teleprompter, Bensen began his briefing before the group assembled in the NASA conference room. Stacks of folders were in front of each of the attending participants. For the next four hours, Bensen called on different scientists to give their eye witness accounts of the Paris conference, Pandora's Box, the equations, ones and zeroes. He presented dossiers on all of the other world scientists present at the event. All the pieces of the puzzle pointed to Dr. Palmer and Dr. Guyion.

When Bensen was asked the obvious question of why the two parapsychologists were not present, he readied a short video, giving the back story of where they were and the condition both of them were in.

"This is a one and a half second video recorded by our Tactical Team when they approached the two doctors," Bensen said.

The video showed Dr. Guyion in her igloo, followed by a similar video of Dr. Palmer in his. Both were hovering in mid-air.

The Secretary of Homeland Defense asked, "Why is the video so short?"

Bensen replied, "Because our probes began freezing over in a second and a half. Not only that, the ice began traversing through the cables to our equipment. We had to cut the cable since we didn't know if the freezing effect would spread beyond their rooms. When we cut the cables, the ice stopped under the doorways."

"Do we know what the temperature was inside the rooms?" the Vice-President asked.

One of the scientists who specialized in thermo dynamics spoke up. "As near as we can tell, the temperature inside of both Dr. Palmer's office here at NASA and Dr. Guyion's room at the Bay Hilton, across the street, is nearly minus one hundred degrees Fahrenheit."

"Is that possible?" asked the President.

"Science is not exact, Mr. President. That's all that we can determine at this point."

"Tell us more about this Dr. Helle Guyion," the Vice-President said.

Bensen got out her files, told the group that she had worked with Russian cosmonauts, was a suspected drug trafficker but they had no evidence to support that charge and she was the European High Priestess of Satanical worship, plus, she had diplomatic immunity from the country of Belgium.

"And we cannot penetrate her room to bring her in for questioning, Agent Bensen?" the F.B.I. Director asked.

"Sir, short of using explosives to blow a hole in her wall at the hotel, no sir, we cannot. Plus, we don't know if the icy conditions would spread into the open atmosphere around the hotel. And, we don't know if Dr. Guyion's life would be put at risk if we did. The same applies to Dr. Palmer here at NASA."

Everyone was looking at the teleprompter awaiting the President's assessment of the situation, wondering if he would order going to DEFCON 2.

The head of the N.S.A. broke in. "The video of Dr. Palmer and Dr. Guyion's trip to this unknown dimension that you call Betwixt was like a scene out of *Star Wars*. Did it provide our astral scientists with any kind of roadmap to this dimension? Do we know how to get there or even if we can get there in the future?"

One of the scientists spoke up. "Sir, even when we played the video at super slow speeds we were unable to determine a path. We're not even sure that we believe what we saw. There's no way to authenticate it."

"There seems to be much more information we need to gather before making any rash decisions here," the President said. "The missing element to this 'Dooms Day Weapon' is important so I'll ask Congress to authorize more probes going to outer space to find it. We will not go to DEFCON 2. If we did, other nations would do the same thing. We need calm heads right now and greater intelligence. Until then, keep me informed of any new findings…"

The briefing was over and left many more questions than answers. Bensen decided to make a quick trip home to get a shower and more clothes since the Space Center was on lock down. On the way, he dropped by Clear Lake General to see what Dr. Tom Maley had mentioned to him and to get further intel from the men he had sent over to the ER.

As Agent Bensen entered the ER, he immediately noticed the entire area was glowing with a reddish light. Without saying a word, his agents led him over to Bella's hovering body. He could see the source of the light coming from the ruby embedded in her forehead. All the agents' training at Quantico, Virginia, had never prepared them for a situation like this. Dealing with supernatural events was not on the curriculum.

Agent Bensen took a brief moment to speak to Robbie Cantrell, Wayne Tyler and Abby, more so to offer a bit of comfort than for giving explanations. He gave each one of them his card and said to call him anytime and that he may want to talk to them later. Bensen introduced them to his agents and told them they would be standing by to offer any help or protection they needed.

Robbie came up to Bensen just before he left and said, "Agent Bensen, we're not dealing with flesh and blood here. You saw my daughter. What're we going to do?"

"I don't know, Miss Cantrell. I really don't know…"

No one mentioned to Agent Bensen about what was going on with Hank Hawkins. So far, Belinda Sealy's secret on the DNA had not been discovered. It was time for everyone to re-group. It was a time for prayer for those who believed in it.

The Tequilaville group at the hospital had no idea what was going on at NASA or what had happened at the Paris conference. Their focus was on Hank and Bella.

"Liz, I'm going out to my car and get my Bible. I want to place it on Bella's body. Somehow that may help. Do you think it will? I don't know what else to do!" Robbie was crying and trying her best to be strong. She felt helpless and wanted to do something to save her only child.

"Robbie!" Liz gathered her courage. "You can try that but I have to tell you the truth. Bella has not accepted Christ as her savior. I don't know what is going on but I do know that she alone must make that decision. All of our prayers will help but they can't save her…"

19

Warrior
"I Am the Storm!"

When Robbie returned from her car with her Bible, Mr. Elroy had arrived with a slew of bikers from the Cowboy Church. He was a welcomed sight even being escorted by such a rough, tough-looking group. The F.B.I. agents on the scene saw the bikers and wondered why they were there. This only added tension to the situation.

Dr. Maley decided to move, or float, Bella to a private Intensive Care room to get her out of the busy emergency room area. He assigned his best nurses to monitor her there.

Robbie ran over to Mr. Elroy, crying, about to fall apart.

"Mr. Elroy! What's going on? Do you know?" Robbie said falling to her knees before him.

"Oh, Miss Robbie, you just get on up and trust in the Good Lawd! That ole dragon is certainly in this place but The Almighty is here, too."

"Do you think it will help if I put a Bible on Bella's chest, Mr. Elroy? She isn't saved..."

"Miss Robbie, it sho can't hurt. I'd go ahead and do dat if I wuz you. Ya know, the prayer of a mother for her chillin is mighty powerful. Never forget that! The Lawd hears every single word." Mr. Elroy was always calm. He had on his usual bright smile that just added a little light to this dark situation.

Robbie and Mr. Elroy along with several of the bikers went to Bella's room in the ICU. Robbie used the step ladder by her bedside to place her Bible on Bella's hovering body. Instantly as she stepped back, a two-foot-thick wall of ice began forming over Bella's levitating frame except where the Bible was placed on her chest. The ice did not or could not form over this Holy book and left an open pathway straight up to the top of the newly formed ice. The nurses quickly called Dr. Maley to tell him what was going on. Robbie fainted.

"Can you get our instruments into the hole and attach them to Miss Cantrell's body?" Dr. Maley asked.

"Yes, Dr. Maley, there's barely enough room for us to attach them."

"Then monitor the patient, especially for hypothermia. If we need to, we can always attach IVs through the open hole leading down to her torso."

Dr. Maley informed the F.B.I. agents on scene as to what was taking place with Bella. They reported back to Agent Bensen.

"I'm going to send a tactical team to assist you there. Is Miss Cantrell alive?" Agent Bensen asked.

"Yessir! She's alive. So far, all her levels are okay according to the ICU nurses. But there's a group of bikers here from some kind of church. We're not sure what to do with them, sir. Should we tell them to leave?"

"No. Just observe and keep me informed. Could you ask her mother if she would allow us to send a team of NASA technicians over to monitor her daughter?" Agent Bensen asked. "We can't get any information on the other two subjects but we need to see what we can find out from Miss Cantrell's situation. I'll hold."

"Yessir, Mrs. Cantrell actually had to be revived; she had fainted but said she would take all the help she could get. Send the technicians, sir."

Within a few minutes, Hank Hawkins was moved to the ICU cubicle next to Bella's. About twenty people from the Cowboy Church were gathered outside in the waiting room. Pastor Randy led them in prayer for this strange situation as Robbie stayed at Bella's bedside and Liz, Abby and Wayne stayed close to Hank. Periodically, they would leave the rooms to take a little mind break and keep each other informed as to what was going on with their two beloved patients.

The NASA technicians arrived and began reaching down to Bella's body, plugging in more wires, monitoring devices and setting up a video camera. The glow from the ruby embedded into Bella's forehead began to glow brighter and brighter. Out of sheer fright, the technicians backed away.

The rotund pixie punkin demoness Mama Che's spirit appeared before Bella's sleeping body, unseen by anyone.

"Time to come with me, Bella! Wake up, child. It's your big day."

Bella's soul arose from the ice castle where she was entombed. Bella yawned and looked over to Mama Che.

"My big day? Who are you?" Bella said imagining she was just having another one of her weird dreams.

"I'm Mama Che, you know, Irma Chemoth, who is buying a whole lot of real estate from you. You've been talking to me over the phone about your book deal and working with my assistant, Trikki Sanders…"

"Oh, yeah. So glad to meet you in person, Irma. You don't look anything like I imagined. Uh, are those real little pixie wings on your back? Is this another dream?" Bella was confused.

"Oh, it's real, baby. Now let's get you into some beautiful clothes. You have a big date!" Chemoth said.

"A date? With who, Irma? I don't remember having this on my social calendar."

"Bella, how would you like to become princess of the entire world?" Che was manipulating Bella with temptations again.

"The whole world? Like a real princess? Rich and famous? Who would be my prince?" Bella was so choosy.

"That's why I'm here, Bella. I'm a match maker for the rich, the powerful and the famous. Here to introduce you to your angel of light. He's the richest, most powerful man in all the world. Now put these purple gowns on and let me fix up your hair. You're going to love this, child."

"Ooh, I'm excited, Irma. Where're we going? Is this real?" Bella asked.

"Very real! Hey, that glowing ruby in your forehead just sets off your beauty, Bella. Where did you get it?" Chemoth asked.

"Oh, uh, just something I picked up from another suitor that I called Adonis." Bella knew she had stolen it and didn't want to confess the act of theft. "How do I look, Irma? Are we ready yet? By the way, where did you say are we going?"

"To Mount Zaphon to meet your prince."

"Where's that? I never heard of it," Bella said looking at the fine, sheer ancient apparel that she was wearing.

"No more questions, child. Close your eyes…" Chemoth instructed.

Without traveling through space or time, Chemoth and Bella immediately arrived at the base of Mount Zaphon. It was beautiful. The setting was not at all like when Dr. Palmer and Dr. Guyion had visited. There were no weird creatures flying overhead.

Satan had prepared his realm to be beautiful with flowers and pots of gold and precious stones adorning his great ebony throne to entice Bella to accept him as her prince. Her acceptance really didn't matter to him; he was going to have her no matter what but he did want to show off his worldly kingdom, his power over life and death and his possessions. Bella was about to become another possession. He burned with lust for her.

Satan, in another form, appeared to Bella as an angel of light, perfect in almost every way. He was fantastically charming. His charisma drew Bella closer to him.

"Bella, my beauty, you have been chosen to be the princess of this world. Will you accept the hand of Satan?" He reached out to Bella.

"Satan? You're the devil?" Bella was taken aback at the name. "Hell, no I won't accept your hand! Everyone is scared of you!" Bella experienced immediate fright at the sound of his name and began to hyperventilate. "Why do I feel like I've been in this place before? Where are all your evil demons? How do I get outta here?"

"Bella, my lovely, calm down. Do you know what I'm offering you? No one turns me down. I have power over life and death and that applies to you." Satan was not used to being rejected by mortals. He tempted them and they fell before him.

"You think you're so smart, Mr. Devil." Bella's defiant nature kicked in as her only defense in this scary situation. "I remember last time I was here and saw what you did to Wayne Tyler. You can't kill my soul. It's immortal, and this is just another bad dream. I, uh, what's the phrase? I reject you, devil. No, that's not right. Uh, oh yeah, I rebuke you in the name of, uh, uh, me, Bella. Get me the hell outta here!"

Satan's laugh could be heard all over the realm of Betwixt. He barked like a howling coyote. The sound of his piercing voice scared Bella even more. She was trapped with no way to escape. She looked over at Mama Che with a glare that could kill.

"You tricked me, Irma. Are you real or are you a demon, also?" Bella started to cry, feeling helpless.

"Oh child, I'm a demoness, not a demon. I thought you would like to be princess of the entire world. How have *I* failed you?" Chemoth began flapping her little pixie wings, lifting her rotund figure above the cowered soul of Bella.

"Okay, Mama Che, can you get me back? Will you take me home or just wake me up from this terrible dream?" Bella was desperate.

"Can't do that, honey child. You may want to negotiate with the master. Your life is in his hands..."

"He can't kill my soul, Mama Che..."

"But he can kill your body, Bella. Do you remember where your body is at present? Is it surrounded by ice in the ICU at Clear Lake General? Think Bella, if you ever want to walk out of that place alive. Your very life hangs on your next decision," Chemoth said in a clear, authoritative voice.

"So you're telling me that I'm trapped in a dream in another dimension with no way out unless I submit to the devil?" Bella said between sobs. "Submission is not in my vocabulary, Irma! Someone help me! Please, someone help me!"

"There is no help on the way for you this time, Bella," Satan said. "You are my perfect mate. Your language is so much like the language spoken here, full of blasphemies. You're so self-centered, so promiscuous. You lie and you steal rubies from my fortune. You are so full of pride, Bella, and that's why I have chosen you to be my forever concubine. Besides, you have no choice. Either agree or die!"

"Then I'll die!" Bella screamed. She was horrified and unable to think. She could see no way out.

"All the better, Bella. Let's set your time of death for exactly one second after I send you back to the hospital. Choose your own kind of death, Bella. How about cancer or a heart attack or even better still, how about I make some of that equipment you are hooked up to in the hospital short circuit and burn you to death. What's your choice?"

"Someone help me!"

"Let me continue, lady fair." Satan had Bella in his grips. "When you die, your soul will be judged. You don't believe in Jesus, so He will send your soul to me. Either way, Bella, you are mine—for all eternity!"

Mr. Elroy walked into Hank Hawkins' cubicle and told Wayne, Liz and Abby to take a break. He would sit with Hank for a while. Even though they didn't want to leave Hank, the break seemed welcomed just to gather their wits.

Shortly after they were gone from the cubicle, Mr. Elroy seemed to drift into a little nap as old men often do. He changed his persona from an old man into Gordon, the mighty guardian angel, and began speaking to Hank. As Hank's mortal body remained in a coma, lying on the hospital bed, Hank's soul sat straight up in the bed, listening to every word the angel spoke to him.

"Hank Hawkins, The Almighty is with you, mighty warrior. You have been chosen by Him to defend against the evil forces of darkness that are present in this place. A soul, a very precious soul is at stake. Will you accept the challenge to defend Bella Cantrell from all the Evil Ones?" Gordon asked.

"Bella is in danger? Yes, I accept the challenge. What is His will?" Hank's soul asked.

"The Lord your God is in your midst. The Mighty One will save; He will rejoice over you with gladness," Gordon said.

Hank answered, "For He has armed me with strength for the battle; You have subdued under me those who rose up against me. The Lord is my strength and my shield. Lead me into battle, Gordon."

Satan changed the image of Betwixt to the hell hole he loved. Millions of demons began flying overhead, swooping down on Bella, blistering her skin with fire and inflicting her with boils. She could feel the pain. It was hopeless. All she could do was to ball up in a fetal position to avoid the atrocities flying all around her. She wanted to faint but couldn't. Satan again assumed his position on his throne, surrounded by smoke so that no one could see his face.

"STOP!" Came a booming voice from above. "YOU, EVIL ONE, WILL NOT HAVE BELLA WITHOUT A BATTLE. ONCE AGAIN YOU HAVE BROKEN MY LAWS AND YOU WILL NOT PREVAIL!"

Satan looked up toward the sound of the booming voice.

"Oh, it's you again! You're always messing in my business. What laws of yours have I broken this time?"

"NOTHING YOU DO HAPPENS WITHOUT MY KNOWING. I AM OMNICENT! YOU CANNOT STEAL THE SOULS OF MORTALS IN THIS PLACE. PREPARE YOUR DEMONS FOR BATTLE.

"FOR I KNOW THE PLANS I HAVE FOR BELLA. PLANS FOR GOOD AND NOT EVIL…"

Bella heard the booming voice from above and looked up from her crouched position. For a moment, the pain of the boils was gone. A brilliant fifteen-foot angel appeared before Satan's throne. Bella looked toward the light and instantly recognized the dazzling image of Gordon, Wayne's Angel, whom she had seen on her last visit to Betwixt. She was speechless and afraid, but now she had hope.

Gordon spoke directly toward the throne of Satan.

"Because you have broken The Almighty's laws, this battle will be costly. You can choose seven demons to go into mortal combat with the chosen champion of God. If they are defeated, they will be sent to the pit to join Ishtar in her hellish kingdom, never to return…"

"I will not agree to such terms, you lowly angel. I set the terms in my domain!" Satan said defiantly.

"You set nothing, Evil One. The Almighty always has and always will rule the universe. He created it, He created you. His Word is law!" Gordon spoke with a clear soft voice.

"Show me your chosen one, lowly angel, and I will choose my demons for mortal combat."

Hank Hawkins appeared before the throne dressed in white, glorious battle gear used by The Almighty's warrior angels in heaven. He was calm, fearless and prepared himself for battle.

Bella called out to him, "Mr. Hank, please save me!"

"What weapon will your warrior choose?" Satan asked, trying to decide how he would do battle and which demons to select to overcome this mortal warrior. "I heard him say when he was here before that he wanted a double-edged sword fifteen-feet long. Is that your weapon of choice?"

Gordon spoke. "A sword indeed is the choice of weapon for this mighty warrior. It will be the Sword of the Spirit, which is the mighty Word of God. It will be light as a feather in our warrior's hands. He will be given many powers to use against your powers of darkness. Prepare your demons for battle, Evil One. A battle to the death. A battle to the pit!"

Satan began planning his strategy, choosing from a variety of demons that he thought this Sword of the Spirit would have little effect upon.

"My first demon is Tartak, god of darkness. You can't fight darkness with a sword. Let the battles begin!"

The area around the throne became pitch dark. Hank had no idea who his opponent was, from which direction it would come or what weapons it would use. Suddenly, he raised his fifteen-foot double edged sword and it began to glow like the sun itself, piercing the darkness, filling the entire area with light.

As he held the sword high, Hank exclaimed, "The people who sat in darkness have seen a great light, and upon those who sat in the region and the shadow of death, light has dawned. Can darkness walk with light, Evil One?"

Once the darkness turned to light, on the floor before the throne perched Tartak, god of darkness. It appeared to be a foot-long cockroach with the head of a rat. It cowered beneath the mighty warrior.

"So you're the tiny demon that causes so many to fear the dark, huh, Tartak? I step on you and send you to the pit!" Hank crushed the tiny demon under his foot and the black marble floor opened up, fire belched out, swallowing up the small creature and enveloping him in flames as he fell deeper and deeper into the pit. His shrieks were soon gone as the floor covered over for the next battle.

"You want a sword fight, mortal warrior, I will give you a sword fight. Prepare to die!" Satan screamed at Hank.

Suddenly the floor was turned to an ocean. Hank had no fear of the raging waters and actually walked on the surface with his special God-given powers. From beneath the waves, Tannin, god of the depths of the sea, emerged. He looked like a combination of a giant squid and a giant octopus formed into one creature of the deep. He was the spitting image of a Kraken that was conjured up in the minds of ancient mariners. He had twenty-four long tentacles, each bearing a variety of razor sharp swords, daggers and knives.

Tannin began to swirl around so fast that the blades in his tentacles were like a giant lawnmower bearing down on Hank. As Tannin came closer and closer to Hank, some of the blades found their mark on Hank's torso. He had cuts on most of his body within seconds of the battle. He was bleeding badly even though Hank tried to parry the bevy of blades coming at him. There were just too many slashing him from all directions. His eyes began filling with blood dripping down from the cuts on his head.

Back at Clear Lake General, Liz began to scream for a nurse to come into Hank's ICU room. Mr. Elroy was sitting in the corner, seemingly asleep.

"Nurse, get a doctor, quickly! He's bleeding! My husband is bleeding all over! Wounds are forming all over his body. You've got to help him!" Liz screamed in a panic. Wayne and Abby ran down the hall to seek additional help for Daddy Hank.

The ICU doctor rushed into Hank's room. Seeing wounds forming on Hank's body right in front of him, the doctor ordered Hank to be sent to the operating room. No one had any idea how the wounds were being inflicted or from where or whom. They just knew that Hank Hawkins was losing a lot of blood in his comatose state.

"Get a team of trauma surgeons up to O.R. number three!" the doctor ordered. "Let's get some four-by-fours on those cuts. We've got to stop the bleeding! Get four units of blood started. Stat!"

In the midst of the mêlée at Betwixt, Gordon spoke, "For Hank Hawkins is God's minister to you for good. But if you do evil, be afraid, for he does not bear the sword in vain; for he is God's minister, an avenger to execute wrath upon him who practices evil!"

Hank began swinging his mighty sword as he spun into Tannin. With supernatural speed, Hank dodged the oncoming bevy of blades as the kraken spun towards him. Hank thrust out his mighty sword before him and as each of the tentacles holding various blades swirled past him, they were severed by Hank's sword. One by one they were cut off until finally all Hank had to do was to walk over to Tannin and thrust his blade into the head of the sea monster.

The ocean boiled and opened up revealing the fiery pit below. Tannin was gone. Hank stood motionless with blood dripping from his body. *Two demons down, five to go,* Hank thought to himself. He looked over at Bella.

"Remember the booming voice of The Almighty, Bella. He said he had plans for good and not evil for you. Be thankful and praise Him. Don't give up!" Hank said, turning to face the next demon. Bella was still too frightened to talk.

As the surgeons began sewing up Hank's many cuts and wounds, a large gash appeared in his stomach area, almost like he had been gored by the horns of a bull. Blood was spurting out into the faces of the doctors and nurses around the operating table. The trauma docs were confused as to what was happening but kept their focus on mending the wounds and stopping the bleeding as best they could. Everything in the O.R. was being recorded on video cameras. They would try and figure out what was happening later. Right now, the surgeons had a dying patient on their hands.

The wounds were the result of the current battling demon, Nebo, an ancient bull god. Nebo was huge, had razor sharp horns and moved faster than any normal bull could. Hank was dodging the mighty demon creature as best he could, even trying to out-run him at one point but to no avail. Nebo caught up with Hank and flipped him into the air with his long, pointy horns. As Hank was falling, Nebo gored Hank in the stomach. With mighty supernatural strength, Hank grabbed Nebo by the horns and wrestled him to the ground.

Quoting scripture, Hank declared, "And you shall offer a bull every day as a sin offering for atonement. Nebo, you are Bella's sin offering for today!"

Hank cut the throat of the giant bull right in front of the throne of Satan. Fire came down out of the sky above and consumed Nebo. The

Almighty accepted the offering for Bella's sins. Nebo was gone forever. As the doctors back on earth raced to stop the bleeding of Hank's wounds and gashes, it gave Hank the life that he needed to do battle at Betwixt, to stay the course and fight the good fight.

Satan witnessed every defeat of every demon he threw up against God's mighty warrior, Hank Hawkins. He noticed that Hank grew stronger with every battle despite the crushing wounds he bore. Satan decided to tip the scales in his own favor, breaking all the rules as usual and chose three demons to go against the mortal warrior at the same time, demons that feared little danger from the thrust of a sword.

Satan called on the names of Nergal, god of the underworld, Yam, an ancient river god, and Kaiwan, a star god. However, what Satan failed to understand or accept was that the Sword of the Spirit was more than a sword. It was the Holy Word of God. The Word that created the heavens and the earth from nothing when God said, "Let there be light!"

The setting before Satan's throne at Mount Zaphon changed from a raging sea to a dark chasm with a river running through it which spewed from Satan's mouth upon his throne. Hades was on one side and Paradise on the other. The three demon gods began surrounding Hank as he stood his ground in the center of the great rift between the two dimensions. Hank walked upon the river, ready for battle.

Nergal, god of the underworld, challenged Hank to come across the great chasm as flames burst forth around him from the underworld.

"Nergal, false god of the underworld. You cannot trick me to cross the chasm. For it is written, 'And besides all this, between us and you there is a great gulf fixed, so that those who want to pass from here to you cannot, nor can those from there pass to us.' You are where you are supposed to be, in the fiery pit and there you shall remain."

Yam, the river god rose up looking like Leviathan, a creature that no sword can penetrate, nor any man or weapon defeat. He was enormous, fierce and had no fear of God or man. He moved swiftly through the river toward Hank.

Kaiwan, better known as Worm Wood, began descending toward Hank from the sky in the form of a massive, frozen comet. Kaiwan screamed with an unearthly roar as the tremendous chunk of ice weighing countless tons bore down on God's mighty warrior. Hank's fifteen-foot sword would do no good against these supernatural ghouls.

Yam, Leviathan, stirred up massive waves that poured over Hank causing him to breathe in the filthy water. Hank gurgled and gasped for air as the Leviathan came closer and closer to him.

Back in the O.R. at Clear Lake General, the surgical staff noticed Hank spitting and coughing out large amounts of water. Hank's lungs were failing due to a lack of oxygen as they began to fill with the dirty river water. The trauma team began giving Hank oxygen, holding his nose and pushing air into his mouth. The monitors were going crazy. Once again the surgeons and nurses were being overwhelmed with all that was going on with Hank. But the worst was yet to come.

Hank faced the false river god, Yam, who had taken the form of Leviathan. The mighty warrior spoke these words, "But the earth helped the mighty warrior, and the earth opened up its mouth and swallowed up the river which the dragon had spewed from his mouth."

The mighty Leviathan was swallowed up when an earthquake opened up below the raging river. Yam was sucked under, never to be seen or heard from again.

Quickly, Hank looked toward the massive comet coming toward him. It was much too big to be ripped apart by his sword. Hank prayed.

"Father, by Your strength, defeat this demon called Kaiwan who rides upon the comet. I pray that you, Lord, will give me the power to reduce Worm Wood to vapor. Show your mighty strength to those who would go against You!" Hank shouted.

As the comet got closer and closer to him, Hank pointed his sword directly at Kaiwan. A blinding bolt of lightning burst from the tip of Hank's sword and blew the comet into millions of tiny slivers of ice which then melted into a fine mist. Kaiwan fell from the comet at Hank's feet, pleading for mercy. No mercy was shown as Hank struck the formless demon, sending him to join the others in the pit of fire.

Bella began to see hope in Hank's God-given heroics and yelled to him, "Save me, Mr. Hank! You're my champion! You're my hero! Don't give up! I'll be good from now on…I promise you, Mr. Hank! I'll be good."

Still bleeding profusely from his stomach wound inflicted by the bull god, Nebo, with deep cuts all over his body and trying to catch a breath of air, Hank was hurting. His energy was practically gone and his pain was great despite the work of the trauma team patching him up back on earth.

Satan was furious at losing six of his demons to a mortal like Hank Hawkins. He planned the last battle carefully and began to psych-out Hank.

"A storm draws nigh, mighty warrior, that you cannot overcome!"

Hank, stooped over, bleeding, holding his sword, looked up into the smoke surrounding Satan's throne and said, "I AM the storm! Bring it on, Evil One!"

20

"Go and Sin No More!" Debt paid!

A liaison nurse from the trauma team came out of the operating room to give an update on what was happening to Hank Hawkins. She found Liz, Abby, Wayne and the rest of the group in the waiting room.

"Mr. Hawkins is still in surgery. He has sustained some massive abdominal wounds which we cannot explain but our team of surgeons and technicians are doing their best. I don't want to give you any false hopes, but I don't want you to give up on us, either. We almost lost Mr. Hawkins a couple of times but for the present he's still hanging in there. He's a strong, determined man. Everyone should be very proud of him. We're doing everything we can, but with new wounds appearing spontaneously, we have no idea how long these surgeries will last."

Abby was crying and tried her best to keep it together. She turned to Mr. Elroy.

"Mr. Elroy, do you think what's happening to Bella and what's happening to my dad are somehow linked together?"

"Sho could be, child. Jesus said, 'In this world there will be trials and tribulations, but I have overcome the world. I will never leave you.' Let's just concentrate on our faith. Keep prayin! He will send The Comforter to you."

Wayne pulled Abby and Liz close and put his arms around them. Mr. Elroy looked concerned.

Back at Betwixt, Bella found herself chained hand and foot to the throne of Satan. He was not going to let her escape his grasp. As the surgical team back on earth tried to mend his wounds, Hank's soul stood upright in defiance, waving his mighty sword, waiting for the final challenge to free Bella from the Evil One's grasp.

Satan let out a mighty howl and chose his final demon.

"Marduk, god of wind and storm, swoop down upon this lowly mortal with the force of many tornadoes. Lift him out of my sight so that I may claim my prize, my new concubine, Bella Cantrell! His sword cannot defeat you."

The entire scene at Mount Zaphon changed to one of a boiling gray and black sky. As Hank stood in front of Bella, four tornadoes began forming all around him. Within the twisting madness of the four tornadoes was every type of blade, snake and scorpion coming at Hank in a swirling mass from all sides. Bella shrunk down behind Hank, too scared to utter a single word. She was gasping for breath. It looked like her end was near.

As the massive live debris came closer to Hank, he began to feel more cuts all over his body. The snakes in the tornadoes began biting him and the scorpions stung him from every direction. At one point, Bella could only make out the figure of Hank's form, completely covered by cuts, snakes attached to him and scorpions stinging him.

Back at the O.R. at Clear Lake General, the trauma doctors began seeing the massive cuts, stab wounds, swelling stings and reptile bites occur on Hanks body. He was covered with them.

"Quick! Get the anti-venom. Our patient is being bitten and stung all over his body," the head surgeon screamed.

"Which anti-venom do we use, doctor? We don't know what kind of bites we're trying to counter," asked one of the trauma nurses.

"All of 'em!" shouted the doctor. "Just give him all of them!"

As Hank began to parry the deadly creatures coming at him with his sword, he looked up into the heavens high above Betwixt and said, "Behold, a whirlwind of the Lord has gone forth in fury—A violent whirlwind! It will fall violently on the head of the wicked."

As Hank spoke these words, he began spinning around and around with his sword outstretched in front of him. Faster and faster he spun in a counter-clock-wise direction. The snakes, scorpions and daggers that were stuck into his body were being whisked away by centrifugal force. All of the clouds and thunderheads in the skies above Betwixt were drawn into Hank who stood in the center of them.

He became the eye of a tremendous hurricane with wind speeds that could not be measured. Bella's chains were the only thing holding her fast as she was blown by the wind to a horizontal position, barely clinging to life. Satan's own throne was blown over by the forces of the wind and lay in shambles on its side.

The hurricane that Hank had become was so powerful, so consuming, that it sucked the four tornadoes down into it like a black hole consuming everything in its path. Marduk went screaming and hollering into the abyss created by the massive hurricane, never to be seen again. The seven challenges had been met and defeated by the Sword of the Spirit which was the Mighty Word of God.

With little life left within him, feeling every stab, every snake bite and every scorpion's sting, Hank looked up in agony into the smoke that covered Satan's now fallen throne.

"Your demons have all been defeated, Evil One! You will free Bella Cantrell and return her to her mortal body. Now!" Hank shouted.

Hank walked over to Bella and removed her shackles. He gently took the ruby from her forehead and tossed it on the slate floor before the cluttered throne of Satan. When he removed the stone, he could see a slight indentation in Bella's forehead.

"I believe this stone is yours, Evil One. The stolen property has been returned to you. Bella's debt has been paid in full!" Hank exclaimed.

In desperation as he hovered above the debris of his kingdom, Satan motioned to his high lieutenant, Baal. In a cowardly attack from behind, Baal swooped down on Hank, sinking his massive claws into his back with such force that they went all the way through Hank's back and exited through his chest.

At the O.R. in Clear Lake, Hank's chest blew open and spewed blood all over the operating room, almost blinding the trauma team from the sudden, massive, lethal wound. The team recovered from the macabre site and began stuffing Hank's chest with towels, trying to seal the open cavity of his chest.

Bella shrieked in disbelief, "No! That isn't fair! Mr. Hank defeated your demons!"

With the massive claws still in his back, knowing his time had come, Hank never lost the grip on his sword and looked up skyward and silently prayed the prayer of Samson.

"Oh Lord God, remember me, I pray! Strengthen me, I pray, just this once, O God, that I may with one blow take vengeance on this demon for my wounds."

With his last breath, Hank swung his mighty sword around just as the scale-covered dragon Baal lowered his two heads to finish off Hank's existence. With one slash, Hank sliced off both heads of Baal, Satan's mighty lieutenant of all the demonic forces of darkness. The two heads fell to the black marble floor before Satan's toppled throne. Hank's legs gave way, his heart back on earth stopped beating and his body gave up its spirit.

Bella cried out, "Oh Mr. Hank, I love you so much. Please don't leave me!"

As the words poured from her mouth, a portal suddenly appeared and hovered above the realm of Betwixt. It was lined with a single mother of pearl. As the portal swung open, a dazzling light shown down on Hank Hawkins. Standing in the portal was Jesus Christ, Holy Son of God. Abigail Green was standing next to her Savior.

Jesus spoke, "Well done, my good and faithful servant. Come to Me and receive your just reward. You have run the righteous race, stayed the course and fought the good fight. Now share in the Kingdom of The Almighty. Your sister, Abigail, will show you the way."

Hank was in complete awe of the love he felt surrounding him, the warmth, the security. His wounds were immediately healed and he looked as though he were thirty-three years old again. The sight of Jesus caused him to fall on his knees before the opened portal. Hank had no words. As he was drawn into the pearly doorway, Abigail took his hand and led him into the light.

Jesus then turned to Bella as she cowered on her knees.

"Bella, I know the plans I have for you. Plans for good and not evil. Hank Hawkins, my mighty warrior, showed the greatest love a man can show. He laid down his life for you. Go and sin no more."

Satan was hiding his eyes from the brilliant light that streamed down all over Betwixt from the open portal above. He knew better than to challenge the Holy Son of God and kept perfectly quiet. Jesus pointed down at Satan.

"Soon, Evil One. Soon! The day is coming when every knee shall bow, of things in heaven, and things in the earth, and things under the earth. I will cast you into the Lake of Fire. Your time is almost done!"

Satan turned himself into a serpent and crawled on his belly into a crack underneath his crumpled throne to escape the light and the admonishment by his victorious adversary, Jesus.

The portal closed as Hank walked into the light. Bella's soul returned to her body back at the ICU at Clear Lake General. The ice around her melted and partially flooded the room causing many of the instruments to short out. She woke up screaming.

"Oh Mr. Hank! Oh Jesus! I saw Jesus! Mom, where are you? I believe! I believe..!" Bella was shaking, scared to death, soaked in water from the melted ice that had entombed her. The Bible was still laying upon her chest.

Back in the O.R. the surgical team had done all that they could to save Hank but to no avail.

"Call the time of death," instructed the head trauma surgeon. "We'll never know what happened to this man, but you can all be proud of yourselves for doing the best you could to save him. I'll go and talk to his family. Prepare Mr. Hawkins' body for viewing by his loved ones."

As the doctor took off his surgical mask, he looked down on Hank. His silvery hair was clotted with blood, his face and upper torso filled with cuts, bruises, stings and bites. Right before the doctor's eyes there appeared a brilliant white streak of hair just above Hank's right ear. The doctor just shook his head and walked out to tell the family, not knowing how to explain what had happened.

Abby, Wayne and Liz ran up to the surgeon as he approached them. They could tell by the look on the doctor's face that the news was not good. Abby's eyes began to fill with tears. Liz stood firm, waiting for the doctor's report.

"We did everything we could..." the trauma surgeon said. "I'm sorry to say, it wasn't enough. We lost him." There was a long pause. "Mr. Hawkins will be in room 1111 in about ten minutes. You may want to spend some time with him..."

Abby fell to her knees, sobbing uncontrollably. Wayne held her and offered his hand to Liz who stood stoically, trying to understand what had taken place.

"What happened to my dad, doctor? What happened to him?" Abby blurted out.

"We don't really know, Mrs. Tyler. All of a sudden a huge gash protruded through his..." The trauma surgeon, hesitated, not wanting to go through the horrid details. "Let's just leave it at that. We tried everything..."

Mr. Elroy joined them and prayed for strength.

Liz, Abby and Wayne entered the viewing room for a last good-bye.

"You're the greatest dad a girl could have, Daddy Hank. I'll always love you," Abby said, running her fingers through Hank's hair and kissing him on his scarred forehead.

"Oh, baby, my beloved husband. I, too shall love you forever. You have my heart. Take it with you. I'll see you soon. I know right where you are..." Liz had tears on both cheeks as she bent over to kiss her husband— of one day—on the lips.

"Mr. Hank, I remember what you told me before you gave me the honor of marrying your daughter. I will always love her and take care of her. I love you too, buddy!" Wayne said as he finally realized what a great man Hank Hawkins was.

He reached down and shook Hank's lifeless, scarred hand and noticed the white streak in Hank's hair. Wayne had a feeling of where his father-in-law had fought his last battle. As they left after their final good-byes, Wayne pulled the sheet over Hank's battered head.

Robbie was dozing in the waiting area right outside of Bella's room. When she heard her screaming, she immediately saw water rushing from underneath Bella's ICU cubical and rushed in, wading through ankle-deep water.

"Oh, Mom! God bless you…I saw the devil, he tried to kill me…I saw Jesus, Mom, He is real. I saw him! That ole two-headed dragon Baal sneaked up behind Mr. Hank and killed him…but Mr. Hank killed him back! He cut off both of his dragon heads just like he said he would, Mom! Mr. Hank is in heaven now with Abigail. I saw them Mom, I saw them! Mr. Hank battled demons for me! He gave his life for me, Mom! I am so scared, Mom, help me!" Bella was screaming, hyperventilating, shaking from her horrid experience.

Robbie held Bella tight, trying to calm her down. "Slow down, baby. Praise God, Bella! You're safe now, baby girl, you're safe. What did you say about Mr. Hank?"

"Mom, Mr. Hank fought off all the demons…he became a hurricane, he caused the darkness to become light…he toppled the throne of Satan at Mount Zaphon. I remember it all, Mom. This wasn't a dream! Mr. Hank is in heaven now. I saw him go through the pearly portal…! Irma Chemoth is a demon, Mom! She tricked me. Satan wanted me for his concubine, but I said, 'hell no!' I never want to go back to that horrid mountain again, Mom. Promise me I'll never go back!" Bella was shaking all over, clutching her mom's Bible close to her chest. "Oh my god, Mom, look at my wet hair!"

The ICU staff carefully removed all of the monitor wires from Bella and moved her into a dry room down the hall. Robbie refused to leave her side.

After Abby, Wayne and Liz went back to the waiting room, they noticed that Robbie was not there. For about twenty minutes, they all sat there, numb, with a thousand things running through their minds. Their hearts were broken but not their spirits. In their scrambled reflections, Liz broke the silence.

"I promised Hank that I would never leave him. We only had a night, one night together, a wonderful night. I waited a lifetime for my God-given soul mate and we only had one night together. How can I go on without him? I'm not sure I can go on…" Liz finally broke down and sobbed. Wayne and Abby held her and cried with her.

The group of bikers from the Cowboy Church each walked up to Liz, Abby and Wayne to offer their hugs and condolences then began to disperse. Pastor Randy and Pat stayed to offer encouragement and talk about final preparations.

Robbie heard the crying down the hall in the ICU waiting room and told Bella she'd be right back. She walked in to see the devastation on all their faces.

"I know about Hank! When you're ready, you may want to come down and talk to Bella, she's back. She was there and saw the whole thing. Hank gave his life for her. They were at Betwixt. Baal killed Hank. With his last breath, Hank killed Baal. It's a long story. I'm so sorry."

After about half an hour, the group gathered around Bella's bed. She told them in detail what had happened at Mount Zaphon. They hung on her every word. Bella gave them closure to the life of a great man, a great and mighty warrior of God.

"Abby, sister, I saw your mom! You look just like her! In her dazzling light, she was the most beautiful woman I have ever seen. She loves you, sister!" Everyone could see that Bella was overwhelmed at what she had witnessed. They believed every word she spoke.

"Pastor Randy, I saw Jesus in that dimension called Betwixt. He told me to go and sin no more and that He had plans for good and not evil for me. I accept Him as my Lord and Savior. Will you baptize me?" Bella said with her whole heart.

"Yes, I will, Bella. I want you to know that Mr. Hank will be given several crowns in heaven for what he has chosen to do for you and for The Almighty. He will be greatly exalted. You have made the greatest decision that anyone can make during their entire lifetime," Pastor Randy replied. "You, Bella, now have eternal salvation and have nothing to fear. Satan can't touch you ever again. Today your name is written in the Lamb's Book of Life, never to be erased."

As the events drew to a close at Clear Lake General with Bella and Hank, other phenomena were taking place at the NASA offices of Dr. Eric Palmer and at the Bay Hilton where Dr. Helle Guyion was staying. The Agent in charge there put in a call to Agent Bensen at his NASA office.

"Sir, this is Agent Dooley with the S.W.A.T. team over at the Bay Hilton. The ice in Dr. Guyion's room is gone. I think we can get in there. Do you want us to arrest her and bring her in?"

"That's affirmative, Dooley. Just be careful and don't harm her in any way."

Dooley and the team entered Dr. Guyion's door. Her room had no water in it or any signs of damage. She was sitting on her couch as if nothing had happened.

"M'am, I'm Agent Dooley of the F.B.I., you're under arrest. Would you come with me?"

Helle began her red laser stare directly into Agent Dooley's eyes. "I will not come with you, Agent. And you will vacate my premises, now!"

Confused, his thoughts suddenly scrambled by the penetrating stares of Dr. Guyion, Agent Dooley and the rest of his team simply turned around and walked out of her room. When they got back to Agent Bensen's office across the street at NASA, Bensen questioned them.

"Where's Dr. Guyion, Dooley?"

"She's in her room at the Hilton, sir," Dooley replied.

"Why didn't you arrest her and bring her in as you were ordered to do?"

"Did you tell us to do that, sir? I don't remember your saying anything but come back to your office. We're all here, even the men on the perimeter and the roof." Dooley was obviously completely confused. It was written across his dazed face.

"Get back over to the Hilton and bring her in, Dooley. Take all the men with you," Bensen ordered.

"I don't think we can do that, sir. I'm certainly not trying to disobey a direct order. It's just that, uh, I don't think we can and I don't know why. It's like when this albino woman stared those laser-like glances at us, well, sir, she had us all in some kind of a trance. We were helpless, like she has some kind of strange power over anyone that goes against her will. Could I speak freely to you, sir?"

"Go ahead, Dooley."

"Sir, I'm not sure that we should have only scientists trying to figure out all of these 'X-File' things. I believe we should have a group of theologians to give us some answers. That woman is evil. I don't know where she gets her power of suggestion, but I think it's beyond scientific. I think it's some kind of a biblical thing, sir."

Bensen ordered a new team to guard Dr. Guyion's room with instructions to keep her there. He then asked some of the NASA psychologists to talk to Dooley and his men to determine what had happened. He wasn't going to destroy their careers for lack of understanding of all the supernatural events that were going on.

"Agent Bensen? This is Belinda Sealy, Dr. Palmer's assistant. You may want to get down here. Water is gushing out of Dr. Palmer's office. I think I can use my key to get in now."

When Bensen arrived at Palmer's office, the outer office where Belinda sat was flooded with ankle-deep water. His men were still posted outside the door.

"Let's get in there, Ms. Sealy," Bensen ordered.

She took her key, inserted it and unlocked the door. Bensen and his agents swarmed inside to find Dr. Palmer sitting at his water-soaked desk, completely drenched and holding his face in his hands.

"Are you okay, Dr. Palmer?" Bensen asked.

"I...I don't know. I'm wet. What happened in here?" Palmer appeared dazed, like he had just awakened from a bad dream.

"I was hoping you could tell us, Dr. Palmer. What did happen in here?" Bensen asked.

"I, uh, I was sitting here at my desk preparing the reports you wanted, then, uh, I was all wet. Why am I wet?" Palmer asked with a strange look on his face.

"Get Dr. Palmer to our medical facilities here on premise," Bensen ordered. He could tell that Palmer was confused. "After they check him out, I want him poly-graphed as soon as possible. Get this place cleaned up and secure all of Dr. Palmer's documents. Miss Sealy, you're in charge of them."

Bensen's cell phone began to ring. It was Dennis Colley, head of security at NASA.

"Yeah, Dennis. What ya got?"

"John, some weird things have been happening over at Clear Lake General. The young lady, Miss Bella Cantrell, is no longer entombed in ice and she's okay. She just told us where she thought she'd been. It's a long story. If you have time, I'll drop by and fill you in."

"Was she wet, shaky and confused, Dennis?"

"Yeah, she was. How'd you know?"

"Don't ask. It's been a crazy day." Bensen clicked off his phone, rocked back in his swivel chair and took a deep breath.

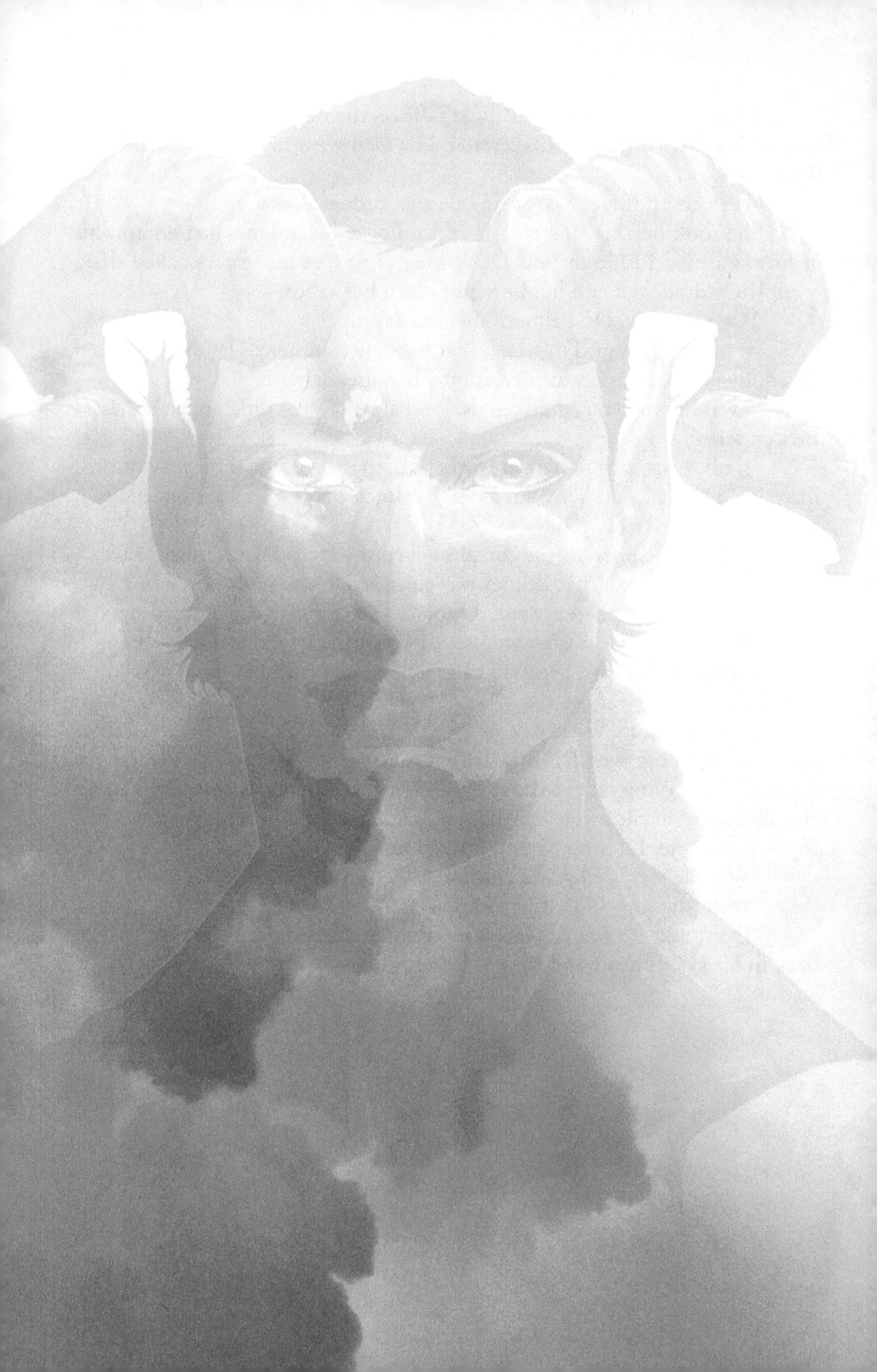

21

WORLD WAR III
YOU WILL CALL HIM...

Before leaving Clear Lake General, Liz walked over to have a private conversation with Wayne and Abby. They were all drained, heartbroken and still had much to do.

"Abby, we all need some sleep and some nourishment, but I need to ask a favor…"

"Anything, Liz," Abby said, picking up her purse.

"I don't think I'm ready to spend a night alone at your Dad's condo and the hotel is closed down. Do you mind…"

"Oh, Liz," Abby interrupted. "Come with Wayne and me and stay at our place. You're family now, Mrs. Hawkins."

"Thank you, Abby. Maybe we can all talk in the morning about all the arrangements and what has to be done…"

Again, Abby interrupted Liz.

"I don't even know where to start, Liz. I've got bills to pay, payroll to do, the club is failing and I don't know how much longer we can hold out."

"We can discuss that in the morning. Let's get some rest."

After sleeping for about ten hours, Liz was in Abby's kitchen cooking bacon, eggs, pancakes, and brewing a fresh pot of coffee. The aroma from the kitchen awakened Wayne and Abby. They put on some shorts and T-shirts and joined Liz in the kitchen.

"Good morning!" Liz was trying her best to lift all their fallen spirits.

Abby and Wayne just nodded and poured themselves a cup. Abby reached into one of the kitchen drawers and pulled out a legal pad and some pens.

"We should start making arrangements, Liz. Do you feel up to it? My Dad and I have always made lists of things to do and to tell you the truth, I can't get settled until we complete everything. I guess you know you're now half owner of Tequilaville—for better or for worse, Liz."

"Yes, I know, Abby. Since we're all family now, we'll deal with this together."

They began their list with Hank's funeral arrangements. Liz and Abby decided that he would have wanted a simple funeral and burial at the Cowboy Church followed by a wake at the club with close friends and family to celebrate his life.

"For the meantime, I'll call Scott Wood, T-Bone and Tito to hang out at the club to provide security in the event some of the weirdoes out there want to rob us blind," Wayne added. "I just don't know what to do with the band and the rest of our employees. Abby, you handle the check book. Got any ideas?"

Liz broke in.

"Abby and Wayne, I don't know what all your Dad told you about my finances. It may be a good time to talk."

"He never told us anything, Liz. He just told me that he was giving you half of his interest in the club and now that he's gone, under Texas Law, you own half."

"Abby, I was very successful on Wall Street before I met Hank. To the tune of millions. We don't have to worry about finances and we have plenty of time to come up with a plan. For now, I'd suggest that we give most of the employees a two-month severance and encourage them to find other employment until we decide what's to come of Tequilaville. I'll finance that."

"Thank you, Liz, but you really don't have to do that," Abby replied.

"I'm family, remember? Yes, I do have to do that. Let's move on. I can't stay here with you and Wayne forever, but I don't feel comfortable moving back to the condo—too many memories." Tears began forming in Liz's eyes. "I want to purchase a small home near here. We can put some of Hank's belongings there for the time being. You can have anything that is special to you, Abby. You're his daughter. I was just his wife for a day."

"Liz, don't think like that. We all love you very much. After we get my Dad's things out, I'll see if Bella can sell the condo. It's paid for and the location on the lake is wonderful. It should sell quickly," Abby said. "But what are we going to do with Tequilaville? We still owe a lot of money on it and with no revenue coming in, I just don't have a direction right now, Liz."

"You know, Abby, God does everything for a reason. You can be sure of that. I've got some ideas for that property, a completely new concept. But we can discuss that later. Just leave that part to me."

Agent-in-Charge Bensen convened an early morning meeting with members of the State Department, Justice Department, C.I.A., the Deputy Director of the F.B.I., and N.S.A. officials. Bensen's men had given poly- graph tests to Dr. Palmer, Belinda Sealy and Lieutenant Stan Stark. They attempted to polygraph Dr. Guyion's staff but each refused, claiming diplomatic immunity.

"Let's go over the polygraph tests first," Bensen began. "What are the results?"

"Dr. Palmer, Miss Sealy and Lieutenant Stark all passed with flying colors," said the man conducting the tests. "They all told some pretty wild stories about having visited this unknown realm called Betwixt, but none had any proof whatsoever. There were no falsehoods that showed up on the polygraph tests from any of them. Every detail that each gave in separate interviews all corroborated the others' stories. Believe me, sir, I drilled them hard on several tests.

"Dr. Palmer was especially talkative. His breathing revealed that he was absolutely fearful of his colleague, Dr. Helle Guyion. He said she had powers that were unexplainable. He's no kind of a spy or anything like that, sir. He was completely honest and helpful with the entire interview."

"So what does our representative from the State Department have to say about the situation?" Bensen turned to one of the men at the table.

"We contacted the Belgium government officials and talked to them through our attaché in Antwerp. The Belgians, uh, well, they have no idea how Dr. Guyion obtained her diplomatic immunity status but were hesitant to make any charges against her. To tell you the truth, they seemed frightened of her, also. They told us that she had a lot of friends in high places in Russia, China and the Middle East.

"At this point, State has decided we should just make some *unofficial* apologies to Belgium, to Dr. Guyion and her staff and get them the hell out of our county. We did kill her head of security. Her staff we are holding has already lawyered up with some real heavyweight firms. They could sue the U.S. government into decades of lawsuits. Our position is to give them seventy-two hours to leave the country and hope nothing else comes from this."

After several hours of discussion around the conference table, the Deputy Director of the F.B.I. began wrapping things up.

"If State will send a representative to Dr. Guyion's hotel room with an official document giving her seventy-two hours to vacate U.S. airspace, I'll release her staff immediately. No charges will be filed. I think we'll all feel better when she's gone. We should all convene here again in three days to see if our scientists figure out anything new on the ones and zeros from the conference in Paris."

"What about the media camped outside of the NASA premises?" asked Bensen. "We've done an excellent job of keeping them in the dark so far. Should we just say that this was a drill for national security and let it go at that?"

"Yes. The State Department will hold a short news conference. No one is to say anything further. Is that understood?" said the legat from State.

Mr. Elroy dropped by Tequilaville to check on the small group that was holding down the fort. He walked over to Scott Wood.

"Mr. Scott? I sho think me and you should write a song for Mr. Hank to play at his memorial service. A song to honor him for his gallantry in serving The Good Lawd and saving Miss Bella. Got a song left in ya, my boy?"

"Maybe I have one more song left in me, Mr. Elroy. Let's write it."

Just before the band walked up on stage for rehearsal, T-Bone motioned for Mr. Elroy to join him in the back of the club. T-Bone was wrapped up in rage and wanted revenge for the death of his boss.

"Mr. Elroy, I know that witch Dr. Guyion had something to do with Mr. Hank's death. I'm burning up with hatred. I truly want to kill her, and I'm not sure I can help myself, but I wanted to talk to you first."

"Mr. T-Bone, the Good Book says that vengeance is mine says da Good Lawd. You just need to calms down and let Him handle this. No sense in getting yoself into a whole lot of trouble. The Almighty don't miss nothing, Mr. T-Bone. He's got a list better than Santa Claus and He checks it twice. Now you just look to the future and put the past behind you, ya hear?

"Mr. Scott, you got them guitars tuned up yet?"

Throughout the rest of the day and the next, Liz and Abby made all the arrangements for Hank Hawkins. Obituaries in the paper, funeral arrangements at the Cowboy Church and burial in the small little cemetery owned by the church. After grave site ceremonies, all the family and close friends of Hank would gather at Tequilaville for a final wake in his honor. They decided that only red wine would be served at the wake with each guest receiving a single small cup of wine, resembling a communion service.

"Pastor Randy said there is never a charge for burial plots for its members at the Cowboy church, Abby. I think that's where your Dad would want to have his final resting place. Is that okay with you?" Liz asked.

"It's perfect, Liz. Can we do this tomorrow? I love Daddy Hank with all my heart and soul but honestly, I just want to move on. I can't stand my own grief," Abby said with tears rolling down her cheeks.

~~~~

The eulogy delivered by Pastor Randy was touching. He spoke of Hank Hawkins being a loving father and a man used by God to accomplish His will. The eulogy was entitled, "No Greater Love," and continued about Hank being a mighty warrior for The Lord, fighting for Bella's soul in the very realm of the devil himself. There were many outbursts of grief during the ceremony. Many people loved Hank Hawkins.

In an unorthodox move, after the eulogy, Pastor Randy baptized Bella into the Royal Family of God as a tribute to her champion and fallen warrior. The small church was packed with bikers, cowboys and employees of Tequilaville. During the grief, there was joy. Robbie smiled as her daughter was baptized. She had thought that she would never see this day.

After the grave site services were completed, only T-Bone and Mr. Elroy remained by the grave.

"I can't help myself, Mr. Elroy. I'm going to kill that woman, Dr. Guyion, if it's the last thing I do. Please forgive me." T-Bone had waited until the crowd was gone to finally let it all out.

Mr. Elroy didn't say a word and put his arms around the huge bouncer and led him back to the parking lot. Everyone headed over to Tequilaville to celebrate the life of Hank Hawkins.

After the group had assembled, Abby, Liz and Wayne raised their small glasses of wine and toasted the life of "Daddy Hank." Mr. Elroy gathered the band, *South*, and began to speak to the crowd from the bandstand.

"Mr. Hank was a loving father, a husband and had a warrior spirit. He was the storm of the good Lawd and laid down his life for sweet Ms. Bella. I loved that man…" A tear ran down Mr. Elroy's ole brown eyes. "Mr. Scott and I wrote him a song and would like to play it for you now…"

"I AM the Storm"

When a man has to face his demons.
When the world is getting him down.
He has to reach inside of himself
And hear that roaring sound…

That's telling him to stand up tall and proud
And to gather all his grit.
It's telling him to be a warrior
And fight his way out of the pit.

No storm draws nigh, no fear to great
That the warrior cannot overcome.
He draws his sword and waves it high
And says, "Let the demons come!"

I AM the storm! I have no fear!
I'm gonna bring you down.
My mighty Spirit sword of light,
HIS strength have I just found.
I'll cast my demons to the pit,
That's just where they belong.
As I praise the Mighty God of Light
And sing my warrior's song,
And sing my warrior's song…

People were clapping and singing, crying and laughing at the same time. Shortly afterwards, the crowd dispersed in silence, humming parts of the song and went home for some much needed rest and restoration. Hank Hawkins had been duly honored. It was time to move on.

An F.B.I. SWAT team escorted Dr. Guyion's staff back to the hotel, led by a member from the State Department, who delivered the seventy-two-hour notice for her to leave and vacate U.S. airspace.

Helle, who was completely unshaken and un-amused at the order, looked at the man from State and said, "So now I'm considered *persona non grata*, huh? No worry, I'm getting bored with this place and your petty, supposedly brilliant, scientists. I choose to leave, but you haven't heard the last of me yet. There's more to be discovered in the conference video if your scientists ever figure it out. I'll be back! You'll beg me to come back to explain the last tape."

That night, while everyone was asleep, the supernatural once again began to explode.

Abby was snuggled in next to Wayne when she thought she heard Wayne call her by name. When she awoke, Wayne was sound asleep. She could have sworn to have heard her name called out in the night. She drifted back to sleep and twice more she heard her name…"Abby!"

Finally, she sat up in bed and simply said, "Here I am, Lord!"

Gabriel, the Holy Messenger angel was hovering in brilliance at the foot of her bed. Abby was shocked and scared as she pulled the sheet over her eyes upon viewing such brilliance and beauty.

"Fear not, Abby. For you have been chosen. You will bear a son and you will call him Billy! He was conceived during your honeymoon in the Garden. It is the will of The Almighty. He will be a mighty speaker of the Holy Word. He will shout boldly, accurately, in loving kindness and without ever being judgmental. He will lead many to salvation. The end times are near…" the angel declared and then disappeared.

Abby had no breath to speak back. She felt overwhelmed, honored and much loved. She was filled with joy as she drifted back to sleep.

Shortly thereafter, the same night, Gabriel appeared for the second time to Liz Hawkins. Her heart was broken, she was exhausted and hadn't slept in several days. She had finally drifted off into a deep sleep in the guest bedroom at Wayne and Abby's house.

"Elizabeth Hawkins!" Gabriel spoke in a small, still, loving voice.

Liz heard her name clearly the first time and raised up in bed. She too exclaimed, "Here I am, Lord. What would you have me do?"

"Liz Hawkins, you are truly loved by the Almighty. Your husband is with Him and on the only night of your marriage, you conceived a son. Your son will be a voice shouting in the wilderness for people to repent. He will lead the way for another. You will call your son Johnny. You will love him and train him in scripture. He has an important role to play. The end is near. Be Blessed, Liz Hawkins."

Liz saw Gabriel's brilliant light streaming all around him. She bowed before him but Gabriel lifted her up. "Worship only the Almighty," Gabriel said as he disappeared from her sight. Liz was almost breathless as the words of the angel ran round and round in her mind.

"Oh Jesus! Thank You, kind Lord. I am truly blessed of women. I will obey all of your instructions. As for me and my house, we will follow The Lord…" Liz instantly fell back into a deep sleep.

Back at the Bay Hilton at 3 A.M. Dr. Helle Guyion was far from sleep. She could go weeks without it due to her Satanical powers. She put herself into a trance and appealed to her master for directions on her next assignment.

Immediately, Tammuz, Babylonian goddess of fertility appeared before her, impersonating an angel of light. She instructed Helle on her next move.

"You will return to Europe. You will be elevated by your master, Satan, who has sent me with this message. From your trip to Betwixt and your union with Dr. Eric Palmer, you will bear a son. You will call him 'Helel,' which means 'son of the morning, who has fallen from heaven.' He will establish a kingdom on earth. You, Helle, are most honored of all the evil women of the earth," Tammuz stated.

"A king on earth?" Helle mused again, unimpressed. "So my reward is to be like a queen mother?"

"You will send him to the finest schools. He will speak many languages. You will introduce him into all the diplomatic circles of world governments and he will be known as a man of peace. He will be from the line of the ancient Canaanites with traits of the Nephilim, who the One Above tried to destroy in the great flood.

"Do you understand, Helle? The master has spoken!" Tammuz asked as her eyes pierced the very soul of the darkness within Helle.

"Got it, Tammuz. So now I'm going to get fat with this child, huh?"

"No more lip from you, lowly mortal. You will obey or die! The One Above has blessed the seeds in Abby Tyler and Liz Hawkins. Their sons will battle with your son, Helel, until our master rules his kingdom on earth." Tammuz pointed directly at Dr. Guyion as the demon slowly disappeared.

Helle called to her assistant, Natasha Patski. "Get everything packed, Natasha. Get the plane fueled so we can leave this place...Oh, yeah, get me the address of Wayne and Abby Tyler. I'm going to pay them a final visit before we leave. I can't wait to tell them my good news...I'm going to have a baby!"

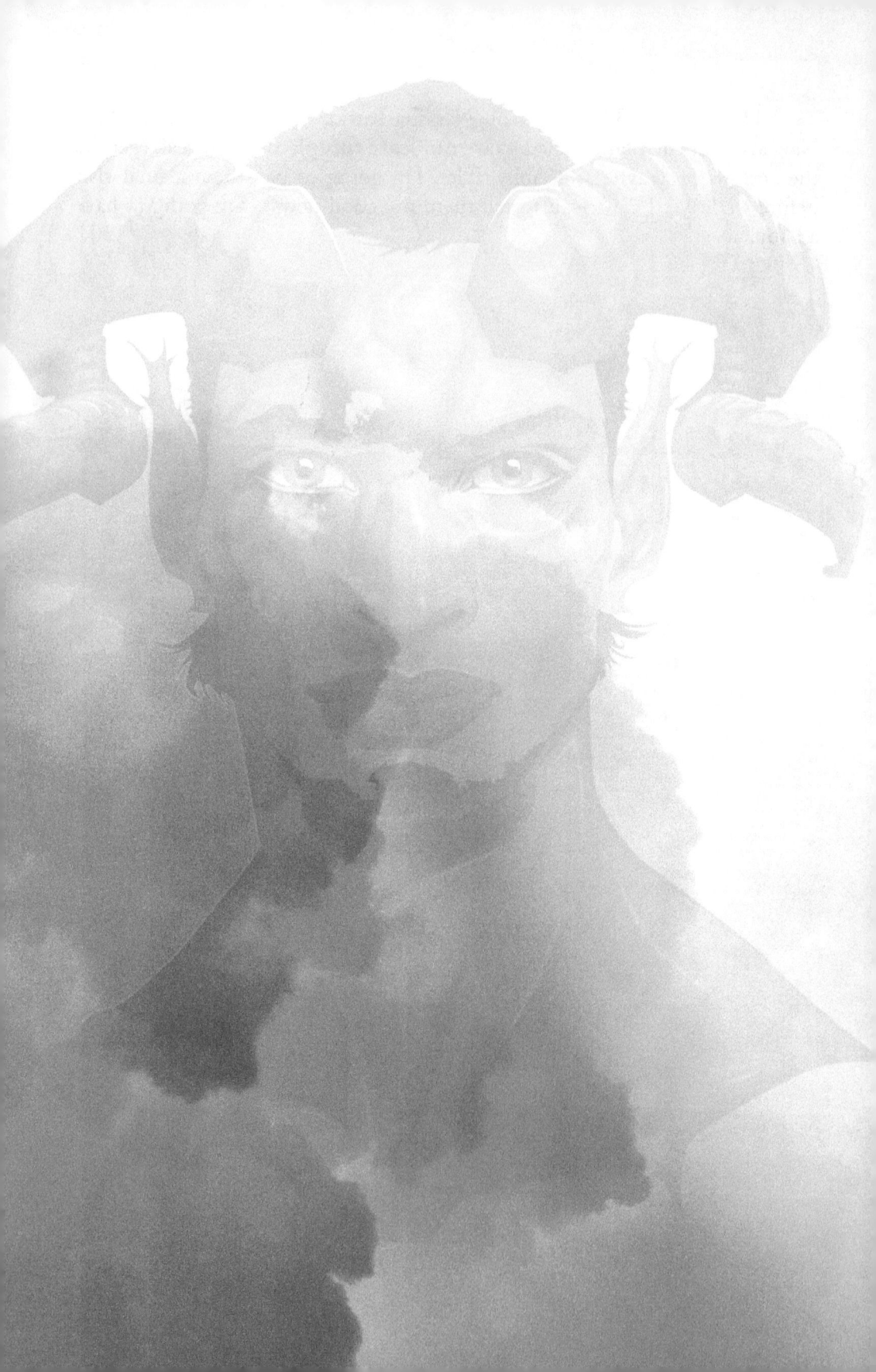

22

I'm Pregnant! I'm Pregnant! Me Too!

The chief astrophysicist leading the team at NASA to break the codes of the Paris videos walked into Agent Bensen's office. He was distraught, tired and obviously trembling.

"Agent Bensen, call the cabinet together. We've cracked another video that is going to scare the hell out of us!"

Once the cabinet and the head of the Joint Chiefs of Staff were convened, the senior astrophysicist began his presentation.

"Mr. Vice President, cabinet members, ladies and gentlemen. Before I show you this video which our scientists have just produced from the images taken at the Paris conference that emerged from the so called Pandora's Box, let me do some background.

"For three weeks, our scientific group here at the facilities have called in some of America's leading prophetic theologians to get information from them on what some call the End Times prophecy. Here are a few brief points that are taken from the Bible that we can neither confirm nor refute. These events seem to be ever present in our world today but scripture says 'The end is not yet.' Scripture says that Israel will be made a nation again which happened May 14, 1948. This is a key date, honored guests. Remember it. Another key date is 1967, when Jerusalem was joined to Israel for the first time in thousands of years.

"Prophecy goes on to say that when people go 'to and fro across the earth,' as in jet travel, and 'knowledge and communication are greatly increased'—make special note of this—'Then the end shall come!' Prophecy also states that the generation on earth that sees these events unfold, will be the generation to see the second coming of Christ at the end of a seven-year tribulation period. From what the theologians have shown us, our scientists—whether agnostic, atheists or believers—have reached a decision that we may be in the midst of these times if any of this is true. The evidence is overwhelming and should at least be considered.

"Scripture also tells of World War Three in vivid detail. It says, peoples' tongues and eyeballs will melt before their skeletons hit the ground. That, my colleagues, is a first century description of nuclear weapons."

"Hog wash! Biblical mumbo-jumbo!" said the Chairman of the Joint Chiefs of Staff. "If you believe this, I've got some seaside property in Arizona I want to sell you."

Partial laughter filled the room. Some laughed but others had stern looks on their faces. The Vice President was one of them.

"Continue with the presentation!" commanded the Vice President.

"Since there seems to be apprehension as to what this video taken from the ones and zeros at the Paris conference shows, I will simply play it for you. Make up your own minds." The astrophysicist was obviously ruffled at the laughter in the room.

As the video began, it showed, in detail, major cities on the eastern sea board. New York, Washington, D.C., Norfolk, Virginia, Miami, Florida, all major financial, government and military facilities based in the eastern United States. Then, a brilliant white flash. Almost all of the North American continent was reduced to rubble in a split second as depicted in *before and after* scenes from each state and cities across the lower forty-eight states. The entire room of officials gasped in horror. There was no laughter.

The video continued to show limited neutron nuclear weapons hitting various downtown city areas throughout the rest of the United States. Dallas, Houston, Omaha, Denver, Seattle, Los Angeles, and San Diego. All complete with the *before and after* scenes. There were more gasps and shouts of 'oh my god' coming from the attendees. Then the video ended.

The astrophysicist continued. "Mr. Vice President, our scientists have studied this video in every detail and have determined that the effects we have seen are exactly what would happen if these weapons were used…"

The Vice President broke in. "The devastation on most of the United States would be the effect of this so-called 'Dooms Day' weapon?"

"Yessir! The exact effect as near as we can determine."

The Vice President asked more questions. "Even the cities in the West. What are the effects of the neutron weapons?"

"Mr. Vice President, neutron nuclear weapons were originally designed to deter any tank and ground personnel attack coming from the Warsaw Pact nations against western Europe. They have an effective range of only a few hundred meters with heavy radiation that would consume and annihilate small areas, not the entire population of these cities. We believe that these scenes would be to break the will and spirit of the American people in the surrounding areas and cause immediate surrender to the attacking forces. This tactic certainly worked for us when we dropped the atomic bombs on Hiroshima and Nagasaki."

"Were you and your group able to determine the source of the 'Dooms Day' weapon? From where was it launched?" questioned the Vice President as the rest of the room went dead silent.

"Sir, we don't have a launch point of this particular weapon, but it is safe to assume that the missing ingredient needed to produce it did not come to us. As close as we can determine, it may have come from China, Sir."

"And what about the neutron weapons, from where did they originate?"

"They're ours, Mr. Vice President!"

"Are you saying that we nuked ourselves?"

"Mr. Vice President, from the signatures and trajectories on the video, these weapons were fired from inside the United States. We know this for a fact!"

"That's impossible! It's preposterous and insane!" said the Chairman of the Joint Chiefs. "We would never fire weapons against our own people!"

"General, of course *we* wouldn't fire against our own nation. But biblical prophecy says that there is going to be something called a *rapture of the church* prior to the End Times when all believers and children from all over the world will be taken up into the clouds. They just disappear. Without going into detail, Sir, if eighty-five percent of Americans profess to be Christians, when and if that event occurred, the United States would be left defenseless. Most any nation could take us over."

The Vice President turned to the four star general. "General, I know you have military think tanks that try to figure out every scenario of attack against the United States and come up with defenses against them. Have you studied this scenario?"

"Of course not, Sir. Who could ever have imagine this...?"

"Then I suggest you begin a study immediately, General, and that's an order!" said the Vice President. "Are there anymore videos on the ones and zeros that supposedly came from this realm called Betwixt?"

The chief astrophysicist hung his head, sighed and replied, "No, Sir. That's the end of it. This video seems to either be a warning or some kind of evil prophecy. We have no more to report."

The meeting ended. A copy of the Top Secret video was rushed to Washington, D.C., for the President to view. No one had a clue as to what his reaction would be. For the first time in U.S. history, government officials didn't feel very secure in their own nation after watching the detailed annihilation of their beloved country, state by state and city by city.

Just before noon, Liz awoke and went to the kitchen. She put on a fresh pot of coffee and started to cook bacon, eggs, biscuits, and gravy. The aroma awakened Wayne and Abby. As they entered the kitchen in their jammies, Wayne noticed that Liz was singing, smiling and she had a glow on her face that he could not explain.

"Liz, you're glowing, like you're completely happy. I haven't seen that grin on your face for several days. What gives?" Wayne said.

"The most wonderful event in my life took place last night. The angel Gabriel visited me!" Liz could hardly contain her joy. "He told me that on the only night I had with your father, Abby, that we conceived a son and that we would name him Johnny. Hank's legacy will live on through me. He told me Johnny would be crusty and tough like Hank and that he would be a man of God leading the way for another!"

Abby got up from the breakfast table and ran to Liz, hugging her, crying tears of joy with her.

"So what did Gabriel look like, Liz?" Wayne asked, noticing that Abby also had the same glow and joy in her face. "Abby, what are you so happy about? Seems you two ladies know something I don't. C'mon, give!"

Liz looked at Wayne and said, "Wayne, I thought you said that you'd seen Gabriel when you went through your trials at Betwixt."

"I didn't see him. I was out if you remember me telling you about that. So what did he look like, Liz?"

"He was…"

Abby interrupted, unable to contain her own joy. "Maybe I can shed some light, Liz. Gabriel also visited me last night. He was brilliant, beautiful, awesome…I can't really describe what he looked like."

"He visited you, Abby? Why didn't I see him?" Wayne was confused and overwhelmed by what he was hearing.

"Yes, Wayne, he did. We are also going to have a male child, conceived while we were in the…you know, on our honeymoon."

"I'm going to be a daddy?" Wayne shouted.

"Oh, yes, Cowboy, you're going to be a daddy to our son who Gabriel said to name 'Billy'. He will bring many people to Christ according to what the angel told me. We are all so blessed! Our sorrow has been turned into hope and joy. No matter what happens at the club, we have a future and a hope!" Abby was gleaming. Wayne was dumbfounded.

"Wow, a little Billy Wayne Tyler, huh? I can't wait to teach him how to play and sing. Was that a stupid thing to say, Abby? I'm just overjoyed and I didn't mean to complete his name without you having a say…"

"I love the name. Billy Wayne Tyler it is," Abby said.

All three forgot about their breakfast and just toasted with their cups of coffee. They were relishing their special moment of sharing such a divine experience. The moment consumed them with tidings of great joy to everyone. They were giving birth. Their families were expanding. No problem seemed too great to overcome at this fantastic moment. The house was filled with almost uncontainable excitement.

"I think I'm going to name my son, Johnny Hank Hawkins," Liz said. What do you think about that?"

"Billy Wayne and Johnny Hank! What a pair they'll make. We can raise them together. They'll be best buddies," Wayne said.

"I just hope there are no complications," Liz said. "I'm a bit past my child bearing age, but Sarah, Moses' wife, had children when she was ninety years old. I guess I'll be okay."

"Liz, there have only been a few divine births announced in the Bible. You and I are truly blessed of God. Everything will be just right according to His will," Abby said as they all gave each other a group hug and laughed and laughed.

Helle Guyion's staff had left for Houston Hobby airport to load up and make preparations to leave the United States per the State Department seventy-two-hour demand. Helle and Natasha got into the limo.

"Driver, drive us to Wayne Tyler's residence. I want to share my joy with them before departing this horrid place. Natasha, did you get the address as I commanded you?" Dr. Guyion feared nothing, not even a confrontation with people she knew hated her guts.

Natasha gave the address to their driver and within fifteen minutes they rolled into the driveway at Abby's home. Helle told Natasha to stay in the car as she got out and walked boldly to the entrance and rang the doorbell.

Wayne walked to the door and looked stunned and angered when he saw who was there.

"What are you doing here, Dr. Guyion? You're not welcome in my house. Please leave and never return or bother us again!" Wayne was mad at the sight of this evil woman.

"Oh, Wayne, I just wanted to congratulate your wife and Mrs. Hawkins on their pregnancies…"

"You couldn't know about that! How did you know, you evil witch?" Wayne lashed out.

"Wayne, darling, I know many things and I have some news of my own that I would like to share with Abby and Liz. Could I talk with them for just a minute or two and then, I promise I'll be on my way?"

"Two minutes. That's all you get." Wayne showed Dr. Guyion into the kitchen where Liz and Abby were sitting.

"I gave Dr. Guyion two minutes to say what she wants to say," Wayne said with a snarl. "Somehow she knows about our news. Figure that one out. She said she has some news for us. Go ahead, Dr. Guyion, the clock's ticking."

"Congratulations on your pregnancies, ladies. I'm sure you are both very happy at such a sad time…"

Abby shot back at Dr. Guyion, "You couldn't have known this! You're a witch, an evil person. Say what you have to say and get the hell out of our house. Now you have one minute." Abby's eyes were blazing.

"Okay. Since you all are so impatient and defensive. I just wanted to tell you that I, too, am pregnant with Dr. Palmer's child. It's a boy and I will call him 'Helel'…"

"Of course you will. It rhymes with hell." Wayne began moving toward Dr. Guyion to escort her back outside.

"Don't touch me if you know what's good for you, Wayne!" Helle's eyes turned bright red. "A final thought before I leave. Your family legacy will continue and so will mine. I have a feeling that our offspring will not be good friends. We will all meet again. You can be sure of that. I will be back with my son, Helel, one day. Get ready! And by the way, tell Eric that he has fathered my son…"

Daniel 4:17, "This decision is by the decree of the watchers, and the sentence by the word of the holy ones, in order that the living may know that the Most High rules in the kingdom of men."

IMAGINE THAT...BELIEVE THAT!

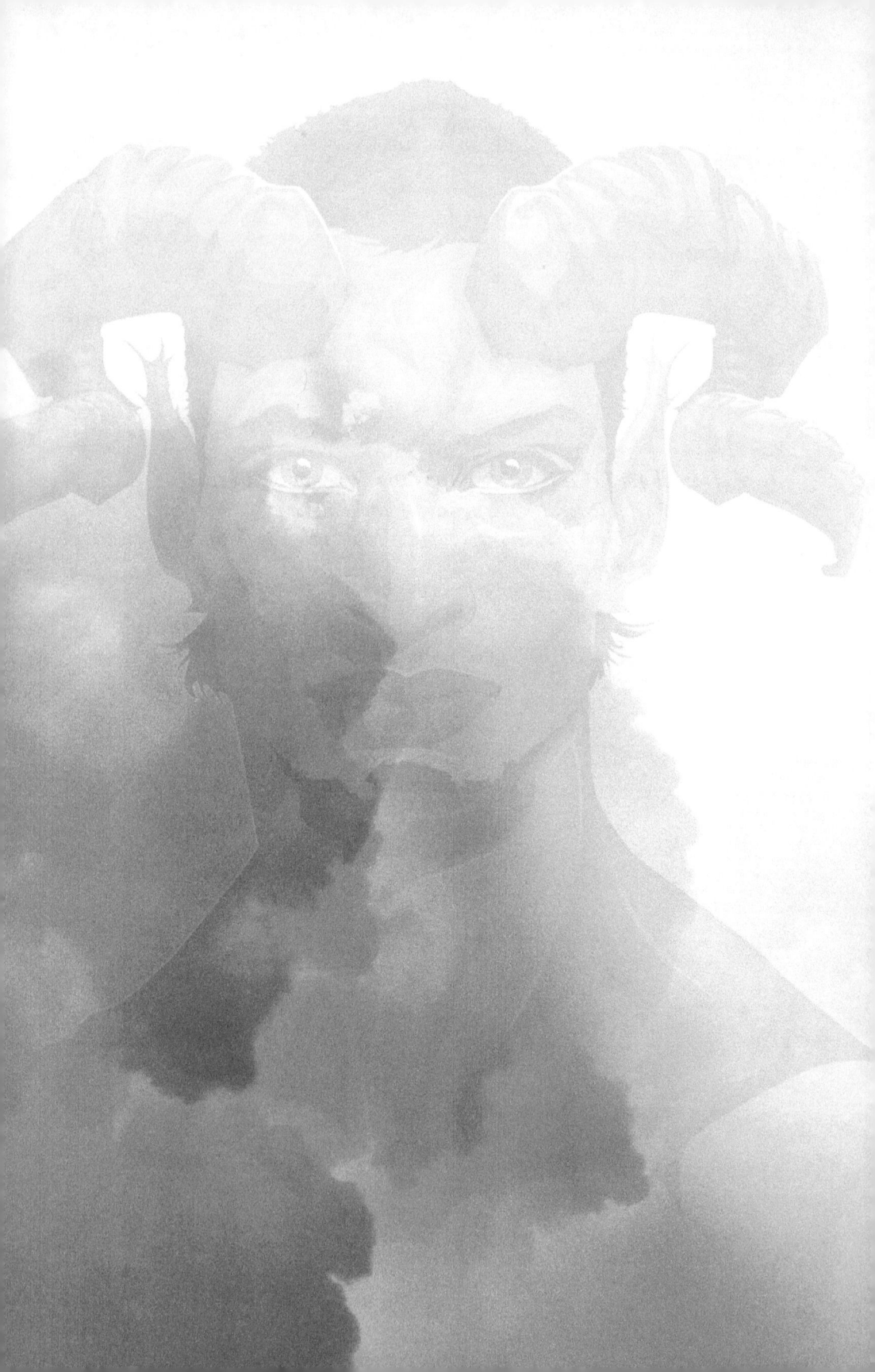

LOOKING FORWARD

Book three of the *Wayne's Angel* trilogy, entitled, "Z-Gen,, The Last Generation," will pick up right where *Betwixt* left off. It will be like the beginning of World War III, literally.

The club, *Tequilaville*, owned by Daddy Hank Hawkins, now deceased, and his daughter, Abby Tyler, his wife for one night Liz Hawkins, is in dire financial straits due to the super natural occurrences that took place on their lake-side docks. People around the lake are avoiding the club in droves. But Liz Hawkins, being a lady of means, has an idea.

There is a new generation on the way to continue the fight of good versus evil. Dr. Helle Guyion will give birth to Helel Guyion, a son conceived in the very presence of Satan's throne. He will represent the explosive evil of the next book in ways you can't imagine. Further and further out of the box but within the reason and beyond the beyond.

Liz Hawkins will conceive a son from her wedding night with Daddy Hank that will be named Johnny Hank. Will he be a warrior like his dad? Then along comes Abby and Wayne giving birth to Billy Wayne Tyler. Will Billy Wayne follow in his dad's footsteps and be a musician, a song-writer and a ladies' man? Oh, the possibilities that will cause these three young sons to change the course of the entire world. And that's exactly what they'll do. Fasten your seatbelts for a very explosive ride to what may just end the world. But, for the better or for the worse?

There will be some new characters added to book three. Some will be funny, others, terrible, almost beyond belief as they begin telling their stories and searching for their destinies. I promise not to let you down. We're going to go where no soul has ever been before.

Wayne's Angel, Mr. Elroy, A.K.A. Gordon, is being spotted in different places around the world. If you have seen him, go to www.ronwmumford.com and leave a message as to the time and location of his sighting.

Ron Mumford

You can contact me at ron.mumford1111@gmail.com for questions and comments.
Be Blessed,
Ron W. Mumford

About the Author

Ron Mumford was a journalism major at the University of North Texas and has worked for many newspapers and magazines. During his time in the U.S. Army, he was a Combat Correspondent (P.I.O.) and a Combat Photographer. He was awarded two Bronze Stars for his service. During his time in combat, he too, had his own super-natural experience…

Later, Ron got into sales and marketing, started up his own company and took it public on NASDAQ only to see the government change some regulations and the wealth that he had accumulated went up in smoke. He became a licensed financial consultant with two of the nation's largest investment firms, helping people do retirement planning and choosing smart investments.

"At some point in my life, I wanted to be like John Grisham, write a best-selling novel, get an agent who would present my first novel to one of the Big 5 publishing houses and get a million dollar advance…Wishful thinking! But I have written five books and every minute I've spent on the writing and creating has been sheer joy!"

Now I write full time, go fishing a lot on Lake Conroe and live in Montgomery, Texas, northwest of Houston. I'm a member of the Lone Star Cowboy Church (I'm not a cowboy) and teach the Bible to a small group. Just doing the three things I love doing most besides being with family. That's the key to life…spending time with family and enjoying God's creation.

I'll have several other books available at www.ReadersCloud9.com and on Amazon in the near future. My first novel, *Gray Justice* is a court-room, action thriller that does away with drugs, organized crime and cleans up congress…Okay, go ahead and laugh but just try to put it down!

On Amazon now is a Christian non-fiction entitled *Finding Your Soul Mate, God's Way* and due to the high divorce rate makes the point, "You've tried it your way, now try it God's Way!" There are over sixty verses that will teach all of us a thing or two about our choices of life-long mates. Plus, it will guide you to your soul mate, guaranteed. Complete with a study guide at the end of each chapter, great for small groups.

Got to get back to writing the third book of the trilogy, *Z-Gen, The Last Generation* which will be out soon. Contact me at www.Ronwmumford.com. Be Blessed today and every day!

www.ingramcontent.com/pod-product-compliance
Lightning Source LLC
Chambersburg PA
CBHW030051100526
44591CB00008B/102